AF654369

CONTEMPORARY SOCIETY: TRIBAL STUDIES

CONTEMPORARY SOCIETY: TRIBAL STUDIES

Edited by

DEEPAK KUMAR BEHERA

and

GEORG PFEFFER

VOLUME ONE	—	STRUCTURE AND PROCESS
VOLUME TWO	—	DEVELOPMENTAL ISSUES, TRANSITION AND CHANGE
VOLUME THREE	—	SOCIAL CONCERN
VOLUME FOUR	—	SOCIAL REALITIES
VOLUME FIVE	—	THE CONCEPT OF TRIBAL SOCIETY
VOLUME SIX	—	TRIBAL SITUATION IN INDIA
VOLUME SEVEN	—	IDENTITY, INTERVENTION AND IDEOLOGY IN TRIBAL INDIA AND BEYOND
VOLUME EIGHT	—	STRUCTURE AND EXCHANGE IN TRIBAL INDIA AND BEYOND
VOLUME NINE	—	HEALTH IN THE CONTEXT OF TRIBAL CULTURE

The Editor

Deepak Kumar Behera is Vice Chancellor, Berhampur University, Odisha, India.

CONTEMPORARY SOCIETY: TRIBAL STUDIES

VOLUME TEN

TRIBAL CHILDREN AND THEIR CHILDHOOD

Edited by

DEEPAK KUMAR BEHERA
Vice Chancellor
Berhampur University
Berhampur-760007
Odisha
India

CONCEPT PUBLISHING COMPANY PVT. LTD.
NEW DELHI-110059

© Author

All rights reserved. No part of this work may be reproduced, stored, adapted, or transmitted in any form or by any means, electronic, mechanical, photocopying, micro-filming recording or otherwise, or translated in any language, without the prior written permission of the copyright owner and the publisher. The book is sold subject to the condition that it shall not, by way of trade or otherwise, be lent, resold, hired out, or otherwise circulated without the prior publisher's written consent in any form of binding or cover other than that in which it is published.

The views and opinions expressed in this book are author(s) own and the facts reported by them/her have been verified to the extent possible, and the publishers are not in any way liable for the same.

ISBN-13: 978-81-7022-640-6 (Series)
ISBN-13: 978-93-5125-142-2 (Vol. X)

First Published 2015

Published and Printed by

Concept
Since 1974

Concept Publishing Company Pvt. Ltd.
A/15-16, Commercial Block, Mohan Garden
New Delhi-110059 (India)
T: 25351460, 25351794, *F*: 091-11-25357109
E: publishing@conceptpub.com, W: www.conceptpub.com
Editorial Office: H-13, Bali Nagar, New Delhi-110 015, India.

Cataloging in Publication Data--Courtesy: D.K. Agencies (P) Ltd. <docinfo@dkagencies.com>

Contemporary society : tribal studies / edited by Deepak Kumar Behera.
volumes cm
Includes bibliographical references and index.
Contents: volume 10. Tribal children and their childhood
ISBN 9788170226406 (series)
ISBN 9789351251422 (vol. X)

1. Ethnology--India. 2. India--Scheduled tribes. 3. India--Social life and customs. 4. India--Social conditions. I. Behera, Deepak Kumar, editor.

GN635.I4C66 2015 DDC 305.800954 23

ACKNOWLEDGEMENTS

I am grateful to all the contributors to the volume for their timely help and co-operation in completing this project. Without their scholarly contribution, the volume would not have seen the light of the day. I am thankful to Concept Publishing Company Pvt. Ltd., New Delhi for agreeing to my proposal to make this as another felicitation volume in honour of Professor Georg Pfeffer. Professor Pfeffer was the co-editor of all the earlier published eight volumes of **Contemporary Society: Tribal Studies**. In fact, I miss him very much by not seeing him as the other editor for this volume. I take this opportunity to express my deep sense of gratitude to him as he has been a constant source of inspiration for me both in my personal life and professional career. I, on behalf of all the contributors, take this opportunity to offer this volume to Professor Pfeffer as a token of our love and respect for him who has made such enormous contribution to the study of tribes in Middle India.

DEEPAK KUMAR BEHERA

Bio-note of Professor Georg Pfeffer

Professor Georg Pfeffer

Georg Pfeffer was born in the year 1943 during World War II in the German capital of Berlin. Later he moved to Hamburg and studied in Freiburg (1963-1970). He married Monica Grosskinsky in 1966 and later had four children and by now six grandchildren. In 1979 he became an associate professor of socio-cultural anthropology at the South Asia Institute of the University of Heidelberg and in 1985 a full professor of the Free University of Berlin. Altogether he has spent almost ten years in South Asia (India, Pakistan, Sri Lanka) and written or edited many books and articles. At the moment, he is writing on his favourite subject KINSHIP AS CONSTITUTION.

CONTENTS

SECTION III

PLAY AND LEISURE TIME ACTIVITIES

SECTION IV

YOUTH: LIFE STAGE, RULES OF MARRIAGE, IDENTITY AND RIGHTS

INTRODUCTION

DEEPAK KUMAR BEHERA

The meaning and concept of childhood is debated within and across various disciplines such as anthropology, developmental psychology, pedagogy, sociology, and cultural history. The idea that childhood has been and is always changing and that we need therefore to recognize and document this.

Close scrutiny of numerous well-known anthropological studies over several decades would reveal the notable absence of children. A careful review of literature reveals that children have not been given adequate coverage in the writings of the noted ethnographers. This is more visible in a country like India where childhood as a "cultural construction" has hardly been studied by anthropologists and ethnographers. Why did anthropologists not take children and their childhoods seriously? Why were children missing from the ethnographic literature? Why did children's voices remain silent in anthropology? If anthropology is scientific study of man and his work, how can we exclude children from the study of anthropology? Are children not human beings? Are they not part of the social structure and network of social relationships? If anthropology is the study of man and its culture, how can we ignore studying children who constitute around 40 per cent of the total population? What children themselves think of the social worlds in which they are growing up? In fact, Indian anthropology and anthropologists have much more to offer to the study of children and childhood. Therefore, those children have been referred to by me as "missing children in Indian Anthropology".

Until recently, the scientific study of childhood was the exclusive domain of developmental psychologists. Influenced by evolutionary theory and logical positivism, they tend to see childhood as a biological category and children as isolated agents who need to proceed through a logical sequence of stages towards adulthood. Children are held to be initially immature, irrational, asocial, and in need of a long developmental journey towards becoming mature, rational, and social adults. Developmental psychologists still see children as incomplete adults and have endorsed a strong separation between childhood and adulthood. However, the work by Skolnick (1976) provided a new perspective to childhood studies in developmental psychology.

This stance of earlier developmental psychologists is increasingly questioned by anthropologists and cultural historians, who critique its neglect of the influence of history, society, and culture (Behera, 1996, 1998, 2005, 2007). Most of those scholars propose instead a social-constructivist approach and hold that childhood is a historical, social, cultural construction, rather than a biological category. In general, this approach views the child not in terms of what s/he is lacking, but rather as active agent who contributes to his/her own linguistic construction of meaning and reality. Children should not be defined as incomplete adults, nor as miniature adults, but rather as unique persons in their own right (Watson and Behera, 2011; Behera and Trawick, 2007).

Childhood as a "cultural construction" has hardly been studied by Indian anthropologists. Further such sporadic writings on children do not include the voices of children on matters affecting their lives. Those analysis best represent adults' perspective on childhood rather than children's perspective on childhood. Anthropologists study exotic cultures by immersing themselves in an environment so that they become accepted as an insider. While doing so, they unknowingly ignore to include children as important members of the community. A much neglected area of traditional ethnographic research is certainly the discovery into the cultures of childhood, where children create their own social structure and influence one another in ways that adults cannot. Children just have their own rules for doing so. It is important to study how children deal with different situations and make adjustment to adult rules.

Though of late children and childhood have been studied in social and cultural anthropology, yet they have not been central to the overall development of the discipline. In recent years, slowly a distinct "anthropology of childhood" has emerged. Ethnographies those make up this subfield suggest a great diversity in definitions of and ideas about childhood and the different roles and expectations placed on children according to their cultural backgrounds. They also highlight the heterogeneous nature of childhood and the impact that gender, age, birth order, and ethnicity have on children's experiences and daily lives. Many childhood researchers advocate that childhood should not be considered as time of universal dependence rather it must be understood as culturally constructed, social phenomenon which changes over time and place (Jean La Fontaine 1986; Allison James and Alan Prout 1997; Chris Jenks 1996; Berry Mayall 1994; Frances Waksler, 1991). Children are no longer viewed as a homogenous group whose views and priorities depend only on their physical advancement. There are many childhood(s) across time and space. The little "s" has a great deal of significance in understanding childhood in different cultural contexts.

Children are first and foremost individuals, born with indivisible and inalienable human rights. They also belong to families and communities that need to have access to resources and services, as well as capacities to ensure realization of their rights. Policy approaches are needed that address both the income and non-income dimensions of children's deprivations. Continued neglect of material, human and psycho-social dimensions of child well-being can prevent children from living a full life and from making informed decisions later on in their life. India too would miss out on the dividends that can accrue from a full expansion of children's capabilities.

Anthropology of Childhood and Related Matters

As the "anthropology of childhood" has coalesced into a distinct field, various overviews have appeared that look at how this has happened and how this theorization might progress in the future. Lancy (1996, 2007, 2008, 2010) has made significant contribution to anthropology of childhood. His volume Anthropology of Childhood: *Cherubs, Chattel, and Changelings* (2008) provides the first comprehensive review of the literature on children from a distinctly anthropological perspective. Bringing together key evidence from cultural anthropology, history, and primate studies, it argues that our common understandings about children are narrowly culture-bound. Whereas dominant society views children as precious, innocent and preternaturally cute "cherubs", he introduces the reader to societies where children are viewed as unwanted, inconvenient "changelings", or as desired but pragmatically commoditized "chattels". Looking in particular at family structure and reproduction, profiles of children's caretakers, their treatment at different ages, their play, work, schooling, and transition to adulthood, this volume provides a rich, interesting, and original portrait of children in past and contemporary cultures. Lancy (2012) argues that "childhood is not static - patiently waiting for us to improve our methods and theories. We cannot turn back the clock and study aboriginal childhood. To build a comprehensive anthropology of childhood, we must use whatever windows on children in culture are available, even if the windows are old, cracked and dirty".

LeVine (2007) looks at the study of childhood within anthropology over the last 150 years, paying particular attention to studies of socialization and child rearing. Montgomery (2008) also provides the best historical backgrounds to the subject, and looks at how studies of childhood have changed over the past years. She focuses on the difference between American and European studies of childhood. She presents an up-to-date discussion of child-focused anthropology. Schwartzman (2001) complements this work by focusing on the way childhood was portrayed and discussed during the same period in one particular anthropological journal, *American Anthropologist*. She argues that anthropologists used children to explore other issues such as socialization or kinship but rarely looked at them as worthy of study in their own right. Trawick (2007) makes an interesting anthropological study on warfare, childhood, and play focusing on children engaged in war in Batticaloa, Sri Lanka. She explains as to how children exercise agency – they knowingly act on their worlds to change those worlds. Sharon Stephens (1995) suggests in the introduction to her groundbreaking volume, *Children and the Politics of Culture*: "children creatively live from the inside complex mixtures of languages and social domains that are external structures for many adults" (1995: 24). We take this to mean that children through their experiences know something, or many things, that adults do not know or fail to grasp, because adults' experiences are compartmentalized while children's are not just hybrid, but fluid. More recently, Lawrence Hirschfeld in the aforesaid article makes a similar if more radical claim in somewhat different terms: "Children not only live in the cultural spheres of the adults with whom they share a life space, but they create and maintain cultural environments of their own" (2002: 615). Where Stephens sees "complex mixtures" inaccessible to adults, Hirschfeld suggests we may locate unique cultures created by children.

Eickelkamp (2010) looks at how theories and ideas about anthropological approaches to childhood have changed in relation to aboriginal childhoods. It is an excellent, comprehensive overview of anthropological literature on aboriginal children. It deals with classic and more recent ethnographies and is an essential starting point for all work on aboriginal childhoods. The late 1980s and early 1990s saw an upsurge of interest in childhood among anthropologists and a realization that children had been somewhat marginal to previous anthropological work. La Fontaine (1986) and Benthall (1992) persuasively set out the case for why the anthropology of childhood should be its own field. La Fontaine (1986) one of the pioneers in the field of anthropology and childhood, sets out why children need to be studied by anthropologists and why they have not been properly discussed in the past. Benthall (1992) identifies gaps in the study of childhood. While many of these have since been filled, his writings served as a rallying call for anthropologists wishing to devote attention to children's lives. While they saw neglect in the past, however, Hirschfeld (2002) saw animosity, and the question asked in the title (Why don't anthropologists like children?) has been much debated ever since. In his controversial and much-disputed article he argues that anthropologists have systematically ignored and sidelined children because of the embarrassing parallels drawn by early anthropologists between primitives and children. He argues passionately that children's daily should be taken seriously. The controversies over anthropological accounts of children have now died down somewhat, and Bluebond-Langner and Korbin (2007) and James (2007) look to the future, examining the methods and ethics of bringing children into the anthropological mainstream.

Mead in her book *Coming of Age in Samoa* [1971 (1928)] analyzed the daily lives of Samoan girls from infancy through early childhood until adolescence. She rejected the idea that adolescence was necessarily a stressful and disruptive experience for both the child and the society, and claimed that behaviour in adolescence was caused by cultural conditioning rather than biological changes. In another major work, Mead in a different study (1830) discussed about the process of growing up in New Guinea (Montgomery, 2008).

Following Mead's pioneering work, there have been more descriptive anthropological studies on childhood socialization, with many focusing on education. Meyer Fortes' examined the social and psychological aspects of education of the Tallensi people in Northern Ghana. In the absence of formal education, Tallensi children were taught by their kin and learned to acquire interest, skills, and observances through their interactions with adults and their participation in social organization. Education was a primary means of socialization as the children reproduced the patterns of cultural practices and social organization [Fortes, 1970 (1938): 38].

Raymond Firth in his study of the Tikopia of the Western Pacific analyzes education as a vital part of social life and as process which "serves to fit human individual more adequately for his social environment" [Firth, 1970 (1936): 76]. His description highlights as to how the parents taught the children etiquettes, discipline, family rituals, religious customs, as well as gender-specific skills from early childhood.

The six cultures study by Whiting (1977) provides a wealth of detail about children's lives, how they were treated, and their place in the life-cycle. This cross-cultural study is a systematic naturalistic observation of children in their routine "behaviour settings" as a method for recording the interactions of children with their environments in diverse cultures.

Christina Toren (1993) in her studies on children's cognition in Fiji analyzed children's and adult's concepts of ritual space, and the differences between them. She argued that children's cognitive development is a micro-historical process that transforms concepts and practices as well as people. She gave an example of how the Fijian children gradually change their understanding of the relationship between space and hierarchy. Based on their knowledge and observation of public spaces, children understand that adults have differential positions and that these are linked to their use of space. In contrast, Fijian adults suppose the spatial position to be important because a higher status person is there, so that "meanings made by children may be direct inversions of adult's meanings" (Toren, 1993: 462). She argued that children are not wrong in their beliefs and that such assignments are not the result of incomplete socialization, but part of the processes that transform them into adults, when they can deny their earlier knowledge and cognitively construct hierarchical relations in a socially mature way.

Child-centred ethnographies place children at the heart of ethnographic research, taking their agency and importance as a given. However, one of the inherent limitations in this form of research is that focusing exclusively on children overlooks the importance of the relationships between adults and children and the ways that these relationships are understood and negotiated by both sides.

Taking inspiration from Aries social constructionist perspective (1962), Alan Prout and Allison James published a seminal piece introducing a new paradigm for the sociology of childhood (Prout and James, 1997). According to this new paradigm, "childhood must be understood as a social construction distinct from biological immaturity and as a variable of social analysis. It also claims that children must be conceived as active subjects who participate in the making of their own lives as well as those of others around them. Hence, it concludes that children, their practices, and their social relationships are worth studying in their own right and also in relation to the larger context of social structure".

Researching on and with Children

From the 1970s onwards there has been a major shift in childhood studies and children have been seen as central participant and reliable informant in research studies. La Fontaine emphasized that research on children should be done by treating them as worthy subjects and not just immature being. She wrote that "in general, anthropology has retained an outdated view of children as raw material, unfinished specimens of the social beings whose idea and behaviour are the proper subject matter for social science" (1986: 10).

James (2007) looks at the specific issue of children's voices in anthropology, how children can best be used as informants, and the problems of interpretation faced by adults when working with children. Some anthropologists even claimed to have built good relationship with children, who in turn helped them in the research process (Bird-David, 2005). In all these studies, children were treated as informants with knowledge about their lives and their participation was highly encouraged. This new perspective entailed changing the emphasis within studies of childhood from socialization, and how parents raised their children, to how children themselves perceived their lives, surroundings, parents, and upbringing.

Anthropologist Mary Ellen Goodman (1970) argued for a "culture of childhood" approach that recognized children as cultural beings capable of social interaction, understanding interpersonal relations, and coping with frustrations, tensions, and troubles. Moving away from socialization and enculturation, Goodman proposed a "child's eye view of society and culture".

Through this shift in perspective, it became apparent that children possesses agency, which could influence their lives, and also the lives of their family members, friends and community (Waksler, 1991; James and Prout, 1995).

From the beginning of 1990s many anthropological studies focussed on children's lived experiences as narrated by the children themselves. Although childhood has been recognized as a social construction, there have been debates with regard to the problems and constraints of conducting research with children (Friedl, 2004). These problems are most often related to the ethical concerns especially when studying older children. One of the ethical issues is about the power differentials between the adult researchers and the child participants which could create particular problem at the field site. Myra Bluebond Langer and Jill Korbin (2007: 243) have pointed out that even if children give informed consent, that problem remains. According to them, emphasizing children's voices, or their right to participate in research, does not necessarily solve all the difficulties: "In using quotations from children we have to be cognizant of all the following: selectivity of representation, uncritical quoting, polyphony of voices, whose point is being made (e.g. anthropologists or the children being quoted), whose agenda is being served (e.g. the human rights community or the people of the community in which child lives)" (cited by Montgomery, 2008).

Many researchers who have worked with children have developed specific techniques which take into account children's attention spans and daily activities. Some of these involve interpreting children's paintings and drawings, which allow younger children to participate in research. These techniques have clearly helped in getting new insights about children's lives and making them an active partner and participants in research conducted about and among them.

The ethical and methodological issues related to children's participation in research have been debated by researchers. However, with more rigorous focus on methods and approaches on doing participatory research with children (Greene and Hogan, 2005; Solberg, 1996) the childhood studies have come a long way.

Children's Play and Leisure Time Activities

Play has an overall developmental influence on children. Play is associated with socialization including the acquisition of gender roles, values and understanding about social institutions. Play and especially outdoor play is absolutely crucial for the child's development, health and well-being.

It is the interplay of multiple factors, such as the child's disposition, the role of play partners and the contextual nature of play, which stimulates the various developmental domains of the child. Piaget saw play as a behaviour that emerges as a result of combining skills, knowledge and understanding to create a learning experience. Play continues to get more complex as children grow, helping to gain mastery and coordination.

Play is often synonymous with childhood and has early beginnings. An infant watching an object over the cot and responding in delight is often the beginnings of play. A toddler improvises and explores objects for innovative play. Older children engage playfully with strategy and planning in complex games. Researchers show that play is a social process through which children produce their own orders and how those orders are related to society at large. Adults refer to instances of child-chosen activities as play. Children spontaneously utilize acts of fun to experiment in the worlds they inhabit. Simultaneously, processes of socialization rush to "teach children", putting social pressures on childhood. Most often, children engaging voluntarily in activities with spontaneous interest are instances seen as "play", which at times may be in tandem with socializing norms. Despite indulging in children's activities, parents begin to regulate childhood play, which slides to a disputed domain as adults begin to see children's play as transgression (Singh and Gupta, 2011).

Research has shown that adult-directed play tends to lose its spontaneity and dynamism (Corsaro, 1997). Play is often a result of the contexts people live in and the environment they are able to provide for their growing children (Pellegrini and Smith, 2003). Children's play depends on familiarity with people, safety and minimal intrusion by adults.

From early childhood children play imitating the adults, invent their own kinds of games, rules, they are very creative. Role plays are social plays in which the child switches to social role like playing doctor or mother and father wild animals, etc. Children play these type of games in order to overcome frustrations if they slip into the role of an aggressor or the opposite. Role plays also follow the social rules of the worlds of peers and adulthood. Problem solving might be trained here or having the chance of being a hero. The children's fantasy, their adopted values, their fights and wars, all this appears in the role plays. Construction games are done by children either in single or in group situations. Construction games start as soon as children do have imagination and planning capabilities. They follow a goal, finish a plan. Children can use their experiences from the phase of functional plays. The know already about materials. The child develops the capacity of imagined action. So again another kind of play which prepares the human being implicitly for adulthood when all these skills and knowledge are necessary for the different types of work and socializing. Here Evaldsson could also see that with the older children gender oriented playing is not the subject of games.

Marble games focus the value of objects. They vary in this and the chidren's acivity is attached with trading in playing. The trading is accompagnied by verbal exchange of verbal negotiation which constantly changes and therefore increases the verbal communcative skills. And if a child has a surplus of marbles s/he shares the marbles with other children who do not have that many. The sharing of objects opens up the possibility of change in economic status and therefore creates an economic and social balance withing the peer.

Studies on children's play, language, and identity have shown that children are a social category in their own rights and capabilities hence disapproving the earlier socialization studies. Opies' research work on children's language, games and knowledge established how children are social beings with their own cultural world, separate from that of adults [Opie and Opie, 1992 (1959)]. Although they also noticed spatial regularity and generational continuity in the basic knowledge and language of the children (*ibid.*, 174-175), they pointed out children's active participation in creating as well as spreading specific types of lore such as rhymes, jokes, games, tricks, and slang expressions.

Opie and Opie [1970 (1959)] compiled children's rhymes and different forms of games in their seminal work *The Lore and Language of School Children*. They discuss the culture of childhood through the rites and rhymes, jokes and jeers, laws, games and secret spells of childhood play, which shows no sign of dying out.

Major theorists agree that the child uses play for self-teaching. The child plays through situations very much like an adult thinks through a situation. Children learn to live within self-imposed rules during their fantasy play; play allows the child to practise self-regulation. Also, fantasy play is a manifestation of symbolic representation – the child represents objects and ideas through play situations. In play the child is always behaving beyond his/her age and above his/her usual everyday behaviour.

Formal and Informal Learning

Education varies widely from the perspective of time, space, context and requirements. Different aboriginal communities possess their own systems of informal education. The dimensions of their informal education emphasize acquisition of competence, subsistence techniques, and values as effective members of society. Children learn to master these skills from the very beginning, but there are no special institutions or personnel or rigid timings for such instructions. In such situation, education is an informal process of learning skills maintaining continuity with tradition (Behera, 2007). The process of formation of modern nation-state through absorption of smaller and weaker cultural entities, and imposition of formal education, common national language, culture and identity have severely threatened the existence of aboriginal people as viable collective entities.

Most tribal societies traditionally had the institution of dormitory, which was separate for boys and girls. Dormitory played an important role in socialisation from adolescent to adulthood. Although boys and girls had the freedom of meeting and knowing each other, there were norms and values in terms of which they were guided in their behaviour, including that pertaining to their sexual life. The traditional social and cultural practices concerning their care and rearing would illuminate the understanding of issues and problems surrounding the tribal children. Division of work based on sex was important and hence the family from the very beginning socialised their children into roles, norms and values associated with such division (Xaxa, 2011).

The social life of tribal children has to be viewed taking into consideration their ecological and cultural contexts that place very different demands on their day-to-day life. Because of differences in the demands of tribal ecology, the patterning of their cognitive abilities shows considerable variation from those of other groups. Tribal children are neither culturally inferior nor cognitively less competent than the children of other groups. Instead many of their skills and abilities are highly developed and extremely sophisticated.

A worldwide emphasis on schooling situates children to be on their own, leaving them to negotiate with school systems in addition to neighbourhood and family norms to pursue any self-chosen activity (Corsaro, 2003). The school as an institution not only provides an ordered temporal passage from child to adult status, but at the same time, on a daily basis, restricts the ways in which children can spend their time. The curriculum is strategic in mapping out the whole in-school experience of the child through a combination of space, time, location, content, proximity, isolation, insulation, integration and hierarchy. The tyranny of educational timetabling has invaded out-of-school time of tribal children.

Even in the sphere of education, the status of tribal children is far from satisfactory. Enrolment is still a problem. However, over the last decade, enrolment of tribal children has increased progressively, clearly winning an edge over other social categories in enrolment in primary and upper primary sections. The GER is taken to bolster the claim for progress made in expanding school education in India. But enrolment is a very unreliable basis for assessing the degree of access to education (Dubey, 2010); the important figures are those for attendance and drop-outs. The enrolment of tribal children in school is not that low, but drop-out figures are still very high. The issue of drop-outs is the most serious as far as tribal children's education is concerned.

The enrolment of tribal children in school is not that low, but drop-out figures are still very high. The issue of drop-outs is the most serious as far as tribal children's education is concerned. The important question is why attendance is low and drop-out rates so high among tribal children. These issues have been attributed to poor curriculum and syllabus, deficient pedagogy and negligent teachers in case of the general population. Parents too, are held accountable for drop-outs and poor quality of students (Dubey, 2010). Now, if this is the case with the larger population in whose language and ethos, school education is imparted, whose history and culture, the school curriculum and syllabus represents, even teachers belong to same cultural group as the students, then imagine the state of tribal children for whom education imparted at all levels is alien to their life, history and experience. The vital question is how to explain this poor and deplorable state of social development among the tribal population. Can it be placed in a perspective so that we have a better understanding and analysis?

An increasing number of researchers strongly advocate the use of the mother tongue or home language as medium of instruction in early stages of education. This assumes greater significance in the context of education of tribal children because their mother tongue is often quite distinct from the prominent languages in the state or regional languages. Tribal children face problems wherever teachers do not speak their dialect at all. Similarly, a clear policy for language use in schools has to be developed. Research evidence suggests that significantly fewer students drop out of schools in which the language of tribal groups is used for instruction at the primary level. Development of primers in the tribal dialect involving content from the local context will go a long way in ensuring children's active participation in the learning process in school. The presence of tribal teachers, especially from the same community, has shown and improved school participation of tribal children. Coming from the same community, it is believed that the teachers would understand and respect the culture and the ethos with much greater sensitivity. Studies suggest that teacher motivation contributes more to teaching-learning process than teacher competence.

The implications of schooling of tribal children are clear. A programme of schooling, which does not pay attention to the ecological, cultural and psychological characteristics of tribal children, is highly unlikely to make any significant impact. The educational system of the dominant non-tribal population is of very limited value in the tribal cultural milieu because it does not match with the lifestyle of individuals and the needs of the tribal community. Linking school education with life in general and the needs of the tribal communities in particular is a most important step that requires serious attention.

Tribal children have very low levels of participation and success in school education programmes. It points to our failure to develop a sensitive model of education that is rooted in the psychological strengths of tribal children. Studies indicate that, in comparison to other groups, hunters and gatherers possess a high level of visual and tactual differentiation; they demonstrate capacity for fine judgment of shape and size of stimuli as well as spatial relations and they produce fine categorization of an array of objects. These abilities are required for success in science, art, music, dance, athletic activities, and vocations like carpentry, tailoring, wood and stone crafts. These skills need to be utilized not only for education of tribal children in schools, but also in the broader economic spheres of tribal life. Such attempts will be helpful in generating and promoting the sense of competence, self-efficacy, self-respect and positive self-image among tribal children in general. Such attempts are also highly likely to provide tribal children with a culturally meaningful, ecologically valid and economically viable alternative to life by reinforcing the dignity of their culture and identity. Ever increasing contact of tribals with the outside world over the years has introduced several changes in their culture and life. These changes are reflected in their psychological characteristics also. Studies indicate that their ways of perceiving the world, categorizing objects, interpreting pictures, and strategies of learning and memory become more similar to those with whom they interact and negotiate their life in these changed circumstances. This suggests that tribal children can acquire all those skills that the members of other groups of the society possess. What is important on our part is to develop a positive frame of mind about tribal children. This is possible only through sensitivity to tribal culture and life, recognition of the cognitive strengths of tribal children, and appreciation of their personality qualities. Efforts in these directions will be very helpful in organizing the programme of tribal education as well as promoting economic and other aspects of tribal development.

While there is a general need for improvement in physical facilities in all schools in remote tribal regions, change in perceptions and outlooks of teachers about tribal children are equally important. Teachers must be sensitized to the cultural and behavioural strengths of tribal children and motivated to do their best for them in schools. Incentives should be initiated to attract effective teachers to work in tribal schools and to retain them there. Only such motivated teachers are likely to generate interest among tribal children towards schools education by attempting to link the contents of the curriculum with the existing realities of tribal communities through the use of innovative technologies.

Tribal Youth

It is very difficult to separate children and youth in a tribal society. There are many overlapping areas wherein we find the participation of children and youth. A growing child becomes a youth with the passage of time. Therefore, any analysis on tribal children will be inadequate without covering the life of the youth. However, tribal/indigenous youth have not received due attention in India anthropology like the tribal children. It is very important to gauge the perception of the youth to the development of globalisation and modernity in a fast changing world. Issues related to youth, viz. life stages, rules of marriage, attitudes toward marriage, marriage practices, identity and rights, family, language, origin, awareness of one's own culture and traditional practices, etc. are very important to be studied from anthropological perspective. Therefore, the volume covers a section on tribal youth so as to provide better understanding of various aspects of the life of the tribal youth in India and abroad.

The IUAES Commission on **Anthropology of Children, Youth and Childhood** has come together to promote childhood and youth research in which children and young people are active participants in the research process rather than objects of study as was most often the case in the past. It has come together to promote a number of guiding ideals. One of its initial and most important aims is to encourage research about children and youth in which they themselves are active participants as opposed to being just objects of study as they were most often in the past.

In recent years a growing number of anthropologists have either studied childhood/youthhood or included children/youth in their broader descriptions of society. Studies today show how children and youth make meaning for themselves by bringing their own unique forms of agency into being. Instead of relying on adult-imposed meanings of childhood/youthhood, as anthropologists we need to continue to give due attention to children/youth as social actors in their own right, actively producing their own worlds while recognizing the multiple constraints within which their agency takes place.

Both the Commission and the community of anthropologists, who are specifically interested in studying childhood and youth, have gathered around a common driving objective, namely to address the relative absence of children and youth (some would argue their almost complete absence) from mainstream anthropological research. This common driving objective is to be met by encouraging the development of research programmes around the common realization that children and youth are a constitutive element of any society and that anthropology needs to attend to this seriously. Today, scholars interested in human evolution and development acknowledge the importance of studying the role of culture in shaping the life course (Behera *et al.*, 2014: i). During this time, anthropologists have contributed a great deal to the ongoing debates in what has come to be known as childhood studies. Ethnography, once an anthropological trademark, is today one of the most-widely used approaches to studying children and youth while anthropological concepts and theories are clearly visible and play an important role in the interdisciplinary study of childhood and youth (*ibid.*, i).

Tribal Children in India

Children below the age of 18 years account for nearly 40 per cent of India's population. It goes without saying that enabling all children to realize their full creative potential is critical for sustaining India's economic growth and accelerating human development. Not all children have benefited equitably from the remarkable progress and transformation that the country has witnessed in recent years. Tens of millions still face basic challenges of survival and healthy development (Xaxa, 2011).

Tribals are one of the most exploited and deprived sections of the Indian society. All development indicators show them to be the most excluded from mainstream Indian society despite the fact that various kinds of policies and programmes have been pursued and executed for their social and economic upliftment in post-Independence India. Needless to say that exclusion from the fruits of development has adversely affected the quality of life of the tribal people.

Tribal children often integrate work, play and school, moving back and forth between child- and adult-centred worlds in more flexible patterns than those allowed by the disciplinary regimes imposed on non-tribal children with driving parents.

Scheduled Tribe constitute 8.2 per cent of the total population of India. Of the total tribal population of 10,42,81,034 in India 5,24,09,823 are male and 5,18,71,211 are female (Census 2011). The distribution of Indian tribal population in various States and Union Territories as per 2011 Census is presented below.

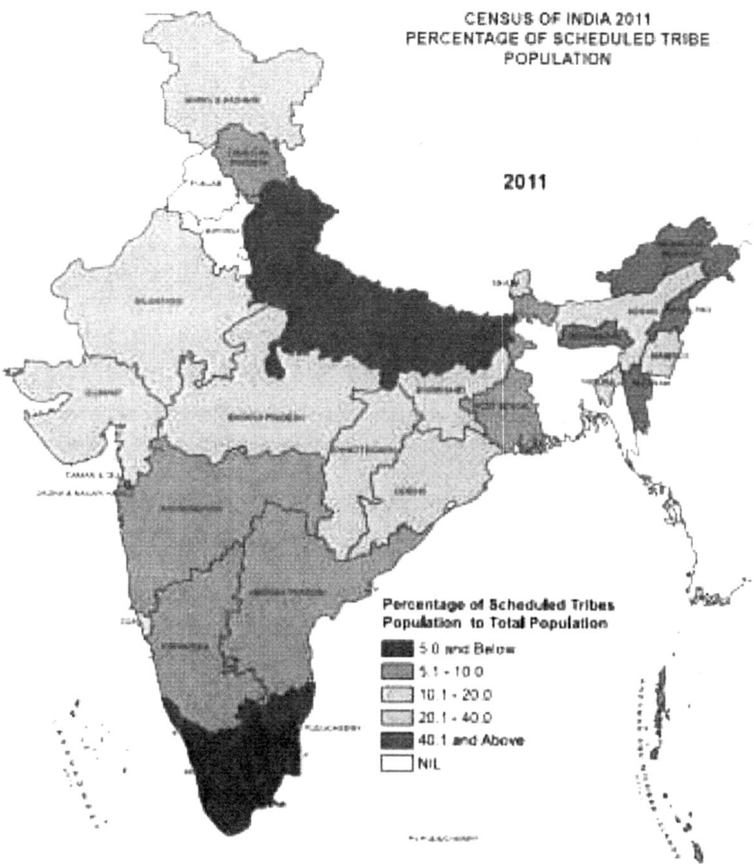

It goes without saying that enabling all children to realize their full creative potential is critical for sustaining India's economic growth and accelerating human development. Not all children have benefited equitably from the remarkable progress and transformation that the country has witnessed in recent years. Tens of millions still face basic challenges of survival and healthy development. Children are first and foremost individuals, born with indivisible and inalienable human rights. They also belong to families and communities that need to have access to resources and services, as well as capacities to ensure realization of their rights. Continued neglect of material, human and psycho-social dimensions of child well-being can prevent children from living a full life and from making informed decisions later on in their life. India too would miss out on the dividends that can accrue from a full expansion of children's capabilities (Xaxa, 2011).

Such a state of development in tribal society is a combination of various factors that have a bearing on the well-being of tribal/*adivasi* children. Malnutrition is one malaise afflicting the tribal children. Poverty, low literacy, unsafe drinking water, poor environment, lack of sanitation, lack of basic health services as well as traditional beliefs and customs add to malnutrition among tribal children. Widespread malnutrition exposes these children to infection and infectious diseases, resulting in high mortality among them.

Tribal people also have scored low on health indicators. Health indices like birth-weight, life-expectancy at birth, infant mortality rate, prevalence of various diseases have been pointers to it. The tribal population is also affected by chronic energy deficiency in school going children, adolescent boys and girls and women of reproductive age. Around 70-80 per cent of the tribal population seem to suffer from various stages of anaemia – mild, moderate or severe.

The Volume

Though Indian anthropology revolves round tribal study, yet tribal children/youth have not received due attention by social anthropologists. This is a much neglected area of Indian anthropology. "Anthropology of children and childhood" is yet to form a sub-discipline in Indian anthropology. Being a researcher of "tribal studies" and "anthropology of children and childhood", I thought of bringing out this volume on "Tribal Children and their Childhood" as a felicitation volume in honour of Professor Georg Pfeffer.

Some of such issues of tribal children and youth have always been the concern of Georg Pfeffer, in whose honour this volume (and the previous one) has been published. The retired professor of social and cultural anthropology at the Free University Berlin/Germany has been the co-editor of the earlier eight volumes in this series and a long-term student of tribal India, being associated with the subcontinent from his early age onwards.

This felicitation volume has 15 chapters arranged under four sections. Using recent ethnographic fieldwork with children, the contributors to this volume will examine the ways in which concepts of "children" and "childhood" are understood and deployed in different cultural contexts in tribal societies. It will highlight the place of childhood by looking at the social representations of children in different tribal and aboriginal communities.

The volume will also discuss the ethnographic complexities of studying "children" as a structural category. It will argue for the importance of anthropological accounts to situate the study of childhood and children's lives broadly in cultural contexts. The volume will make an attempt to provide an understanding of "tribal children and their childhood" through ethnographic analyses.

The first section of the book titled, "Concept of Childhood and Related Matters," contains four chapters. The first chapter titled "Are Children Individuals?" by **Vinay Kumar Srivastava** is rather an unconventional chapter. It notes ruefully that anthropologists and fieldworkers pursuing other disciplines disregard children as "fully-formed respondents" or worthy of study. Children are viewed as "innocent and ignorant adults", who are at the bottom of the evolutionary ladder. They can at best be observed and appreciated, but not taken seriously in terms of what they think, say or do. Contrarily, Srivastava puts forth the argument that children are highly creative, displaying exemplary autonomy, and this is clearly visible in their plays, interactive sessions, episodes of conflict and friendship. For knowing what they are, it is imperative that we begin forsaking popular beliefs and assumptions about childhood and look at children as "individuals". Srivastava examines the meaning(s) of the term "individual", exploring the utility of this concept in understanding children. Anthropology of children, he argues, needs to develop as a sub-discipline in its own right.

Eva Reichel in her chapter discusses the concepts of childhood and what it means to be a child. These are hotly debated issues within the anthropology of childhood and the interdisciplinary field of childhood studies. Ethnographically, informed research literature on childhood in the 20th century have quite often are centrally based on developmental psychology. However, ethnographic evidence keeps challenging the assumption of a universal progression from childhood as a state of immaturity and incompetence towards adulthood as a state of being mature and more complete. Reichel focuses on Ho ritual life in a village in Odisha. Young children, in this case, boys, contribute to the recreation of the societal whole in constitutive ways, i.e. they are complete as boys and they can perform their ritual duties only as members of that category. In the examples chosen from her recent fieldwork among the Ho, she argues that young children do perform as competent social actors and knowing subjects. Although they are quite young in biophysical terms, they act in quite grown-up ways in socio-cultural terms. In this vein this chapter by Reichel illustrates that the concept of childhood as opposed to that of adulthood is not a universal given, but narrowly culture bound.

The chapter by **Baktygul Tulebaeva** contributes to the current anthropological debates on defining children, their status and role in a society and their childhood. Studies on childhood usually touch the comparative issue of the history of childhood and try to draw a line between a child and an adult. Comparison can be used for methodological purposes to construct an idea of a "child" and "childhood" in general. However, as soon as cross-cultural comparisons are made in defining a child or "judging" childhood of a particular society, misrepresentation emerges. This chapter by Tulebaeva is based on findings of her recent ethnographic fieldwork and reveals what Kyrgyz people themselves think and what values they hold about their children and their proper development. She claims that a child is of great importance to Kyrgyz people and holds positive interpretations of some practices that outside scholars would estimate as having negative effect on children and their development.

The next chapter by **Geetika Ranjan** explores the child rearing practices among the Khasi of Meghalaya, India. Bringing up children involves a gamut of beliefs and practices and these are community/tribe specific. Khasi is a matrilineal tribe. The chapter discusses various child rearing practices prevalent among the Khasi and the beliefs behind those, which range from notions about "protection" to "socialization" of children. The chapter by Ranjan presents "dos and don'ts" attached to the Khasi way of bringing up children. It also discusses the role of lullabies and stories in child upbringing.

The second section of the book titled, "Formal and Informal Processes of Learning" consists of four chapters. The chapter by **Marine Carrin** deals with Santal children as guardians and interpreters of indigenous knowledge. Today, Santal adults deplore that "the knowledge of the ancestors, is not shared like it used to be. In the peer groups among youth, knowledge about animals and plants is negotiated through play. This knowledge which is rooted in the cosmology also depends on children's awareness of the environment and is genderised. In times of scarcity, boys learn about small rodents or birds they want to trap or catch, while girls fish with their mothers. Some boys however become the disciples of a healer and learn about plants and animals which are used in the pharmacopeia. While healers reframe their various elements of knowledge to pass it on their disciples, youth learn by observing their peers. Boys and girls develop different kinds of knowledge and become conscious of environmental degradation while they share a common sensitivity as shown in love songs where they develop a language of intimacy with animals and plants. Youth thus develop a relational view of the forest which helps them to avoid the fetishisation of nature as a commodity".

Lidia Guzy in her chapter discusses about the *Nag Bacca* of Bora Sambar region. In this region especially during the month of *Phalguna* (March) *Nag Baccha* rituals take place. *Nag Baccha* literally means the "snake children". It is a local trance and possession cult combining the veneration of the snake god *Nag* — a local deity identified with the Pan-Indian Hindu god Shiva — with male peer group and initiation rituals, indigenous theatre, martial arts performance, music and healing traditions. It is mostly performed by young people from ethnic backgrounds such as Binjhal, Gond, Mali and Telli. A *Nag Baccha* group consists of around 25 to 30 young people, mostly unmarried, often of a comparatively fragile and feminine physical appearance. They join the group on their own and having undergone an initiation, are considered as "snake children". The group is led by an older guru, an experienced master to maintain discipline among *Nag Baccha*. The group members may belong to different communities from one village or from several neighbouring villages. The *Nag Baccha* group is invited by people from other villages to perform healing ceremonies or bring the blessings of Shiva.

Christine Finnan in the next chapter deals with tribal children within the fold of formal education in India. Universal, compulsory education has been clearly linked to individual and societal advancement in a global economy. However, persistent educational and economic inequities, especially for poor indigenous and minority populations, cannot be glossed over. Explanations for these inequities lie in research that turns the focus from the macro to the micro, from the global to the local. This chapter builds on anthropological literature that focuses on the intersection of indigenous and minority cultures and formal schools. It brings anthropological insights into how children learn outside of formal schools, the interplay between the institution of the school and communities, social and cultural traditions, and the potential mismatch between cultural expectations guiding most schools and those held by minority and indigenous populations. Turning to the specific situation of tribal children in India, she outlines the principle challenges associated with relying on formal schooling to address poverty and inequity among Indian tribal groups. These challenges, she feels, include: identifying appropriate languages of instruction and culturally appropriate curriculum and instruction, training and recruiting qualified teachers sensitive to and respectful of tribal cultures, and providing evidence to tribal families that an investment in education beyond basic literacy is justified. This chapter by Finnan ends with a set of recommendations for improving formal schooling for tribal children in India.

In the next chapter **V. Subramanyam** argues that children are considered as one of the excluded groups in human society. The cultural practice of early child care, process of socialization and education reflects largely on the personality development of a child. Large majority of the tribal communities in India are still economically backward and live relatively in isolation. Children in those communities are treated as economic asset by their parents. This results in their exclusion from school education. This chapter by Subramanyam discusses about socio-economic backgrounds, ecological condition and process of enculturation of the tribal children. It covers aspects such as school age children, their enrollment and drop-out rate, functioning of multi-lingual schools, right to education act 2010 and its effectiveness. It also deals with the exclusion of tribal children from formal education, inclusive education policy and its effectiveness in the study area of Visakha agency of Andhra Pradesh.

The next section of the book, consisiting of four chapters, focusses on "Play and Leisure Time Activities" of the tribal children. The chapter by **Zazie Bowen** presents peer play and child subjectivity in tribally dominated areas of Mayurbhanj, Odisha. Squeezed between their school work and other work, children still prioritize unsupervised play with their peers in the village. The different expressions of their peer play provide a special mode of interaction with spatial and social contexts that has important ramifications for children's subjectivities and represents a domain in which adults are not overwhelmingly in control. Drawing upon ethnographic fieldwork with school aged children in rural villages of Western Mayurbhanj, Bowen examines the unsupervised peer play of Santal and Ho school students and how it shapes their subjectivity.

The study by **S. Simon John** tries to understand play, narrative and gender in the context of children folklore. Folklore — the expressive traditions of human beings — is an important subject matter in social science research. Children are the fundamental element of every society and the socialization or enculturation process begins through the medium of folklore, as soon as a child is born. For children, folklore is primarily an amazing and exciting activity which lets them to express their play, narration, singing, dancing, joking, etc. The characteristics and functions of children's folklore need to be understood in a particular socio-cultural context. This chapter by Simon is an attempt to understand the expressive traditions of children belonging to Pallar, an indigenous agricultural community in Tamil Nadu.

The next chapter by **Quinbala Marak** analyses the games played by Garo children. Children learn many aspects of their own societies through the process of enculturation/socialization, of which games are an integral part. Studies have revealed that the kind of games children play and the way they play them, disclose not only the psychological constructs of children themselves but also the unwritten societal norms. This chapter by Marak discusses the games that children in Garo society play, and how much of a social reality it portrays. The Garos are a tribal people living majorly in the Garo Hills region of Meghalaya, and its adjoining areas, and well-known in anthropological circles since they are one of the very few people who follow matriliny. This chapter while discussing children's games focuses on two important situations – the imitations of elders by children in the form of games and mild rebuke by elders when children play games. Marak tries to see how far these two situations go in upholding the societal genderedness in terms of societal behaviour or upbringing of children. Finally, she tries to analyse whether the matrilineal social structure, that Garos follow, plays any role in such a socialization process, and if so to what extent.

In the next chapter by **Nibedita Nath** argues that the general conception of childhood as a period free from responsibility, conflict and full of fluttery, play, leisure and opportunity is quite unrealistic in the context of tribal children living in slum. It is because they are the children who live amid economic stringency, social insecurity, psychological stresses and tensions, environmental pollutions and cultural fission. Childhood in slum is characterized by hard work, absence of leisure and lack of any opportunity. Countless tribal children in slum settings advance almost directly from infancy into adulthood, and if they ever experience childhood, it is only a fleeting stage. The tribal children living in slum experience worst kind of life even at a very early age during childhood. The childhood of those children can be referred to as "ruined childhood" and the worst ages of their life in contrast to the common designation of childhood as best phase of a man's life filled with play, leisure and recreation. Against this background Nath makes an attempt to take a stock of the leisure time activities of the tribal children in a slum setting. She tries to explore the gender differences in the leisure time activities of boys and girls. She also analyses the impact of poverty on the choice of play and leisure time activities of children.

The last section of the book, consisting of three chapter, deals with life stage, rules of marriage, identity and rights of tribal youth. The chapter by **Kumkum Bhattacharya** looks at the concept of youth as a life stage and how youth is to be examined in the context of the Santal community. Among all the life stages, childhood and adolescence are very important especially the tasks that are to be achieved in order to make a smooth transition to young adulthood. However, it is found that there are cultural differences in the chronological age of the (life) stages as well as the pace at which development and maturation take place – thus, it is problematic to decide on the "correct pace or path". There are communities that are relatively isolated and there are communities that are very much in the plural setting; the isolated communities often live within limited dependencies while smaller communities living in plural situations are expected to adapt and adopt the "standards" of the dominant others. There are also differences in the worldview and state of mind of different communities. The special focus of this chapter is the Santal community of Birbhum, West Bengal. Some of the questions raised by Bhattacharya are: Who are the youth in the context of the Santal community? What are the life tasks that these youth are expected to perform? Is the pace of change from adolescence to young adulthood/youth different from that of other neighbouring communities?

The next chapter by **Roseman and Rubel** deals with Feasts of Merit as systems of exchange and related social structures in the geographic areas of Asia. In an area stretching from northern Myanmar to northeast India, societies had what were called "Feasts of Merit". These feasts of merit were similar to the potlatches of the Northwest Coast of North America. This similarity was pointed out by Kaj Birket-Smith and Frederick Simoons. However, these two analysts did not explore how the two kinds of ceremonies related to the social structures of the societies involved. This chapter by Roseman and Rubel, in contrast, will first explore the relationships of "feasts of merit" as systems of exchange and related social structures in the geographic areas of Asia noted above. They will then examine potlatch exchange and social structure on the Northwest Coast. The chapter will conclude with a comparison of these two ceremonies and types of exchange systems, and their related social structures.

The chapter by **Piet Erasmus** discusses the battle at Mamusa between the Korana of David Massouw and the South African Republic in early December 1885, which led to the disintegration and disappearance of the last established Korana community in South Africa. Sarah Taaibosch (née Watersoek) experienced this war as a girl of about ten years. She was one of the many children wounded or killed during battle. In this contribution an attempt is made to construct an understanding of the war's impact on her and on the other Korana children, drawing from the limited idiosyncratic information available about Sarah. It will be illustrated that because Sarah only made limited use of the opportunity to process her traumatic experiences through narrative construals, this ultimately influenced her ontological comprehension of herself. She, for example, decided that the children would not learn the Korana language! Ora, as she feared they would be stigmatised and prosecuted for having fled after the war. In order to hide her Korana identity, she presented herself to the outside as Griqua or Coloured. However, she has become a role model of Korana perseverance and their will to survive. Unintentionally she became instrumental in the revival of the Korana identity which she once rejected.

REFERENCES

Aries, P. 1962. *Centuries of Childhood.* Trans. Robert Baldick. New York: Knopf.

Behera, D.K., S. Spyrou, A. Luithel-Hardenberg and G. Alex. 2014. "Children and

Youth in a Changing World: Anthropological Perspective," *The Oriental Anthropologist,* 14 (2): i-iv.

Behera, D.K. and M. Trawick. 2007. *Children and Youth in Global Metropoles.* New Delhi. Manak Publication Pvt. Ltd.

Behera, D.K. 2007. "Childhoods in South Asia: An Introduction," in Deepak Kumar Behera (ed.), *Childhoods in South Asia.* New Delhi: Oriental Longman and Pearson Education.

_______. 2005. "Aboriginal Female Children in Kanyashram of Orissa, India: A Critical Assessment of the Process of Educational Institutionalization," *Childhood Education*, 81 (6): 321-326.

_______. 1998. *Children and Childhood in our Contemporary Societies (ed.)*, New Delhi: Kamla-Raj Enterprises, 1998.

_______. 1996. *Contemporary Society: Childhood and Complex Order* (jointly with Georg Pfeffer, Free University of Berlin, Germany) New Delhi: Manak Publication Pvt. Ltd.

Benthall, Jonathan. 1992. "A Late Developer? The Ethnography of Children," *Anthropology Today,* 8 (2): 127-38.

Bird-David, N. 2005. "Studying Children in 'Hunter-Gatherer' Societies: Reflection from a Nayaka Perspective," (pp. 92-102) *In:* B.S. HewLett and M.E. Lamb (eds.), *Hunter-Gatherer Childhoods: Evolutionary, Developmental and Cultural Perspectives.* New Brunswick NJ: Aldine Transaction.

Bluebond-Langner, Myra, and Jill Korbin. 2007. "Challenges and Opportunities in the Anthropology of Childhoods: An Introduction to 'Children, Childhoods, and Childhood Studies," *In Focus: Childhood, and Childhood Studies*, *American Anthropologist,* 109 (2): 241-246.

Corsaro, W.A. 2003. *We're Friends, Right?* Washington, DC: Joseph. Henry Press.

_______. 1997. *The Sociology of Childhood.* Thousand Oaks, CA.: Pine Forge Press.

Dubey, Muchkund. 2010. "The Right of Children to Free and Compulsory Education Act: 2009: The Story of a Missed Opportunity," *Social Change*, 40 (1): 1-13.

Eickelkamp, Ute. 2010. "Children and Youth in Aboriginal Australia: An Overview of the Literature," *Anthropological Forum,* 20 (2): 147-166.

Emond, Ruth. 2005. "Ethnographic Research Methods with Children and Young People," (pp. 123-140) *In*: S. Greene and D. Hogan (eds.), *Researching Children's Experience: Approaches and Methods.* London: Sage.

Firth, Raymond. 1970 [1936]. "Education in Tikopia," (pp. 75-90) *In:* John Middleton (ed.), *From Child to Adult: Studies in the Anthropology of Education.* New York: Natural History Press.

Fortes, Meyer. 1970[1938]. "Social and Psychological Aspects of Education in Taleland," (pp. 14-74) *In:* John. Middleton (ed.), *From Child to Adult: Studies in the Anthropology of education.* New York: Natural History Press.

Friedl, E. 2004. "The Ethnography of Children," *Iranian Studies*, 37, 556-663.

Goodman, M.E. 1970. *The Culture of Childhood: Child's-Eye Views of Society and Culture.* New York: Teachers College Press.

Greene, S. and D. Hogan. 2005. *Researching Children's Experience: Approaches and Methods.* London: Sage.

Grindal, B. 1972. *Growing up in Two Worlds: Education and Transition among Sisala of Northern Ghana.* Orlando: Holt, Rinehart and Winston.

Hirschfeld, Lawrence. 2002. "Why Don't Anthropologists Like Children?" *American Anthropologist,* 104 (2): 611-627.

James, Allison, 2007. "Giving Voice to Children's Voices: Practices and Problems, Pitfalls and Potentials," *American Anthropologist* 109 (2): 261-272. (Special issue edited by Myra Bluebond-Langner and Jill Korbin, *Focus: Children, Childhood, and Childhood Studies*).

James, A. and A. Prout. 1998. *Theorising Childhood.* Cambridge: Polity Press.

_______. 1997. *Constructing and Reconstructing Childhood: Contemporary Issues in the Study of Childhood.* London: Falmer Press.

_______. 1995. "Hierarchy, Boundary and Agency in the Experience of Children: Towards a Theoretical Perspective," *Sociological Studies of Children*, 7: 77-99.

Jenks, Chris. 1996. *Childhood.* Routledge.

_______. 1982. *The Sociology of Childhood: Essential Readings.* London: Batsford Academic and Educational.

La Fontaine, Jean. 1986. "An Anthropological Perspective on Children in Social Worlds," (pp.10-30) *In:* Martin Richards and Paul Light (eds.), *Children of Social Worlds*. Cambridge, UK: Polity.

Lancy, D.F. 2012. Why Anthropology of Childhood? A Brief History of an Emerging Discipline," *AnthropoChildren*, 1 (1): January.

_______. 2010. "Learning from Nobody: The Limited Role of Teaching in Folk Models of Children's Development," *Childhood in the Past,* 3: 79-106.

_______. 2008. *The Anthropology of Childhood: Cherubs, Chattel, and Changelings.* Cambridge: Cambridge.

_______. 2007. "Accounting for Variability in Mother-Child Play," *American Anthropologist,* 109 (2): 273-284.

_______. 1996. *Playing on the Mother Ground: Cultural Routines for Children's Development*. New York: Gulliford Press.

LeVine, Robert. 2007. "Ethnographic Studies of Childhood: A Historical Overview," *American Anthropologist,* 109 (2): 247-260 (Special issue edited by Myra Bluebond-Langner and Jill Korbin, *Focus: Children, Childhood, and Childhood Studies*).

Mayall, Berry. 2002. *Towards a Sociology for Childhood.* Buckingham, UK: Open University Press.

_______. 1994. *Children's Childhood: Observed and Experienced.* London: Falmer Press.

Mead, M. 1930. *Growing Up in New Guinea.* New York: Morrow.

_______. (1928/1961). *Coming of Age in Samoa.* New York: New American Library.

Montgomery, Heather. 2008. "Childhood within Anthropology," (pp. 17-49) *In:* Heather Montgomery (ed.), *An Introduction to Childhood: Anthropological Perspectives on Children's Lives*. Oxford: Wiley-Blackwell.

Opie, I. and P. Opie. 1992[1959]. "The Lore and Language of School Children," (pp.173-180) *In:* Chris Jenks (ed.), *The Sociology of Childhood: Essential Readings*. Hamshire, England: Gregg Revivals.

_______. (1970 [1959]). *The Lore and Language of School Children*. Oxford: Oxford University Press.

Pellegrini, A.D. and P.K. Smith. 2003. "The Development of Play during Childhood:

Forms and Possible Functions," *Child Psychology and Psychiatry Review*, 3(2): 51-57.

Qvortrup, Jens, *et al.*, (eds.) 1994. *Childhood Matters: Social Theory, Practice, and Politics*. Aldershot, UK: Avebury.

Roy, S.C. 2004 (Reprint). *The Mundas and Their Country*. Ranchi: Crown Publications.

Schwartzman, Helen B. 2001. "Children and Anthropology: A Century of Studies," (pp.15-37) *In:* Helen B. Schwartzman (ed.), *Children and Anthropology: Perspectives for the 21st Century*. Westport, CT: Bergin & Garvey.

_______. 1979. *Transformations: Anthropology of Children's Play*. New York: Plenum.

Singh, Asha and Deepa Gupta. 2011. "Contexts of Childhood and Play: Exploring Parental Perceptions," *Childhood*, 19 (2): 235-250.

Skolnick, Arlene. 1976. *Rethinking Childhood.* Little Brown.

Solberg, Anne. 1996. "The Challenge in Child Research: From 'Being' to 'Doing,'" (pp. 53-65) *In:* Julia Brannen and Margaret O'Brien (eds.), *Children in Families.* London: Falmer Press.

Stephens, S. 1995. "Introduction: Children and the Politics of Culture in Late Capitalism," (pp.3-48) *In:* S. Stephens (ed.), *Children and the Politics of Culture.* Princeton: Princeton University Press.

Trawick, M. 2007. *Enemy Lines: Warfare, Childhood, and Play in Batticaloa.* Berkeley: University of California Press.

Toren, C. 1993. "Making History: The Significance of Childhood Cognition for a Comparative Anthropology of Mind," *Man* (N.S.), 28: 461-478.

Waksler, Frances. 1991. *Studying the Social World of Children: Sociological Readings.* Basingstoke: Falmer.

Waterson. R. and D.K. Behera. 2011. "Introduction: Extending Ethnographic Research with Children in the Asia-Pacific Region," *Special Issue of the The Asia Pacific Journal of Anthropology,* 12 (5): 411-425.

Whiting, B. 1977. *Six Culture: Studies of Child Rearing*. New York: Wiley.

Xaxa, Virginius. 2011. *The Status of Tribal Children in India*. IHD-UNICEF Working Paper Series. Children of India: Rights and Opportunities.

SECTION I

CONCEPT OF CHILDHOOD

ONE

ARE CHILDREN INDIVIDUALS?

VINAY KUMAR SRIVASTAVA

> "I believe that God can manifest himself or herself through the purest of creatures and that could be children."
>
> —**Kailash Satyarthi**
>
> (*The Hindustan Times*, Lucknow Edition, 2 November, 2014)

Are children individuals? I started mulling over it against the backdrop of the discipline of anthropology, or a comparative study of different social formations. I believe that an anthropologist is always "fieldworking", in the sense that fieldwork is not only an activity that is conducted lengthily and uninterruptedly in a far-flung territory, with the "other", or near home, with the 'self', for a certain number of months or years. It is also an activity that anthropologists (or "anthropologically-oriented researchers") involuntarily carry out everywhere; wherever they are, in whatever state they are, they are always observing, even when they may not like to observe or eavesdrop; observation, which may be pithily described as "conscious sensing", becomes their primary and involuntary nature.[1] They observe – as participant observers – the children they raise, and as non-participant, the children of their relatives, neighbours, and friends, and children in the streets, playing, or at the traffic red-lights, selling magazines, books, food and water bottles, cleaning cars, playing acrobatics, or begging alms.[2]

Their anthropology progresses as a comparative venture; their insights come from comparisons between various forms of "us" and "them". Their anthropology is, in the words of Madan (1982), a "mutual interpretation" of different cultures, practices, and the ways of thought and life. The "other" teaches them about themselves and they also acquire the practice and skill of making their own ways of living "defamiliar", keeping them at distance, and then studying these with as much of dispassion and detachment as is possible.[3] Lévi-Strauss (2013: 30) writes: "To know and understand one's own culture, it is necessary to regard it from the point of view of another."

Speaking to Children

I conducted during an intensive fieldwork with the Raika (also known as Rabari) of Rajasthan, a community of traditional camel-breeders and graziers, a study on the customs and practices of child marriage among them (Srivastava, 2007).[4] Besides the usual anthropological interests, I was particularly interested in speaking to their children, especially those who were married, or were getting married, about what marriage meant to them: What was their conception of responsibilities that would follow marriage? Did they ever accommodate in their thoughts the possibility of falling in love with someone else from their own or some other community? Or, does the concept of "romantic love" exist in their culture? Are they able to distinguish the sentiments of "love" from other psychic states? What did they think of the impact of the encroaching media (television, particularly) on their lives and thoughts? Do they ever think about themselves or do they only think about their community? Besides these questions was the anthropological point: not all communities have the same understanding of love and marriage, although these institutions may bear apparent similarities.

Talking to children – and they were mostly male – was an enriching experience for me.[5] These boys dwelt in two worlds. The first was the "world of reality" that their kinspersons had constructed for them. This world was seemingly immutable. Any defiance of its rules and conventions was catastrophic for them, their families, and their caste community. Not only going against but even contemplating against the wishes of the elders was sacrilegious, invoking punitive sanctions. A family may be ostracized or excommunicated for any action that may be deemed and interpreted as against the norms of the community. To be left on one's own – to bear the stigma of excommunication – was the worst punishment, feared the most. It amounted to being thrown in solitary confinement.

Here, I am reminded of a piece of conversation I had with a man of the dominant caste of the village where I was engaged in data collection. I asked him, rather relaxingly and casually, about the social consequences if his daughter, by the way, happened to marry outside her caste. There was nothing unceremonious about this question, for fieldworkers usually ask hypothetical questions to gauge people's choices and options. The man, who otherwise was gentle and soft-spoken, briskly lost his temper. In a reprimanding tone, he questioned me as to how I could ever imagine (or hypothesize) the possibility that his daughter would ever consider marrying outside her community, thus bringing ignominy to its credit. "How could you think of that?" "How did this vile thought come to your mind?" These were the questions that he asked me whenever and wherever he saw me, even after a lapse of time. He perhaps found it hard to pardon me for I had thought of his daughter as an "individual" rather than someone whose identity was no different from the identity of her collectivity, here in this context the caste to which she belonged by virtue of her birth. Traditional communities want men and women completely assimilated in their respective castes.

If this was the world where the normative order reigned, the other world was of fantasy, imagination, romance, freedom from the shackles of rules and conventions, something unrealizable, something non-materializable in reality. Nevertheless, it was great, mentally and aesthetically satisfying to be a part of that world. From these experiences emerged the strings of poems and songs, the artifacts of creativity, most of which were divinely, or godly, directed or had the mysteries or enigmas of nature as a primary theme. Love poetry was spiritual; it was nothing sort of being blasphemous when one composed verses for human males or females. It is likely that one may have in mind a "particular human female (or male)", one with whom one may be in love, while composing a poem, but its words and symbolism would have the unmistakable divine character. Human lovers melted in divinity. Such disappearances were socially and morally acceptable.

Liveliness of Children

I spoke to a large number of male children. Whilst a number of adults were repetitive, uninteresting, conventional, and uninspiring, for they said what their "community" directed them to say, the children were lively, forthcoming, brimming with energy. They were good respondents; they wanted to talk; and who would lose the opportunity of not listening to them? What related these children was the fact that someone was listening to them, with undivided attention, and was eager to note down what they said in his little field notebook that he always carried with him. In other words, the children derived great satisfaction and a sense of fulfilment from the fact that since someone (who was an outsider, educated and sophisticated) was jotting down in the notebook what they were saying meant that what they were saying (and also doing) was not unimportant, as was the feeling they unvaryingly received from their elders, who paid measly attention to their ideas and thought, and who did not want to listen to them.[6]

Most of the children I spoke to were from middle and late childhoods. They were reasonably matured. Some of them were close to bringing their wives home, a custom locally known as *ânâ* or *gaunâ* ("send-off ceremony"). The world of imagination was fathomless, unshackled; however, the real world was bereft of options, following a particular designated pattern, with no deviations. The world of imagination was expanding, being incessantly fed by media, particularly the television, on which these boys feasted their eyes, and also through interactions with migrant boys, working in Indian cities and towns, who returned home temporarily, and narrated the stories, sometimes sensuous, juicy, and exaggerated, of their lives in the "glittering urban areas", free and unconstrained. The "visiting boys" spoke like "individuals"; they were the rallying points; they were the respondents of the local boys, who quizzed them about everything, from employment avenues to women, from possibilities of making money to spending, from good clothes to soaps and shampoos, from transport to high-rise buildings. The world the adults created for them was different from the world they were creating for them. They unhesitatingly disclosed their worlds, the contradictions of these worlds, to someone who empathetically wanted to learn about them, rather than the one who gave them toffees and chocolates, to woo them so that they could lead them to their parents for the mundane activity of data collection. It is well known that fieldworkers buy lots of gifts for children, since they consider it as one of the initial steps in establishing rapport; it would also spread the message of being a Samaritan, which they want the most. The anthropologists eye on adults, the fully-formed respondents; the children are just a conduit.[7]

The World at Home

By comparison to the world of the Raika is the world at home – my own world. In a group interview I conducted with a set of my relatives on whether the children have an individuality of their own, the answer of one of my participants deserves mention. She said that her children were highly individualistic, whilst the adults were the clones of one another; the children did not conceal their likes and dislikes; they put across all that "without mincing a word", totally unmindful of whether their parents welcome it or not, whether it would sadden their parents or make them helpless. During this lengthy interview, one of the respondents, a female, said that if the name of her child was not mentioned on the invitation card for wedding (or any other ceremonial function), he would refuse to go. "When my name is not on the card, why should I go?" It was the usual (and expected) reply. Not only that, the parents would also be unwilling to take the child along with them if his name had not been mentioned on the invitation card, for they might be uncertain if the hosts had actually extended invitation to the child or not. It is thus not only the children who assert their individuality but also their parents who want them to become individuals and be recognized so by the others.

Against this backdrop, just to write on the invitation card the name of the head of the household "and family" is not enough. The inviters are expected to know the names of the children of the invitees. Modern urban middle class family is nuclear and child centred; everything revolves around them, the children, their education, their career; the parents adjust their schedules according to their children's; the parents will not play television if the child is studying; they will take leave from work when the child has his examinations; the parents are a bundle of worries when the school performance of the child is poor; child's health, child's interests, child's friends, child's TV programmes and games, have priority over every other thing.[8] I know a household in South Delhi where the old grandparents were shifted out of their bedroom, to sleep in a corner in the drawing room, and throughout the day move from one corner of the house to the other, depending upon the guests who had to be entertained in the drawing room, because their bedroom was converted into a "study room" for their grandchildren, who were preparing for their respective competitive examinations. This was interpreted as an altruistic act on the part of elders, receiving encomium from all, although the truth was that they were forced out of their space they had been occupying for years. The members of the family and the neighbourhood seemed to believe that the "children were the future", for whom the elders must be ever prepared to make sacrifice and accommodate them, notwithstanding hardships, to the needs and requirements of children.

Children, fewer in number, are regarded as assets, and their success in life is in fact the upward mobility of the entire family. Look at the sheen on the faces of parents when they say "my daughter is in the Indian Administrative Service", "my son is in Australia", or "my daughter is reading medicine"; it is not only the parents but in a context where the values of the extended family are still alive, the relatives in general take pride in the achievements of their members as if these are in fact theirs.

Individualization of Children

Children in my society have started asserting themselves. They are no more "so-and-so's sons, or so-and-so's daughters", as was the case in rural Rajasthan, where even grown-up boys and girls were known by the names of their fathers or grandfathers. As I noted earlier, the individualization of children was beginning in rural Rajasthan, as was the case with urban middle-class households, especially with those boys who had then moved out of their villages for work or study.

A case I studied will throw light on it. A boy from one of the villages was admitted to a medical college in Jaipur. As is common, he got married in early childhood, but had yet to bring his wife home. Since he was doing well in his school, his kinsfolk delayed the ceremony, which was further deferred for he had joined the medical college, an engagement that would preoccupy him for the next five years. After he completed his study at Jaipur, he came to Delhi in search of a job and found one in a local hospital for a paltry sum of rupees ten thousand per month. All through these years of his education and getting a job in Delhi, the girl's parents continued to intensify pressure on him and his family for an early "send-off ceremony", for it was getting inordinately delayed, but his family, though equally interested in it, being badgered by their boy, kept on postponing it under the pretext of his busy study schedule.

After reaching Delhi, the newly-trained medical doctor started exploring the possibility of studying in the United States for a higher degree in paediatrics. He was successful in his efforts; but just before he was leaving the country, he informed his kin in Rajasthan to cancel his marital tie, "free the girl" (*ladkî ko chuttî karnâ*) and "pay the fine" (*jurmânâ denâ*), whatever it would be, so that he could be liberated from the "fetters of matrimony" and studied peacefully. Sending home his savings, for meeting the settlement amount and the other household expenses, he left the country. Although he had anticipated the painfulness through which his family would go, and indeed it did, with heaps of humiliation, he found it impossible to reconcile his individuality, his differentness from the others of his community, with the demands of his traditional social structure. When this was happening, the elders back home were scathingly critical of modern education, which was making their children infringe upon the social norms unabashedly. They thought that their children otherwise were not disobedient. What they did not concede was the fact that even when their children appeared to be exemplarily obedient and accepted the customs and practices of their respective caste communities, without an iota of dissent, they had within them the streaks of individuality, which thickly precipitated during their play, peer group interactions, and if an opportunity came, it followed the way it did in the case described above.

Perhaps, we may say, the child's life was a biography of the incessant conflict between individualism and collectivism, in which eventually the latter conquered. It was the former that made the difference between children, determining their respective interests and commitment to these in their later lives.

Louis Dumont on the Individual: The Self Studies the Other to Know the Self, the Method of Comparative Sociology

The meaning of the term 'individual' needs to be understood here. For this, I shall lean on Dumont's work (1970, 1992). Dumont's sociology was comparative; he used the Indian case, which he also studied empirically, having carried out his fieldwork in both south and north India, the case of holism and hierarchy to understand the west, the context from which he came, which was an example of individualism and equality.

In his work (1970: 43), he attributes two meanings to the term "individual": the first is empirical – the individual as a unit of society. Each society is first of all defined as a congregation of individuals; in that sense each one of us, whether an elder, an adult, or a child, is an individual, for each one of us is a unit of society. It is generally the meaning that the sociologists adopt – the individual is an empirical agent, the subject of speech, thought, will, and action.[9]

Dumont's (1970: 43) other meaning of the individual is of a "rational being" and of a "normative subject" of institutions. Here, the individual is autonomous, essentially "un-social", moral being, found principally in the domain of modern ideology. When we call the individual "un-social", and not "a-social" or "non-social", it does not mean that he is anarchic, deviant, non-conformist, problem-monger, or the antithesis of an ordered living, which is the primal characteristic of society. As a result of the vast changes occurring in society, which Dumont has analyzed in his publication (1992) following *Homo Hierarchicus*, the individual has acquired the capability to think and act independently, without being a slave to the social thinking, which may be vastly prevalent, and put forth in his deeds and sayings a point of view different from what is socially in vogue. In this way, the individual creates a multiplicity of thoughts.[10] Bygone are the days when an individual putting forward a perspective in contradistinction to what is in currency was subjected to ostracism and reprimand.

Dumont (1970: 36) further thought that while hierarchy, as in India, or any other traditional society, is natural, equality, as in West, is a recent and peculiar phenomenon. Hierarchy, as defined, is a relation between the larger and the smaller, in Dumont's words, between that which "encompasses" and that which is "encompassed". The West has two cardinal principles – equality and liberty; the principle these assume is of the "idea of the human individual". For Dumont, humanity is made up of men (or human beings); and each man is conceived of as presenting, in spite of and over and above his particularity, the essence of humanness. The point is that each individual, even when separated from the whole, is a complete moral being. This is the opposite of hierarchy, where the part has meaning in relation to the whole. In a system of equality, the individual stands away from the whole, which is nothing more than a set of rules, prescriptions and procedures that takes care of all, as an embodiment of his own characteristics, identity, and attributes. Dumont (1970: 280) thought that India, essentially a caste society, did not have "individuals", in the sense of autonomous, rational, and normative beings; and it was only by renouncing the world (which is a caste society) that a caste became the "individual". If caste *collectivizes* the individual (in the empirical sense), renunciation *individualizes* the individual.

Against the backdrop of this rather comprehensive account of Dumont's thesis, I have in mind the following questions: When Dumont says that the West has the "individual", does he apply the characteristics of the "individual" to all "individuals" (in the empirical sense), the children, the adolescents, the adults, the elders? Can one think of a qualitative scale of some being more individualistic than the others? And, is the individual absent in traditional cultures? Anthropologists working on India have refuted Dumont's idea regarding the absence of the individual in caste society. His idea may operate at the theoretical level, at the empirical, the studies point out the presence of individual thinkers, initiators, and the harbingers of change in traditional society. Notwithstanding these, Dumont's idea of encompassing – one that encompasses and one that is encompassed – may be of relevance here.

The Encompassers and the Encompassed

A return to the Rajasthan society, traditional and hierarchical, to which I alluded earlier, pointed out the encompassing of the children's world, the decisions about their lives, by the adults, the encompassers. The latter decided what was good for them and how they should handle the predicaments of their lives. What would they do for their living, whom would they marry, when would they start cohabiting, where would they set-up their household – all these questions about the course of their lives were decided by their elders. It was unthinkable for them that their children would ever deviate from the time-tested path their ancestors had so fastidiously built. The children's voice was their voice; or rather, their voice was that of their children's.

The structures of hierarchy and dominance, coupled with oppression, the existence of which the insiders always denied, had quietened, almost lip-sealed, children. Whenever an enthused child, in the midst of a conversation with the adults, which took place quite infrequently, as most children did not speak to their fathers or the other patriclan men, made a point, slightly different from what they were saying, he was instantly reprimanded, silenced, in words like: "You are a child; your job is to play; it is not right that you speak before the elders; you are expected to listen to what they say; you are expected to carry out their commands."

Against this backdrop, whatever the child had to say, where he exhibited his creativeness, the originality of his ideas, was all done in his peer group. In this group, the individuality of each child precipitated, however, there existed a scale of power differentiation – the older children "bossing" over the younger – but this "bossing" over was phenomenally different from the display of hierarchical values in the adult society; if the latter was "caste society", the "children's society" was "caste-liberated". Children were "just children"; they made no social distinction among them, the only distinction among them was in physical terms (bigger-smaller, taller-shorter), and this was age-related. Although the older children, it was said previously, tried to "exercise their superiority" over their younger members, collegians, so to say, but the latter were not silenced. They protested to any domination/bossism by crying, displaying non-cooperation by retreating, openly announcing their enmity to the others, or vowing not to speak to the others; and soon the older children tried to make peace by relenting from their earlier stand. Protest, hostility, acrimony, not-speaking-to-the-others, lasted ephemerally. Soon they were one, the same friends, with the same sentiments and attachment to one another and to the group, as if nothing had happened in the past. Children experienced all moods, they gathered experiences of all emotions, and were prepared for every eventuality. Children epitomized dialectics of the convivial living, fight and cordiality, "peer groupism" and its dissolution into one, but there was no hatred, envy, jealousy, connivance, deviousness, or any streak that might remind one of the evil.

The model to understand the interpersonal relations among children whom I observed was of participation. The children participated with a feeling of togetherness; they spoke their hearts out; older children listened to their younger counterparts, corrected them as and when they erred, incorporated their points and observations in their collectively-held bank of knowledge; in other words, their peer group – of children of different ages but sharing a feeling of oneness – created its own "culture", and transmitted it within. They did not want to share any modicum of their culture with the adults of their society and their embarrassment was limitless when their parents and the other adults came to know what they were doing, what they were talking, for it was always thought that their "work", their activities, would always be a matter of jest, arousing good laughter. That is why, it has earned the title of the "children's play", not to be taken seriously, but rather jokingly. In fact, in one of the Hindi periodicals (called *Sarita*), a column bore the rubric of *bacchon ke mukh se* ("From Children's Mouth"), to which the readers sent the funny and witty comments their children had made, and most of which were treated as a matter of jocularity. However, some of them were quite profound and deserved mention.

Demythologization and Deglorification of Children: They are Human

This discussion should not lead to the conclusion that I am trying to "mythologize" or "glorify" children, in the sense that they are noble beings, they do not tell lies, or they are uncorrupted, the best souls, in the idiom of *bacche man ke sacche* ("children are truthful at heart"). As said earlier, they also fought, often physically, among them, schemed against their peers and formed factional units, expressed their rights over certain objects (toys, for example), stopped talking for a while, and then became friendly, formed one solid group; they also improvised games and plays. In other words, never was there a moment of tedium, or even rest, when they were together, for they were a creative lot; they were creating their folklore (songs, stories, puzzles, plays and dramas) without ever claiming authorship; they were collectively creating, collectively learning, collectively transmitting, all in a participatory mode.

The same chirpy, creative lot was a prototype of muteness, in the presence of adult men. The mothers (and the other female members) often mediated between them and their fathers and grandfathers (and the others male members of the patriclan and in putative kinship).

The large, powerful, adult world encompassed the tiny children's world. They had to behave as the adults wanted; the adults took all decisions about them. The children were supposed to accept all this, and comply, without winces on their faces. If the adults wanted a boy to drop-out of school and tend cattle, he did, albeit his performance in studies. He might be the topper in his class, but this achievement would fall deaf on ears of the tradition, which was, in words of Weber (1978), "eternal yesterday", inimical to change.[11]

Children did not have an "individuality" of their own when they interacted with adults in the "actual social world"; "child's world", being a matter of play, joke, and fantasy, was regarded as ephemeral. "Grow up" was the *mantra* for children. Transcending "children's world" was considered as the immediate aim of their life; the process of becoming "unchildren" was to be seriously attended. The "individualness" they exhibited in their peer groups, the play groups, was to be buried there and then, to be taken up in the next generation by their posterity. Once, in an adult role, they were encompassers, those who upheld the social order. Today's puppets were tomorrow's puppeteers. The idea of the "puppetized child" may be illustrated with the example of the interaction I described earlier when I asked a local man about the reaction of his family if his daughter wanted to marry a man from some other caste. Not only that he chastised me for asking such a question, or harbouring such a possibility, but, as I learned later, he told one of his kinspersons that I was introducing his children, whom I also coached if they were schoolgoing, to nefarious ideas, one of these being thinking of marrying outside one's community, and that I should be sternly warned, with terrible consequences if I did not mend my ways.

Children are not in the Minds of Ethnographers and Sociologists

The point I wish to put forth is the structural opposition of the children's world, where the individuality of each child precipitated, and the adult world, which was its antithesis. Perhaps when Dumont said that the individual was non-existent in India, he did not have in mind the children, whose autonomy and rationality were the cornerstones of their peer groups. Although each child has his biography, perpetually affected by external factors, including the global, of war and hunger, of prosperity and displacement, they all share a common stage – a common social space of childhood, where they can be their own, the individual, the original and creative lot, and the builders of their culture. And, this individual in them is eternal; it hibernates for the time, which may be one's entire life, or it may be for the time being, and can make its appearance, if the other conditions are favourable, as happened with the Raika physician. Once he became an "individual", he unhesitatingly severed his ties with his family, for it wanted him to be a conformist, which was contrary to the station of life he then occupied. His wife – not then "sent off" – was a helpless victim of the conflict between the individualism of her consort and the stringency of her community. The futuristic Raika were confident about the multiplication of these cases in times to roll; some local men also said that the educated men, employed in cities, might become bigamous, looking for the other "party-going" spouse. It was better, they thought, that the girl became "free" to remarry rather than leading a pitiable and stigmatized life of a co-spouse.

The ideology the traditional Indian culture espouses is that the child is "unformed", "raw", but is malleable, like the flour that has to be kneaded and kneaded with water to yield bread of good quality; the more it is kneaded, the better it would be. Against this background is justified the use of *danda* (staff, punishment) and the *shikshâprada kahâniyân* (moral-tending stories). India has a fabulously rich tradition of folk tales, *Panchtantra* being one of them, the objective of which is to work towards the moral maturation of children. All societies are ethnocentric – the adults in traditional societies regard their ways of raising children as the best, time-tried; so an episode of running astray is dealt with repressively, an extreme form of which has come to be called "honour-killing". The traditional councils have strengthened them on the ideology that also purports to give them an identity of their own. Privately, the youth may controvert the decisions that these councils take, but knowing full well the grievous consequences of any kind of public rebuttal, they have no option but to surrender; their lips remain sealed.

The Structure of Power, Mutedness of Children, and Anthropology

The structures of power in these societies create mutedness among children, as they do among women, disabled, and the deviant and fringe communities. Mutedness is embodied. The anthropologists generally looking for vocal respondents – those who act and also talk – tend to ignore the "silent and reticent" people;[12] and they also become victims – often unknowingly – of the kind of knowledge that the local power structure generates, such as "children know nothing", "they are simpleton", or "women are less informed".

In other words, even when they do not want, anthropologists perpetuate the local, partisan perspectives on knowledge, one of which is that the adults know, so they should be approached, but since rapport-building with them may be a difficult or slow process, why not befriend those who could easily be befriended, the children. Anthropologists like children, perhaps not as respondents, but as instruments, as said earlier, to reach the adults. On the contrary, if one spends a substantial time of his fieldwork with children and learns the local language in their company, he would not only know what they do but this experience will also provide him with several useful leads that may be followed in his fieldwork.

The Contours of the Anthropology of Children and Childhood

As has been detailed out in several studies that although anthropological data on children from different societies are fragmentary and of differential quality, undoubtedly, in the second half of the twentieth century, anthropology of children has continued to grow and diversify (LeVine, 2007). Children have prominently figured in the other collateral studies, like household and family, women and mothering, rites of passage, socialization and education, and violence, where anthropologists have concerned them with the issues of atrocities on children, whether as prostitutes, in pornographic literature, camel-jockeys, their sale and labour, their use as aggressors and soldiers (Rosen, 2007).

The issue of how culture is learnt and how children create their own culture has drawn at one platform specialists from different disciplines, particularly from psychology and education, working with anthropologists or anthropological approaches. The "mainstream" anthropology increasingly feels the need to be inclusive, multivocal, and emic, bringing together diverse views and practices, for it knows that the processes of vast social and cultural changes and those that make cultures resilient go hand in hand, and so does their study. As we have now incorporated gender studies or ethnic studies in our curricula for graduate and post-graduate studies, in the same manner, the studies of children should be a part of our courses. The idea is to have anthropology of childhood integrated with other anthropologies.

This would require us, as the United Nations Convention on the Rights of the Child (1989) says, "to listen to children."[13] This notion has been emphasized in various phrases such as "children's perspective", "children's point of view", or "hearing children's voices"; the submission here is of "representing children" in one's study and juxtaposing this understanding with the other multiple, sometimes contesting, views. Allison James and Adrian James (2004) have discussed the conceptual and epistemological problems that come when we deal with the matter of "giving voice to children", since it is believed that either they do not speak or are unheard; in each case, they necessitate an external help.[14] Here the questions of representation, editorial and selective usage, authenticity, diversity of children's experiences need to be discussed threadbare. On reading an ethnographic account, the first question that comes in our mind is whether, to borrow words from Geertz (1983), it is the "describer's description" or that of the "described". The described are further not a singular, homogeneous category; the "particularity of childhood experiences" goes alongside the "universality of childhood as a social stage." This initiates another question, asked at different times by Giddens (1976) and Obeyesekere (1990), whether there is a "native point of view", or are there *several*?

Listening to Children, Mainstreaming Children, Looking for an Anthropology of All Beings

The agenda of "listening to children" is welcomed, with the result that in academic as well as in the world of policy development and activism, we come across "children's voices", recorded, described, and written up by experts, the adults, who employ these to draw home a particular point or conclusion. However, these voices may be suppressed if it is felt that they are running contrary to the interests of the organizations that the recorders of these voices represent. That children are highly vulnerable to all types of forces is central to all their studies. Any suppression of children's voices to serve the interests of a particular establishment is unethical and unjust, to say the least.

It is also possible that in order to be heard, the children may use the idioms, language, vocabulary, and demeanour that the adults use, so that they sound meaningful and relevant. This will also bring the question of "what kind of listening are we indulging?" Listening to children is recognition of their individuality, but do they tell us what they really feel, think, and believe, or are they like the adult respondents, hued by the indexes of social desirability and political correctness?

The panacea to this lies, perhaps, in what may be termed "anthropological listening", which is ineluctable to a lengthy ethnographic fieldwork. It transcends the reactivity syndrome on part of the respondents and the ethnographer is able to observe and listen to them in a state of nascence, as if for people he is not there. Ethnographic accounts produced thus are valuable both for knowing the diversity and for theorization. Keeping this in mind, many writers have discussed the methods to be employed in childhood studies and the technological gadgets to be used for data collection (James, 2007).

In this context, it has been argued that if children are used as researchers and co-researchers, then the children's voices will be better represented. Or, as Roberts (2000) says that in some quarters, the participation of children in research is seen as "*sine qua non* of a pro-child stance." In fact, a reviewer of Hirshfeld's paper (2002: 624) suggests that one of the reasons why serious interest in children has not emerged could be because there are no "children anthropologists", those who could take up the studies of their kind, and those who could agitate on their behalf.

Arguments have been marshalled on both sides—using children as part of a research team is a pro-child gesture, or it is a sort of exploitation, forcing them to deviate from the work they are engaged in or are expected to pursue, for example, schooling. One of the principal criticisms of the television programmes in which children are engaged is that they disrupt their study schedule; some of them are constrained to dropout from schools to participate in reality shows, and they want to do so because of the glitter of the media world. Financial gains that follow constitute another incentive. After the television show culminates, the children return home and find difficulties returning to the normal schedule, the one they observed before they were selected to participate in a show.

During my fieldwork, I desisted from engaging children as "research assistants", for I did not want them to deflect from the work they were doing or were supposed to do. If time at their end permitted, I expected them to be my respondents, and if they could read and write, I requested them to write a short essay on their community, which they did gleefully. I told them that in addition to rendering me this information, it would also make them reflective about their culture and greatly assist them in improving their writing and linguistic skills. I think there cannot be "children anthropologists", although the possibility of "children field assistants" may exist. By the time the children successfully learn the craft of anthropology, they are no more children. They become adults. Anthropology is not data collection; it is a reflective discipline requiring substantial theoretical and comparative ethnographic understanding. Against this backdrop, some Indian anthropologists think that this subject should not be taught at the level of under-graduation, but limited to master's degree programme and research. Although this view is contested, there is some merit in the argument that a proper understanding of anthropology needs a particular level of maturity.

Autobiographical Approach

Besides the ethnographies on children, another type of writing, an autoethnographic account of one's childhood, a sort of which may be called "autopaediography", is also coming into vogue. Of course, the fictionalized accounts of one's childhood and upbringing have multiplied manifold after the grand success of Arundhati Roy's 1997 Booker Prize-winning novel titled *The God of Small Things*. In 2010 was published an edited volume of twelve essays bearing the title *Remembered Childhood*, in honour of Professor André Béteille. Written by eminent scholars, anthropologists and litterateurs, each essay has a close look at one's childhood. Each essay is an intellectual and academic account – an adult scanning his or her childhood with introspective (and anthropological) lenses, and surely they will be different from those where a child looks at his childhood. However, it is heartening to note that these essays sumptuously tell us about the childhood as it was experienced in the twentieth century. Interestingly, the editors of this volume invited papers from a large number of scholars, but some declined the offer since they thought that their childhood was neither exceptional nor extraordinary. By juxtaposition, anthropologists look for ordinary lives, typical people, from all strata, demythologizing the tenaciously held beliefs. That was the reason why they succeeded in producing fine, empathetic accounts of the lives of Pedro Martinez, Nisa, Tuhami, or Muli.[15] We look forward to reading a life-history account of the same stature on a child, where the entire data come from the subject of the ethnography. In today's anthropology, individual children rarely figure; if at all they do, they are in the form of cases of feral men and wolf children, the veracity of which has been challenged (Ashley-Montagu, 1960).

Individualism is considered as an historically developed process. From Durkheim to Dumont, anthropologists and sociologists have been concerned with it. The main argument in their writings has been that individualism is a characteristic of the modern west, which traditional societies lacked. Had these scholars centred on the study of children and their groups, they could have come face-to-face with their "participatory individualism", by which it is meant that each child is an individual and participates in a group to create a culture of their own. There is a strong probability that our concepts and theories will be revisited when the studies of children and childhood are 'mainstreamed' in anthropology.

Acknowledgements

This paper was presented on 29 November 2012 in the Inter-Congress of the International Union of the Anthropological and Ethnological Sciences titled "Children and Youth in a Changing World" that took place in Bhubaneswar, Odisha. I am grateful to Professor Deepak K. Behera for extending me invitation to participate in the conference. This chapter is a revised version of what was presented in the conference.

NOTES

1. The idea here is that fieldwork is training in observation, which is a key technique to science. Anthropologists are trained to observe. For them, nothing is frivolous, trivial, or unimportant. Subscribing to the idea of the purposefulness and goal-orientation of human behaviour, anthropologists are committed to discovering its meaning in different cultures.
2. We have on record the concept of "primary group" having come into existence from the observations that C.S. Cooley conducted on his children. He regarded his domestic unit as a kind of "laboratory" (Cooley, 1909).
3. Madan (1988: 138) writes: "...our study of 'other' cultures should no longer be a 'distant' enterprise of describing how these 'others' live: it should also illumine

our own way of life." At another place, Madan (1995: 126) says: "Fieldwork...may well be described as the act, or feat, of *living intimately with strangers*...The anthropologist is an outsider trying to become enough of an insider to understand what the insiders do and how they make sense of it."

4. A shorter version of this article was published in a report titled "Child Marriage in India, A Workshop Report, 2007", released by the National Institute of Public Cooperation and Child Development (NIPCCD), New Delhi, in 2007.
5. The Raika, like the other communities in Rajasthan, were sexually segregated. It was impossible for a young male fieldworker to speak to their women and collect data from them. It has been the experience of other fieldworkers as well. Madan (1995: 120), for instance, writes: "I never was able to meet with all the women but only young girls and relatively old women." The Raika men believed – rather confidently – that they knew about the activities and duties of women, and, if one wanted to know, they would be most pleased to share their knowledge of women's works with them; and so there would not be any need for a male researcher to speak to women. Male field workers, spending long time with people, however could establish ties with older women, particularly widows, and in some cases, as happened with me, they could enter into putative kinship relations with local women, accepting one of them as sister, and this would definitely provide an opportunity to have a first-hand understanding of women's lives. See Srivastava (1997: 231-4).
6. I found in my fieldwork that while adults were hesitant to speak to me in the initial days of our relationship, or were unwilling to share many stories of their lives or about the others, or, in other field studies that I have carried out in other parts of the country, they expected monetary favours for parting with information, the children were always willing to share with me whatever they knew. Their happiness was boundless whenever I approached their groups and started conversing with them. Oftentimes, they treated me as if I was one of them. Their collegiality touched me thoughtfully. This might have been the experiences of the other researchers. I read the following in an article on the civil war in Syria (in *The Times of India*, 2 August, 2014) by Lyse Doucet: "I began to realize that, on every visit to cover Syria'a punishing war, it was the children who told the most compelling stories. It was their stories of living with fear, hunger, anger, and resolve that helped us to understand one of the most complicated and consequential conflicts of our times."
7. It is because the children are regarded "as 'not-yet persons', 'not-yet knowing', 'not-yet responsible'...they are viewed not as 'human being' but as 'human becoming'" (Behera, 1998: 2). What impels our choice of respondents is the bundle of beliefs and preconceptions we hold about them. That the children do not know what we want to know forces us not to hear from them what they know. For the anthropologist of children, what is cardinal is to know what the children do and say. How can we assume that they are *tabula rasa*? We may arrive at this conclusion after having studied them, but the truth is that without having studied them we have set up certain conclusions that we regard as binding on us. One will agree with Behera's remark that the children are the "most undervalued entity" in contemporary societies (1998: 2). It is imperative that social scientists change their 'mind set' with respect to children.

8. I discussed some of these issues in an earlier publication of mine (2000), which was on old age. Here I argued that the centripetality of the child in our families was going hand-in-hand with the centrifugality of the elderly. In this process those who really are at the "receiving end" are the parents of the children; they also happen to be the children of the elderly, who are being marginalized. I submitted the need to study those in the family who were truly caught on the horns of dilemma.
9. The other meaning of the "individual" as an "unsocialized complex of flesh and bones" also figures in sociological literature. For instance, commenting on Émile Durkheim's conception of the child as an "unrestrained savage" and Talcott Parsons's description of the birth of a child as a "barbarian invasion", Buehler-Niederberger (1998: 54) writes: "The child was put on the individual side and, therefore, he stood on the wrong side." The child represented the state of the "pure individual".
10. Also see Macfarlane (1993).
11. Weber used this expression in the context of the traditional authority.
12. They also forget that there may be communities where silence is valued and people speak only when it is absolutely necessary for them. Gossiping may be shunned as an act of demerit. Here the anthropologist will have to spend long time observing the acts of people.
13. For the entire document, see Behera (ed.), 1998. For some comments on this, see Bluebond-Langer and Korbin (2007). In this context, one may also refer to the Draft National Policy for Children, 2012.
14. Also refer to Allison James (2007) on this point.
15. These names are of the subjects of the life-history accounts that the anthropologists have produced. These books also attempt to provide a glimpse into the social and cultural life of the communities to which these actors belonged. For Martinez, see Lewis (1964), for Nisa, Shostak (1981), for Tuhami, Crapanzano (1980), and for Muli, Freeman (2004).

REFERENCES

Ashley-Montagu, M.F. 1960. *An Introduction to Physical Anthropology*. Ill.: Thomas, Springfield.

Behera, Deepak Kumar. 1998. "Introduction," *In:* Deepak Kumar Behera (ed.), *Children and Childhood in Our Contemporary Societies*. Delhi: Kamla-Raj Enterprises.

Behera, Deepak Kumar (ed.). 1998. *Children and Childhood in Our Contemporary Societies*. Delhi: Kamla-Raj Enterprises.

Bluebond-Langer, Myra and Jill E. Korbin. 2007. "Challenges and opportunities in the anthropology of childhoods: An introduction to Children, Childhoods, and Childhood Studies," *American Anthropologist*, 109 (2).

Buehler-Niederberger, Doris. 1998. "The Separatist View – Is there any Scientific Approach to Children?" *In:* Deepak Kumar Behera (ed.), *Children and Childhood in Our Contemporary Societies*. Delhi: Kamla-Raj Enterprises.

Cooley, C.S. 1909. *Social Organization, A Study of the Larger Mind*. NY: Charles Scribner's Sons.

Crapanzano, Vincent. 1980. *Tuhami: Portrait of a Moroccan*. Chicago: Chicago University Press.

Dumont, Louis. 1970. *Homo Hierarchicus*. London: Paladin.

Dumont, Louis. 1992. *Essays on Individualism*. Chicago: Chicago University Press.

Freeman, James M. 2004. "Collecting the Life History of an Indian Untouchable," *In:* Vinay Kumar Srivastava (ed.), *Methodology and Fieldwork.* Oxford University Press.

Geertz, Clifford. 1983. *Local Knowledge*. New York: Basic Books.

Giddens, Anthony. 1976. *New Rules for Sociological Method*. New York: Basic Books.

Hirschfeld, Lawrence A. 2002. "Why don't Anthropologists Like Children?" *American Anthropologist*, 104 (2).

James, Allison. 2007. "Giving Voice to Children's Coices: Practices and Problems, Pitfalls and Potentials," *American Anthropologist*, 109 (2).

James, Allison and Adrian L. James. 2004. *Constructing Childhood: Theory, Policy and Social Practice*. London: Palgrave.

Karlekar, Malavika and Rudranghsu Mukherjee (eds.). 2010. *Remembered Childhood, Essays in Honour of André Béteille*. Oxford University Press.

LeVine, Robert A. 2007. "Ethnographic Studies of Childhood: A Historical Review," *American Anthropologist*, 109 (2).

Lévi-Strauss, Claude. 2013. *Anthropology Confronts the Problems of the Modern World*. Cambridge, Mass. & London: The Belknap Press of Harvard University Press.

Lewis, Oscar. 1964. *Pedro Martinez, A Mexican Peasant and his Family*. Random House.

Macfarlane, Alan. 1993. Louis Dumont and the Origins of Individualism. *Cambridge Anthropology*, 16 (1).

Madan, T. N. 1982. "Anthropology as the Mutual Interpretation of Cultures," *In:* H. Fahim (ed.), *Indigenous Anthropology in Non-Western Countries*. Durham, N.C.: Carolina Academic.

____. 1988. "The Son as Savior: The Hindu View of Choice and Morality," *In:* G.N. Appell and T.N. Madan (eds.), *Choice and Morality in Anthropological Perspectives. Essays in Honor of Derek Freeman*. Albany: State University of New York.

____. 1995. *Pathways. Approaches to the Study of Society in India*. Delhi: Oxford University Press.

Obeyesekere, Gananath. 1990. *The Work of Culture, Symbolic Transformation in Psychoanalysis and Anthropology*. Chicago: University of Chicago Press.

Roberts, Helen. 2000. "Listening to Children and hearing them," *In:* Pia Christensen and Allison James (eds.), *Research with Children*. London: Falmer Press.

Rosen, David M. 2007. "Child Soldiers, International Humanitarian Law, and the Globalization of Children," *American Anthropologist*, 109 (2).

Roy, Arundhati. 1997. *The God of Small Things*. Harper Collins.

Shostak, Marjorie. 1981. *Nisa: The Life and Words of a Kung Woman*. Cambridge, Mass: Harvard University Press.

Srivastava, V.K. 1997. *Religious Renunciation of a Pastoral People*. Delhi: Oxford University Press.

____. 2000. Ageism. *Seminar*, 488.

____. 2007. "Cultural Tradition and Child Marriage in India," *The Eastern Anthropologist*, 60 (1): 45-68.

Weber, Max. 1978. *Economy and Society: An Outline of Interpretive Sociology*. Berkeley: University of California Press.

TWO

CONCEPTS OF CHILDREN AND CHILDHOOD IN ANTHROPOLOGY AND IN A TRIBAL COMMUNITY OF MIDDLE INDIA[1]

EVA REICHEL

Ho Children and Fieldwork

In my long-term fieldwork among the Ho, a tribal community in central eastern India, children were my best teachers many times – their acquired competence of socially interacting self-confidently within their Ho universe and their patience with the ignorant anthropologist were simply amazing. Often, when grown-up Ho interlocutors gave up because they had more urgent things to do, Ho children continued to spend their time with me. They taught me Ho, their mother tongue, made me repeat words time and again until they were satisfied with my pronunciation, often motivating me with a big sigh of relief when I got it right – just as the adults did. They shared fruits with me that they had plucked from high up in the tree tops. Often they would take care of their younger "siblings" by carrying them on their hips. They took me to the jungle where they knew their way around as if it was a second home to them. They would inform me when rituals were taking place somewhere, and they would take me along if they happened to be among the protagonists of these performances. They would run off, though, if there were duties waiting for them such as herding the cows which implied chasing them, beating them, calming them down, thus educating them. They demonstrated that they had the upper hand even in risky situations when the cows turned wild. Often they would be busy for a full day.

[Ho] Children are "not only important, in and of themselves, they are interesting"[2], and they can be so funny. The encounter with Ho children as knowing subjects has certainly been rewarding in every sense, but, of course, there is more to it than a personal, coincidental, and emotional experience. Since they are firmly entrenched in their Ho culture the encounter has also been revealing from an anthropological perspective. It has inspired this chapter on children and childhood.

What follows is a selective and general introduction into relevant concepts of children and childhood as they are presently debated in the field of anthropology and beyond, complemented by ethnographic illustrations from recent fieldwork among the Ho in Odisha and Jharkhand, India.

Concepts of Children and Childhood in Anthropology

By now there is quite an impressive, though highly contested body of anthropological literature on childhood offering a wide range of cultural understandings and cross-cultural evidence from a variety of very different societies[3]. However, as yet amazingly little has been published to throw light from a social and cultural anthropological perspective on the concept(s) of children in India[4] and even less of the tribal children of India—beyond educational, nutritional, and medicinal aspects of child care, the context—free collecting and presenting of "data" and the "objective" world of statistics.

While there is no denying that children growing up in Ho country and children growing up in "Western culture areas" equally constitute *Anthropos*, I intend to show that there is an encompassing socio-cultural dimension to account for significant differences in interactional patterns and children's agencies. I will argue that children's aspirations and behaviour in a Durkheimian sense are impacted by the surrounding societal values and norms. How children are raised, how children are expected or tolerated to behave and behave "back", what status, social role and place they are assigned in their community and at what age, and what their futures hold for them is interrelated to how childhood is conceptionalized in their respective societies.

Geertz, Sahlins and the Controversy on Child Development

Clifford Geertz once remarked, "We have the equipment to live a thousand different lives, although we end up living only one"[5]. In analogy this should also be true for children who have the equipment to live a thousand different childhoods although they, too, may end up living only one. Marshall Sahlins refers to the above statement by Clifford Geertz in a pamphlet advertising its position in the title "The Western Illusion of Human Nature" and continues that "this is only possible on the condition that biological needs and drives do not specify the particular means and forms of their realization. Biology becomes a determined determinant" (Sahlins, 2008: 107)[6]. This is a brief and blunt counter position to much (western) contemporary writing on the anthropology of childhood that is at times strongly informed by genetic determinism, primatology, evolutionary anthropology, or psychology. In the course of my fieldwork among the Ho, I, too, found how limiting and limited legally, biologically, or psychologically based notions of children and childhood may prove when it comes to understanding complex cultural situations of which children form a constitutive part. The analysis of my childhood-related fieldwork data in the final part of this chapter will rather reveal the social nature of constructing a Ho child's personhood within the context of Ho society. I also question the usefulness in anthropology of operating with a singular category of childhood characterized by linear processes of developmental progression and, moreover, with notionally distinct domains such as childhood, adolescence, and adulthood. For these reasons I sympathize with Sahlins's position, and I will come back to his argument later.

Geertz's initial statement about humans' "equipment" invites a number of questions. Who or what accounts for diverse trajectories in a human's, in a child's development? Are differences in the concepts of the categories of "child" and "childhood" of a principled, qualitative nature and how are these related to those diverse trajectories? Who or what are the determining determinants? Where and how does *social and cultural* anthropology enter the scene and with what perspectives? Indeed, within contemporary mainstream discourses all of these questions are being raised and controversially dealt with to the extent that concepts of childhood and what it means to be a child have become an emotive, multi-faceted subject matter and a hotly debated issue, also in a number of other disciplines, also often politically charged.

Anthropology and Debates about the 'Universal' Child

Dominant Western discourses of "normal" child development are quite frequently and centrally based on developmental psychology (Montgomery, 2009: 3)[7] with its unshaken claim of presenting universal facts about a supposed universal progression from childhood as a state of immaturity to adulthood as a state of being more complete and representing the norm. Ethnographically informed research literature on childhood, however, has confronted such generalizing assumptions ever since the twentieth century, and continues to do so. Also, the applicability outside the West of standardized legal definitions of a child as any human being below the age of eighteen as reflected in the United Nations' Convention of the Rights of the Child (UNCRC)[8], its organic needs, its best interests, and its rights as a citizen is at stake. Not only within the context of human rights discourses it is D. Lancy who warns not only against the wholesale exportation of ethnocentric definitions, but also against the ethnocentric lens of a "wholesale exportation of culture – specific child-rearing practices" (quoted in Bluebond-Langner/Korbin, 2007: 244) following from this. So what and how, actually, should we study and examine, portray and represent, when we are doing research on children and childhood from an *anthropological* perspective or, more precisely, on culturally constructed concepts of children and childhood rather than biologically informed specific stages of life as static givens?

An anthropology of childhood will have to take into consideration that the very category of childhood has been claimed to be a recent invention in the West and a modern idea. Montgomery argues that the concept of adolescence has been travelling around a globalized world only since its "discovery" in the twentieth century (Montgomery 2009: 13, 15, 51). Such essentializing claims continue to be travelling to this day, sometimes supported by highly specialized discourses[9]. An anthropology of childhood would also have to account for those contemporary scholars who argue from a somewhat reverse anthropological point of view. They envisage children's *agency* as a dominant and unrelated factor to constitute a child-centred anthropology thereby recognizing children as active informants, authentic voices and meaning-makers living in their own meaningful and autonomous culture, producing their own culture and shaping that of their peers as well as that of the adults (Hirschfeld, 1999; Trawick, 2007). On the other hand this approach "to promote children's agency as a cornerstone of research" (Lancy, 2012) is sharply criticized by some as harmful to a scientific approach to the study of childhood. It marginalizes, the argument runs, anthropology because "it focuses attention on the traditional targets of psychology (the individual's mental state) and sociology (social position)" (*ibid.*) and denies the impact of a child's embeddedness within the tapestry of the surrounding culture. Lancy strongly emphasized this criticism in his keynote at the IUAES congress in November 2012.

Indeed, some have only lately deplored the neglect of an empirically grounded anthropology of childhood due to anthropologists' hypothesized aversion to and professional ignorance of children (Hirschfeld, 2002). At the same time others have begun to write out its very history (LeVine, 2007; Montgomery, 2009) and praise "the trove of scholarship" (Lancy, 2012) that already exists. Referring to B. Malinowski, M. Mead, and R. Firth as pioneers – others even go back further to Boas 1901 (Lancy, 2012) or Spencer 1899 (Benthall, 1992)—they claim there has been a well-established tradition ever since the nineteen twenties that was also critical of universal developmental markers as formulated in psychology and biology about the child. In fact, Margaret Mead's ethnographic reasoning contradicted the then mainstream assumptions by G.S. Hall of adolescence (1904) as a specific biologically informed stage in a person's life universally characterized by turmoil. They point to an already existing rich literature grounded in ethnographic fieldwork in diverse cultures and often discussing childhood in the context of kinship and ritual thus underpinning the unity of adult and child social spheres (LeVine, 2007: 250; Benthall, 1992: 1) and focussing on socio-cultural aspects rather than a child's determining innate dispositions. It is exactly this line of argument that I will focus on and return to in my ethnographic examples later.

The debate is on – within anthropology as well as within the interdisciplinary field of childhood studies. Issues, methods, and perspectives on how to study children and childhood continue to be negotiated between the poles of "childhood is about health, vitality, and growth in order to produce a robust animal" (E. Charnov, 2001) and "childhood" is about "culture acquisition" (E. Sapir, 1993). Contemporary anthropological discourse has to come to grips with how to envisage children within a given society and cross-culturally. Do we conceive of them as innocent[10], weak, fragile, dependent, incomplete, immature, naturally good if presocial, and vulnerable? Are they "cute cherubs, preternatural angelic beings" (Lancy, 2008), individual isolates growing up in a *child-centred* neontocracy as opposed to those that are attributed social competence and maturity in varying degrees, reliability, trusted to assume responsibilities, growing up and into what has been called a *child-supported* society (*ibid.*: 11)?

To preliminarily sum up: assuming that generalizing views of the universal child are "antithetical to most anthropological thinking" (Bluebond-Langner and Korbin, 2007: 244), anthropologists have resisted universal and essentializing definitions of children and of childhood as a matter of principle to this day. "There are no separate or autonomous categories of adult or child" (Montgomery, 2009: 55), there is no domain of childhood that is notionally separate from a domain of adulthood the divide between both being complex, permeable, and culture-specific. However, how childhood is *conceptualized* has a direct impact on what "equipment" they are believed to dispose of. Conceptualizations are cultural constructs: the innocent child, e.g. is one such cultural construct among many others; another contrasting one, e.g. is understanding infants as being ensouled by their dead kinsmen and having their "skills, knowledge, temperament and attributes" (Sahlins, 2008: 100). The point I want to make is, "There is nothing *natural* in how children grow up" (Montgomery, 2009: 236; my emphasis).

Human Nature, Children's Nature, and Personhood

This brings me back to the statement by Clifford Geertz which I quoted at the outset of this chapter. Marshall Sahlins has embedded it in his reflexions on Western and comparative notes on other conceptions of Human Nature – implying other cultural constructions of a child's "nature". Both Geertz and Sahlins have been largely ignored in most of the latest publications on childhood although in my view they offer some seminal insights into a child developing personhood – "at home" and elsewhere, and also in Ho society. A similar neglect is true of Marilyn Strathern who finds highly sensitive and differentiating formulations concerning a child's social maturing processes in Melanesia[11]. In his essay Sahlins addresses Christianity and the Christian belief in the concept of Original Sin resulting in the assumption of Man as basically evil or inherently egoistic. In fact, Sahlins develops in much detail, how the contemporary Western conceptualization of the individual, of human nature, of how a child and its needs is envisaged, has been informed over centuries by Christianity, by ancient philosophies, and, now-a-days, by modern sciences. These assumptions have become materialized in the individualizing ideology prevailing in the West of the "selfish gene" (R. Dawkins, 1989)[12], or what Sahlins labels the issue of "biologism", i.e., the supremacy of the genetic imperatives ascribed to be operative, dominant and characteristic of human nature and also an infant's development. The cultural consequence resulting from this, he argues, is the narrowed conceptualization of a child's growth in the organic terms of its bodily achievements, desires, deficiencies, and needs.

Round the planet, in non-western societies, however, "the more common belief is simply that the infant is not yet a full person" (Sahlins, 2008: 101). Children are treated as "humanity-in-becoming" or on their way from imperfect to perfected humanity. Children are "trained" into recognizing social obligations, and they are credited the confidence, sometimes at quite an early age as we would think in the West, in their capacity to perform social duties, and to perform them well. They are conceived to be born human whether incompletely so or fully so in the case of incarnation, but not from some pre-social state and not as an anti-person with inherent either agreeable or disagreeable dispositions. An infant in Hagen, Strathern remarks, is less trained than nurtured to personhood and certainly not considered wild or innately anti-social. A child's maturation is addressed towards developing the mental capacity of assuming social relationships or, in Strathern's words, the Hagen child grows into social maturity, becomes socially competent "through appreciation of what social relationships with others involve" (Strathern, 1988). Sociality is conceived of as the normal human condition, Sahlins argues with reference to topical ethnographic evidence and with reference to contemporary anthropologists who also stress cultural and social aspects as the determining determinants in a child's development. Biological markers are neither denied nor ignored. But as they are always symbolically defined, they are expressions of cultural order and not of some 'irresistible', objectively existing, innate inclinations defined as universal human nature existing unrelated to the world around. Anthropology is about the social and cultural significance given to these inherent dispositions in culture-specific contexts. Children's maturing then may eventually turn out to be an issue of:

> "their progression of mind and soul rather than the regulation of bodily impulses. Personhood is gradually achieved through social interactions, especially those involving reciprocity and interdependence, for these comprise and teach the child's social identities" (Sahlins, 2008: 101).

I have shown in the representation of the anthropological debate that childhood is so much more than a set, separate, vulnerable, and physiologically determined fixed stage in a person's life, an intrapersonal affair, as it were. It is also so much more than a space inhabited by rights-bearing citizens protected by much national and international legislation. In the next paragraph I will illustrate how the Ho's alternative conceptualizations of children and childhood contribute to initiating mutual relationships, categories of behaviour, and, more generally, child-oriented practices.

Children and Childhood in a Tribal Community of Middle India

The following two ethnographic examples have been chosen from recent fieldwork among the Ho, a tribal community of roughly a million people living mainly in the hilly and plateau areas of the States of Jharkhand and Odisha.

Example 1: The Anthropologist as Child

For the sake of participant observation I had found a "family" who accepted me as a classificatory member, addressed me by kinship terms, and taught me to reciprocally do the same. I had made it very clear that I was a novice, as concerned Ho culture and that I wanted to learn everything that I was trusted to learn from somebody competent to teach me. So I was afforded by my classificatory younger brother (*undin)* with his *kaki,* a term for the categories of a father's younger brother's wife or a mother's younger sister, who that way became my *kaki* and who in turn addressed me as "young girl" (*mai*). *Mai* is an address term, but not a specific kinship term.[13] It is a category related to those whose task conventionally is to help and do necessary daily chores in someone's household, also in somebody else's. In the course of my stay it turned out that my *kaki* conceived of herself as my mother, however, she did not address me as *beti* or *kui-hon* (see number 12 under Notes). I had a mother, but I was not "quite" her daughter in the sense of being her *kui-hon*. Obviously there were different shades of being a child, a girl, or a daughter! It took me some time to establish a pedigree from the bits and pieces that were passed on to me in order to trace the relation between her, my younger brother, who was the village eldest (*munda*) in the neighbouring hamlet, and myself. Eventually it was confirmed that our *kaki* was "our" FFBySW. This made socially sense, because in terms of her and "our" pedigree she was one generation ahead of me. However, it did not make sense biologically – which is the reason why I enlarge on this very situation here – because she was clearly so much younger than I was. Even when she learned that l was a grandmother to three grandchildren back home, she continued to address and treat me as "young girl" or *mai*. I was surprised at this, but nobody else was. When after a few months she heard me make a phone call to my husband, she smiled and said: "*aratadi* – after all this time I am going to meet my son-in-law". This clearly identified me as her social, classificatory daughter in kinship terms, and I began to realize that in Ho country kinship was a process rather than a static given, a state of becoming rather than of being once and for all— perhaps. I also learnt that others to whom I was elder sister (*dai* or *ji*), looked forward to meeting my husband because that way they would acquire an elder sister's husband (*teya*), which is a joking relationship. My social identities, as I have argued above, further increased when I was constructed into my Santal assistant's mother, whose wife consequently turned into my daughter-in-law (*kimin*). May be I was socially maturing, slowly, slowly, and becoming more and more complete acquiring more joking as well as avoidance relationships and on my way to a "multiple person, made up through relationships with others", as Strathern has formulated?

So while by some, who were younger than I was, I was addressed as young girl, for others who were similarly younger, I was turned into a mother. The example should illustrate how inadequate our conventional Western dichotomy of childhood *versus* adulthood may prove when it comes to making cultural sense of a simple kinship situation elsewhere. Also, exclusive notions of being either a child or an adult in a biologically informed chronology of a person's life may become meaningless in a culture where childhood and adulthood are socially defined, where the boundaries between the two are known to be blurred and the domains as such are seen as complementary to rather than separate of each other. This is illustrated in more empirical detail in the second example.

Example 2: Unity of Child and Adult Social Sphere in Ritual

Mage Porob, a Ho Village Festival

Mage Porob is a feast that is observed in every Ho village after the harvest work is done. It usually takes place in the course of January or February, and the whole village is involved in singing, dancing, drinking, and, most importantly, meeting kith and kin. In the process of fixing the very days of the feast the village priest (*diuri)* has the decisive say. A lot could be said about *Mage Porob* and its relevance within Ho ritual performances, but this is not the point why I mention it in the context of this chapter.

The case that I want to elaborate here will shed some light on the ritual importance of quite young boys which came to the fore in the course of preparing *Mage Porob* in Pathan Sai, the site of my fieldwork.

The present village priest had decided to step down for a number of reasons that I cannot enlarge upon within the scope of the present article, from an otherwise hereditary post. So, in order to fix a day for *Mage Porob*, a new *diuri* had to be elected first in the course of a ritual designed to serve exactly this very purpose. For the procedure itself about 60 to 70 male adult persons assembled each household of the village being represented that way. Eventually everybody sat down on the ground next to the sacred grove of the village (*desauli*), whereas a few people stepped inside the sacred grove such as the former village priests, two village elders (*mundas)* of two adjacent hamlets plus their helping hands. All were facing east when the ritual called *mad pata:* began.

Mad Pata, the Ritual to Elect the Village Priest

Mad is a generic term for bamboo, and in this case it became notionally important that *buru mad*, i.e. bamboo growing in the jungle, was cut. This was the former village priest's task which he performed after he had taken a ritual bath in a pond nearby. *Pata*: on the other hand carries the meaning "to entwine (e.g. two ropes, two branches), to interlace" (Deeney, 2005: 284). The idea of the ritual is the following: the candidates willing to be elected as village priest needed to be suggested by any of the Ho villagers first and they needed to consent to standing as a candidate. The final say, however, was with the Ho spirits and gods. It was up to them to decide who was going to become the village priest and who his helpers.

For this purpose two boys, perhaps eight or nine years old, functioned as the intermediaries to the divine sphere. They had taken a bath and were dressed in a clean loin cloth (*dhoti*). A dot of vermillion (*sindur)* and some rice grains were put into their palms by the *diuri* who was in charge of the ritual. They stood opposite each other, concentrated and calm, maybe three metres apart from each other, holding the bamboo branches that had been split into two halves, under their armpit, and throughout the ritual they did not move. When their positioning was considered correct, the *diuri* began chanting his *mantras* thereby demanding of the gods to show consent or dissent whenever he called out the name of a candidate. It was interpreted as a sign of divine consent when immediately after a name was called out the bamboo halves that the boys were holding began to entwine or come closer to each other, visibly and publicly. Indeed, this happened time and again. It was considered a sign of godly dissent on the other hand, if the split bamboo branches did not move. This also happened. That way not only the *diuri* got elected. Also those two men (*oron sakowa)* were awarded divine distinction who would be entitled to blow the jungle bison horns on the occasion of all big village feasts just as those men (*da: go:)* entitled to carry on the shoulder the pots of water needed for the sacrifices to be performed at the village grove, (*desauli*). *Desauli* refers to the sacred village locality and at the same time the main protective spirit of a village, to whom sacrificial offerings are made in the course of the main village feasts, of which there are quite a few. Finally divine consent was demanded for those called *ramba rid* who are entitled to grind black lentils, a ritual pulse (*ramba)* for the same purpose. The success of the ritual had literally been in the two boys' hands. At last water was sprinkled on the ground by the preceding village priest thus inviting the gods to leave.

The complete ritual had lasted 35 minutes. When it was finished, the boys – should I really call them children? Was there anything incomplete, incompetent, immature, imperfect, or deficient about them in this situation? - laid down the bamboo halves and left the scene.

Indeed, in terms of age they might clearly be considered deficient if being biologically adult was expected to serve as the norm. However, the boys' integral involvement in this very ritual – and it is not the only one – reveals that their being so young turns out to be the very source of their value, of their purity, of their closeness to and their relatedness with the realm of the divine. As intermediaries they are entitled to cross a bridge that is open to other boys of their age, but certainly not to (male) adults. In this particular situation, I argue, their being a "child" is not a deficiency, but rather a qualification, a marker of excellence, a constitutive prerequisite for the ritual to be performed adequately – or, more importantly, to be performed at all. The example illustrates that Ho children, in this case boys, are entrusted with ritual duties and they experience early in their lives that they are capable of contributing to the (recreation of the) societal whole. As Ho children are usually allowed to witness and participate in all kinds of cultural affairs that accompany the yearly crop cycle, they can perform as competent social actors and knowing subjects when it is their turn. May be Sahlins might have remarked that Ho childhood was a process of culturally informed growing into personhood or social adulthood.

Conclusion

There are many more rituals where Ho children figure in prominent ways which cannot be elaborated here. All of them would have revealed that although Ho persons may be quite young in biophysical terms, they may act in quite grown-up ways in socio-cultural respect. In this vein it has been attempted to illustrate that the concept of childhood as opposed to that of adulthood is not a universal given, but narrowly culture bound. It has at the same time attempted to illustrate, how due to some anthropologists' exclusive advocacy of the innocent child in need of legal protection and nutritional provisioning, a child's impressive abilities and cultural performances elsewhere may easily be underrated or even overlooked. Ho children develop not independently of or against Ho *samaj*, as far as I can tell from fieldwork among the Ho. It may well be that exactly their being socially and ritually competent and active, knowing subjects from an early age within an encompassing meaningful whole, makes them walk tall.

NOTES

1. This is the title of a lecture held at the 2012 Inter-Congress of the IUAES Commission on Children, Childhood and Youth which took place in Bhubaneswar, India from November 26-30. The following paper is a revised and slightly enlarged version of that lecture.
2. Margaret Trawick in her Position Paper for the 2012 Inter-Congress.
3. To give a few examples: Montgomery, 2009; Lancy, 2008, 2012; Bluebond-Langner/Korbin, 2007; Hirschfeld, 1999, 2002; LeVine, 2007; Whiting, 1963, 1988; James, 2007; Benthall, 1992.
4. The monograph by Seymour 1999 is a remarkable exception.
5. Quoted in Sahlins, Marshall (2008: 107).

6. *Ibid.*
7. Montgomery points out the emphasis on psychology in American anthropology going back to the days of Franz Boas under whose aegis the Culture and Personality School was inaugurated, and LeVine (2007) remarks that to his knowledge Boas's assessment of this branch within anthropology has nowhere been documented. Montgomery further argues that British social anthropology, on the other hand, has always been suspicious of this focus on psychology as a determining factor and the perspective resulting from this within anthropology.
8. This convention is also criticized within the West beyond anthropological discourses. It should be mentioned that the United States have signed, however not ratified this convention for a number of different reasons. One reason is that the convention legally binds the state to regularly check or control what is going on within the American family, another one is that the Convention's non-violence approach would disallow children's access to guns and rifles before the age of 18.
9. In a renowned national German journal for physicians, *Deutsches Ärzteblatt* (June 2013: 423), e.g. adolescence is the topical subject matter. It is presented from a neuroscientific perspective as an intrapersonal "developmental period" between the age of twelve to 24. In relation to a person's brain development and other somatic changes the focus includes psychological and legal consequences in terms of a youth's (age of) criminal responsibility, heightened risk behaviours, and emotional disorders.
10. Seeing children as innocent is a view that Montgomery claims to be culture-specific in the West. Moreover, she argues that the reifying concept of the innocent child can be "extremely dangerous to children" (2009: 236) in the case that children act as child soldiers, e.g. thus turning out to be aggressors rather than aggressed.
11. Montgomery, however, does draw from Strathern (1988) when discussing the Melanesian concept of the multiple person.
12. "He argued that, in fact, living organisms are just the means by which genes replicate" (Lancy, 2008: 8, 9 on R. Dawkins).
13. In my area of fieldwork people more often used the Hindi equivalent *beti* or the Ho term *kui-hon* to address their daughter. Also Deeney 2005 does not list *mai* as a kinship term. Bouez 1985, however, relates to *mai* as "younger sister" and "daughter" with both the Ho and Santal (1985: 202) and characterizes the relation between *ma/ kaki* and *mai* as "*legè re hiérarchie*" (*ibid*: 64).

REFERENCES

Benthall, Jonathan. 1992. "A Late Developer? The Ethnography of Children," *Anthropology Today*, 8 (2): 1.

Bluebond-Langner, Myra and Jill E. Korbin. 2007. "Challenges and Opportunities in the Anthropology of Childhoods: An Introduction to 'Children, Childhoods, and Childhood Studies," *American Anthropologist*, 109 (2): 241-246.

Boas, Franz. 1901. "The Eskimo of Baffin Land and Hudson Bay," *Bulletin of the American Museum of Natural History,* 15 (1): 1-370.

Bouez, Serge. 1985. *Réciprocité et Hiérarchie. L'Alliance Chez Les Ho Et Les Santal De L'Inde.* Paris: Société d'Ethnographie.

Charnov, Eric. 2001. "Evolution of Mammal Life Histories," *Evolutionary Ecology Research,* 3: 371-383.

Dawkins, R. 1989. *The Selfish Gene.* New York: Oxford University Press.

Deeney. 2005. *Ho-English Dictionary.* Ranchi: Xavier's Publications.

Deutsches Ärzteblatt. Die Zeitschrift der Ärzteschaft. 2013. "Adoleszenz. Hirnentwicklung und psychische Störungen," Ausgabe C, Heft 25, 21. Juni 2013.

Firth, Raymond. 1936. *We, the Tikopia.* New York: American Book.

Hall, Granville Stanley. 1904. *Adolescence: Its Psychology and its Relations to Physiology, Anthropology, Sociology, Sex, Crime, Religion, and Education.* New York: Appleton.

Harris, Judith Rich. 1998. *The Nurture Assumption: Why Children Turn Out the Way They Do.* New York: Free Press.

Hirschfeld, Lawrence. 2002. "Why Don't Anthropologists Like Children?" *American Anthropologist,* (*New Series*) 104 (2): 611-627.

____. (1999). "L'enfant terrible: Anthropology and its Aversion to Children," *Etnofoor* (Kids and Culture) 12 (1): 5-26.

James, Allison. 2007. "Giving Voice to Children's Voices: Practices and Problems, Pitfalls and Potentials," *American Anthropologist,* 109 (2): 261-272.

Lancy, David F. 2008. *The Anthropology of Childhood. Cherubs, Chattel, Changelings.* New York: Cambridge University Press.

____. 2012." Unmasking Children's Agency," In: www.usu.edu/anthro/davidlancyspages/blog

LeVine. 2007. "Ethnographic Studies of Childhood: A Historical Overview," *American Anthropologist,* 109 (2): 247-260.

Malinowski, Bronislaw. 1927. *Sex and Repression in Savage Society.* London: Paul, Trench, Trubner.

____. 1929. *The Sexual Life of Savages in North Western Melanesia.* London: Routledge.

Mead, Margaret. 1928a. *Coming of Age in Samoa.* New York: William Morrow.

____. 1928b. "Samoan Children at Work and Play," *Natural History,* 28: 626-636.

Montgomery, Heather. 2009. *An Introduction to Childhood. Anthropological Perspectives on Children's Lives.* Chichester: Wiley-Blackwell.

Sahlins, Marshall. 2008. *The Western Illusion of Human Nature. With Reflections on the Long History of Hierarchy, Equality, and the Sublimation of Anarchy in the West, and Comparative Notes on Other Conceptions of the Human Condition.* Chicago: Prickly Paradigm Press.

Sapir, Edward. 1993. *The Psychology of Culture: A Course of Lectures.* Judith Irvine (ed.). The Hague: Mouton.

Spencer, F.C. 1899. *Education of the Pueblo Child: A Study in Arrested Development.* New York.

Strathern, Marilyn. 1988. *The Gender of the Gift. Problems with Women and Problems with Society in Melanesia.* Berkeley: University of California Press.

Trawick, Margaret. 2012. Position Paper for the 2012 Inter-Congress of the IUAES Commission on Children, Childhood and Youth. Bhubaneswar, India.

Whiting, Beatrice. 1963. *Six Cultures; Studies of Child Rearing.* New York: Wiley.

Whiting, Beatrice and C.P. Edwards. 1988. *Children of Different Worlds: The Formation of Social Behaviour.* Cambridge, MA: Harvard University Press.

THREE

BEING A KYRGYZ CHILD

BAKTYGUL TULEBAEVA

Introduction

The purpose of this article is to contribute to the current anthropological debates on defining children, their status in a society, and their childhood by looking at children among Kyrgyz people. If one searches on the internet about Kyrgyz children, s/he first comes across articles on street children, children as workers, children suffering from child abuse, neglect and poverty. Usually, these kinds of topics circle around through mass media and it is understandable that these articles are meant to raise people's awareness of the problems existing in the society and contribute to the improvement of children's lives in the country. However, this is a one-sided description which can create only negative picture of children in Kyrgyzstan.

Even among international anthropological sources on childhood, which has been rapidly developing lately, a Kyrgyz child is mentioned only in David Lancy's book *Anthropology of Childhood: Cherubs, Chatels and Changelings* (2008), where the author mentions in a single sentence how a 12-year old Kyrgyz child left his house for the city to earn money to send it to his family. That was one of the examples, where Lancy wanted to show that there are children in "other societies", like a Kyrgyz child, "where children are viewed as unwanted, inconvenient *changelings* or as desired but pragmatically commoditized *chattel*". I fully share Ennew's point, where she underlines that research on children in non-western countries mostly focuses on children in difficult circumstances, which widens the gap of knowledge about their 'normal' childhoods (see Waterson and Behera, 2011).

I take the above mentioned critique as a starting point and show what Kyrgyz people themselves think about their children and their proper development. I claim that child is highly valued by Kyrgyz people who hold positive interpretations of the enculturation processes that outside scholars would estimate as negative.

In the first part of my article I will discuss what a "child" actually is for Kyrgyz people and where the "line" between a child and an adult lies. The second part of this article is on local concepts of values, which are vital for a proper development of a Kyrgyz child. In the third part, which is on enculturation process, I will raise the issue of upbringing, in a local term called *tarbiya*, which, in its term, circles around the concepts of *yimanduuluk* (well-manner), discipline and work.

A Review of the Literature

Studies on childhood usually touch the comparative issue of the history of childhood, that is, children before and now (Zelizer, 1985; Aries, 1962; James, Jenks & Prout, 1998), children of the west *versus* non-west (Lancy, 2008; Montgomery, 2009; Alderson,1998; Chowdhury, 2007; Christensen, 2000) and note that there is no childhood, but there are childhoods, which lately started to be strongly accented (James and Prout, 1990; Jenks, 2005; Behera, 2007). Scholars generally look at what status a child has in comparison to adults, such as when childhood ends and adulthood begins or that a child is not a becoming, but a being like adults (Jenks, 2005). In all of these scholars try to draw a line between a child and an adult, by stating that "childhood is constructed as separate (conceptually and physically) from the adult world" (James and Prout, 1990), which I claim to be a misleading approach. Bueler-Niederberger (1998) points out that whatever approach we use when we study children, there will be juxtaposition between a child and an adult. However, in my article I show that it is not the case among Kyrgyz people.

Sometimes the focus is only on attempts to define a child and determine what childhood is. It seems better to look at what role and status a child has in a particular society, and how that particular society values the child. A child in each culture is uniquely placed and valued in the context of that culture, and it is difficult to do comparisons.

Comparison can be used for methodological purposes to construct an idea of a "child" and "childhood" in general. However, as soon as cross-cultural comparisons are made in defining a child or "judging" childhood of a particular society, misrepresentation emerges.

In the autumn of 2012, I went to Kyrgyzstan to study childhood and a healthy growth of children. The aim of my project was to research what Kyrgyz people understand by a child, a healthy child and what they do in order to ensure the health and well-being of their children. I started my research by studying "healthy growth" of children in the country. However, as the research progressed, I realized that I was actually studying Kyrgyz people's cultural values through the topic of children. It is not because I lost a track of the initial research plan, but because for Kyrgyz people, childhood and the healthy growth of children are all circled around bringing up a culturally nourished child. Children are like a harvest – parents plant cultural values in their children from the first day of their birth. Implanting Kyrgyz culture and nourishing children turned out to be inseparable topics.

I also argue that studying children needs a holistic approach. In order to analyze any concept related to children such as children's agency or child labour, which usually raise negative pictures of non-western children, one should not ignore local people's perception related to children's development, upbringing and economic conditions. These perceptions are sometimes ignored by outside scholars. Unfortunately, ethnographic work of local Kyrgyz scholars on children and values related to children do not reach an international arena because they are published in the Kyrgyz language and not translated into a language more universally accessible, such as English.

Part 1: The Concept of the "Child" from the Perspective of Kyrgyz People

"A father is a rocky mountain, a mother is a spring that comes out of the chest of the rocky mountain, and a child is light that shines to both of them". This is the proverb that describes a Kyrgyz child and shows its high importance among Kyrgyz families. One of my informants described a child in the following way: "A child is number one for Kyrgyz people. If a bride could not give a birth to a child, then she was sent back. A kidnapped bride stays because of children. Couples who fight get reconciled only because of children. Life without a child is meaningless. It is meaningless, if there is no child who would meet you when you come home, or would cry when you die". From this person's words one can see that a child cannot be defined on its own. A child is carrying a value, a child is creating a relationship, and a child is holding a meaning.

For Kyrgyz people a child is a "relational term" which is based on intergenerational relationships, attitudes, responsibilities, obligations and expectations. A child is not measured or limited by age. A child is always a child in front of its parents' eyes, even if s/he is 40 years old or 60 years old and has his or her own children. A child stays as a child to its parents because of responsibilities, obligations in front of them. In Kyrgyz culture it is especially implied to male children, usually the younger ones, who are the most responsible to their parents. Female children are said to be members of another family upon marriage and they are accepted as guests and are highly respected.

It should be noted that when it comes to responsibility and obligation, it is not children alone who serve their parents, but also parents have their life-long responsibilities in front of their children. According to Kyrgyz tradition, parents stay with the youngest male child in the house and live as an extended family. One of the wishes of parents for the later years of their lives is to have grandchildren whom they would tend and look after. Grandchildren are their joy. In the field I noticed a lot how despite health problems, grandmothers helped their daughters-in-law about the house and served as baby-sitters.

Elderly people also support their adult children financially. In Kyrgyzstan the number of families, where adult children live on their parents' pensions or where grandchildren are raised by elderly people, as their own parents left for Russia or Kazakhstan to work, is not small. Usually, studies on child work and labour (Lancy, 2008; UNICEF, 2011), show how children work for their parents, but they forget the other side, that is, how parents also work for their already adult children. A 50-year old informant mentioned that her 90-year old father once told her that only now he stopped worrying about her, because her children turned out to be good children, who will look after her in her old age. This example shows that a good child is a caring child. At the same time one can see that a child is always under its parents' thoughts and concern, irrespective of its age.

Concerning age, it is not age itself, but relationship that defines a child. Jenks (2005:37) points out that "childhood always speaks of a relationship" for example, adult-child, parent-child, teacher-child, and Bueler-Niederberger (1998) states that studies on children are generally "imprisoned" in the inter-generational juxtaposition of adult-child. Indeed, most anthropological sources on childhood look at child-adult relationship, but very few look at the relationship between children (Alex, 2009), especially between siblings (Gregory, 2010).

Kyrgyz people use *chong* (big) and *kichine* (small) when they refer to their children. It does not depend on age, but on the seniority and juniority among siblings. Kyrgyz families are big, usually three children minimum, and elderly siblings are accepted as big and mature, and younger ones are small and immature. Maturity, which is another indicator of the shift from childhood to adulthood, is also based on the junior/senior status of children in the family. The status of a child also defines his tasks within the household: the elder children in the family are expected to "understand" and accordingly, they have more obligations and tasks that they are expected to do. On the other hand, the fulfilled tasks can also define a child as "big" and "small". In her research among children in Norway, Solberg (1990) compared children at the age of twelve. Some of the 12-year old were accepted as already "big" and others as still "small", depending on the big and small tasks they fulfilled at home.

When it comes to adults, it should be noted that there is no concrete term in Kyrgyz for "adult". Usually, the words *uluu* (elder) and *chong* (big) are used to refer to adults. When I asked my informants when a child stops being a child and becomes an adult, many people took as an example their eldest child as already *chong* and mentioned that the youngest one is still a child. First, it seems that the same categorization of adults and elderly children in the family rejects age as an indicator of child-adult distinction. Second, it indicates the lack of clear division between child and adult. Third, it implies that a shift from a child to an adult depends on a child's junior/senior status in the family, as well as in the community. In a local context not the term "child-adult", but more "junior-senior" or "small-big" is most often used and a child can be senior and big, like adults. But it is also a relative status.

Nevertheless, there are certain indicators according to which a child becomes *chong* – an adult. For some parents it is finishing school and leaving for the city to study, where a child stays beyond parents' control. For others it is marriage and building own family, or financial independence due to work. Now, many people mention that due to work and money children today mature earlier than before. One of the male informants mentioned that before (he means during the Soviet time) only after returning from the Army, which was at the age of 21, a child was accepted as an adult. Only then a child could have voice and be included in adult's circle. According to him, now children start to work earlier and that is why their consciousness is better developed. He mentioned that in his childhood he also worked, but that was housework, which he even did not count as work. I will pause on work more in detail later in this chapter.

Marriage, which is a sign of maturity in most cultures, also shifts a Kyrgyz child from lower stage of the ladder of personhood to the higher stage. As indicated by Otten (2010), it is also a sign of becoming a "full person". Nevertheless, it does not change a child's status as junior in front of its parents and elderly people. Marriage is the last ritual, which parents perform for their children. Before reaching a marriageable status several other rituals are done for a child in order to shape the child with desired qualities and skills. In the following section I will give broader elaboration on the construction of a Kyrgyz child.

Part 2: Values of Kyrgyz Parents in Constructing a Child

The life of a Kyrgyz child is full of plantings, mouldings, buildings, teachings, regulations and expectations. Giving birth to a healthy child is one thing, but bringing up a "proper Kyrgyz child" is a very thorough and important task of each Kyrgyz parent. A child is always a child for its parents and remains under constant watch of its parents, that is starting from babyhood until parents pass away. It is also under the watch of the relatives, neighbourhood and the whole community. The lack of a clear shift from a child to an adult in a Kyrgyz culture might also be explained by the fact that from the very first day when a child is born both parents and the community already start to invest in the child the desired qualities that the child requires when it grows up and becomes an adult. So, the shift is not from childhood to adulthood, but from childhood to a personhood, to a Kyrgyz person.

Most rituals, be they life-cycle or health related rituals, or ritual of protective character, are performed more for children than for adults. Alex (2009) in her study of children in Tamil Nadu, also noticed this tendency. The reason for that could be the purpose of the community to construct a child through rituals (Berger *et al.,* 2010). In this chapter, I would like to analyze the main rituals conducted for Kyrgyz children. I will not pause much about how rituals are conducted, but rather mention two main concepts: blessings (*bata*) and the transmission of qualities (*juguu, ooshuu, beriluu, ötüü*), which I noticed in all these rituals and which play a main role in constructing a child.

The Concept of "the Transmission of Qualities"

When a child is born parents slaughter an animal and conduct sacrifice for their child by inviting relatives, friends and neighbours. They celebrate the arrival of the baby. When the baby is forty days old mothers conduct a 40-day-ritual. It is not a big event, but very important. It is done in an intimate circle, that is within the family, or only by the presence of a mother alone. Mother bathes the baby in forty spoons of water, cuts the nails and shaves the hair of the baby for the first time.

Another ritual, which can precede or follow the 40-day ritual is the ritual of putting a baby in a cradle, a traditional cradle called *beshik*. It is made of wood, with a hole under it, which keeps the baby clean and dry. It has specially made matresses, blankets, covers, which keep the baby warm in winter. A child sleeps well in a swaddled position, gets used to a certain sleeping routine, which also gives time for a mother to do things about the house or to have a rest. Many people still use this traditional cradle in villages, not because of its traditional feature, but because of its practicality.

When a child is around one year old and about to walk the ritual called *tushoo kesuu* is performed. The ritual consists of the actions of tying a black and white rope around the child's feet and which is cut. It is believed that from now on a child will not stumble and will start walking fast. Also in a figurative term a child will not stumble in his life and be successful. The aim of this ritual is to wish a child a broad future.

For a female child the following ritual after *tushoo kesuu* is marriage, when, according to my informant, her fate is determined. As for male children, before marriage they have to undergo circumcision around the age three or five. At least neighbourhood gathers for circumcision and parents organize a party. The scale of the parties depends on the economic conditions of parents and personal interests. Some families organize big parties for *tushoo kesuu* ritual or circumcision by sending specially prepared invitation cards to their relatives and friends and by organizing these parties in restaurants, because of huge number of invited guests. But some also conduct it in a very small circle, just for the sake of conducting the symbolic part of the ritual.

In all of these rituals the concept of "the transmission of qualities" was clearly noticed. The word transmission is translated into Kyrgyz in several ways: *ooshuu, beriluu, ötüü, juguu.* If one analyzes the elements in rituals, the most commonly asked questions would be: "Why is the ritual conducted in this way and not in another"? or "Why is this particular thing used in the ritual"? Many elements used in the rituals for Kyrgyz children circle around the concept of transmission of qualities. Let me elaborate it more in details in the rituals conducted to children.

Each Kyrgyz name has a meaning and Kyrgyz people believe that the name of a person affects his/her fate. People choose names carefully and on purpose. Most names have deep positive meanings. Even the names, which were used with negative meanings, such as slave, bold, dirty nose, were used for positive purposes, such as, to distract evil eye from children and protect them. For a Kyrgyz family having a son is very important. If only daughters were born to a family then parents named their daughters *Burul* (turn), *Jangyl* (get mistaken), *Uulbolsun* (let it be a male child) on purpose, in the hope that the next one would be a son. Nowadays people started to name their children after famous and important people, so that their children would also inherit the qualities of the person, after whom a child was named.

When mothers conduct a 40-day ritual and cut their babies' hair and nails, they usually bury them under a tree or safe place, which cannot be trampled by people. Some people put nails under growing flowers so that the baby's nails grow beautifully like a flower.

The ritual of putting a baby into a cradle holds in itself many nuances, which have an implication of giving good qualities to the baby both in its babyhood and further life. Three, five or seven respected old ladies of the village are invited to conduct the ritual. They must be respected women, who gave birth to and raised many successful children, so that a child's future will be as successful as these ladies'. When one prepares the cradle, the first thing they do is they purify the cradle by smoking it with fir tree. Then they put certain objects that imply certain qualities. People put an axe into the cradle, so that a child's life becomes strong and sharp like an axe, or hoe, so that a child becomes hard-working (Murzakmetov, 2011). Bread is put, so that a child's life be in abundance and sweets are put, so that a child's life be "sweet". One old lady mentioned that previously Kyrgyz people covered the cradle with a sack, so that the child sleeps well, while others mentioned that shirts of people in the village, who like to sleep, were used for covering, so that a child gets a habit of long sleeping. "Objectified social qualities" which mentioned by Platenkamp (2010) are believed to be transferred to a child through using these objects in rituals.[1]

In a *tushoo kesuu* ritual, which is conducted for a child, who is around one year old, a group of boys and girls run and whoever comes first cuts the white-black rope, tied around the child's feet. The rope is made white-black on purpose, meaning that life consists of both white and black sides. And it is cut by a girl or boy who comes first, so that a child for whom this ritual is performed, would be as fast and successful as the one, who stood out from the crowd and came first. Also it is cut by children and not by adults, because it is believed that children's thoughts are white and intentions are clean. Pureness and cleanliness were mentioned by my informants to be the qualities of small children.

The last ritual conducted for a Kyrgyz child is marriage. In some regions, when a bride is brought to her in-laws' family, women spray flour in front of the bride, so that her life will be white and clean.

They also throw *chachala*[2], which consists of sweets and *boorsok*[3], so that the couple's life may be sweet and they may live in abundance. When a bride comes into the house the first person who puts the scarf onto her head should be a respected elderly female person, who has many children. She puts a white scarf, and not of any other colour, so that the life of the bride may be as white as the white scarf. Widows or women, who married more than once, cannot put the scarf, so that the bride does not have the same fate like those women.

The transmission of qualities are commonly practiced in rituals of Kyrgyz people, however these kinds of beliefs are met in everyday practices too. For example, some parts of sheep meat are forbidden to children. Other parts of sheep meat are given to children to eat in order to gain some desired qualities. Girls are not given the tip of a sheep tongue, so that they do not become quarrelsome. Instead, they are given palate of the sheep, so that they become skilful embroiderer, or tendon, so that girls' hair grows long and strong. When distributing meat, which is usually done by an elderly male of the family, a child is openly told why or why not is s/he being given that particular part. This is one of the enculturation processes of a Kyrgyz child, which occur through constant teaching of parents and their comments.

The concept of "*keshik*" among Kyrgyz people is another way of enculturation of a Kyrgyz child. *Keshik* is food which is brought home after a special occasion. It is usually parents, who bring *keshik* to children. As a rule parents bring confection after attending parties, celebrations or funerals, but they especially make sure that they bring something for their children to taste, if the event was special. One of the purposes of the *keshik* is to transfer good qualities to their children. If it is a birthday party of a very old person, parents bring some confection from the party to their children, so that they also reach that person's age; if it is a wedding anniversary of elderly people, then so that their children also have a long happy marriage; if it is a party organized by successful and rich people, then so that their children also have such successful and wealthy life. Mothers bring *keshik* after the funeral of 80 or 90-year old people, so that their children also live that long. By bringing their children things that have connection to good qualities, parents mention where the *keshik* is coming from and openly wish for their children those qualities. In the following section I will pause on blessings, which greatly contribute to raising and educating a Kyrgyz child in a desired way.

The Concept of "Bata"

Bata, a Kyrgyz word that stands for blessings, is essential for each Kyrgyz person. There is a proverb saying: "*Bata menen el kogorot, jamgyr menen jer kogorot*" [People "get green" (develop) with blessings; the Earth gets green with rain]. People try to get blessings as much as possible. They believe in the power of blessings and one of the reasons for conducting rituals in a big circle is that the more blessings they get, the better.

Blessings of the elderly people are believed to be effective and powerful. When giving blessings all people, who are present at that time, open their palms and an honourable, respected elderly person in the group gives blessings and after the blessing words are pronounced all sitting people "wash their faces with the blessings" by going with their open palm from forehead down to the chins. The person, giving blessings, stresses those desired qualities which the community wants to see in a growing child. Blessings are the wishes of the elderly people, which are usually expressed in an instructing tone, such as "Be happy, live long life, be healthy, be well-mannered and caring child to your parents, etc.…", which are followed by many other Kyrgyz words, that mean well-being, abundance, prosperity.

According to my informant, "*bata* is a psychologically influencing power, energy. If the blessings are given by all people, who are present, and if they are given from the bottom of their hearts, the person, to whom blessings are directed, will be in such an aura, where the ideas and intentions in the blessings will be absorbed by that person that s/he will psychologically prepare himself/herself to achieve the values mentioned in the blessings". This implies that blessings have educating character as well. They not only affect the person for whom blessings are directed, but also others, who learn about the values of the community and what the community expects from its members.

Blessings are given not only on special occasions, but in everyday life too, especially when the younger people do something good for the elderly, such as pouring water to their hands, giving places in public transportations, or helping them to carry their bags. According to Kyrgyz tradition, children in the family, usually male children, should pour water to the hands of guests before the main meal is served. The younger children are sent by parents on purpose so that they pour water and receive blessings. It is also one of the ways of contributing to the development and enculturation of children. Further in the following section I will discuss in details what values are praised much in bringing up a Kyrgyz child.

Part 3: Enculturation of Kyrgyz Children in regard to Values

As it is the relationship that defines a child, a Kyrgyz child is expected to have a certain identity, a certain way of acting and a certain place in a hierarchical society. If a child acts in a way that does not fall into the community's expectation, then it is not the child, but its parents, who are blamed for that. That is why parents make sure that the child is brought up with certain qualities. It is not only parents' rights to control the behaviour of the child, but all elderly people feel obliged to comment on a child's good and bad acts. As the whole community invests in a child's proper development through blessings and wishes, in the same way, the whole community expects from the child that it behaves in a proper way.

Tarbiya is a very important concept in bringing up a Kyrgyz child. *Tarbiya* is translated as bringing up a child with good manner. It is informal education full of wisdom, proverbs, prohibitions, skills that teaches a child to what is good and bad, what is right and wrong, what is allowed and prohibited to do in the society. In other words, it is an enculturation process. A child is like a harvest, what you plant, you will get at the end. Giving birth to a child, raising it, educating it and teaching desired skills, all are included in *tarbiya*.

In this section I will pause on three values that every Kyrgyz child should acquire through *tarbiya*. These are *yimanduuluk* (good manner), discipline, and work. These three concepts are not independent; they complement each other, and at the same time they include in themselves many other values, which are essential for the proper development of a child.

Yimanduuluk

Yimanduuluk is a quality of a well-mannered, polite, humble, discreet person, who respects both seniors and juniors. For Kyrgyz people it is quality number one, which parents want to see and expect from their children. When I asked my informants what an *yimanduu*[4] child means, the most common answers I got were: "a child who takes care of its parents when they become old", "who listens and obeys its parents and respects them". Respect to parents holds in itself a hint of fear in front of parents. According to one of my informants before children were *yimanduu* – they feared from their parents, were disciplined and were ready to fulfil whenever parents gave orders.

The elderly people's idea about *yimanduu* child is that the child respects the elderly and gives place to them in public transportation and keeps silence when an elderly person talks or scolds them. If a child says something back to the elder person, that child is accepted as being without *yiman*, and even called "that child is not a child, as it argues with the elderly"!

Yimanduuluk of Kyrgyz people is unique. As an example one of my informants took the way meat is distributed at the table. He noted that the honourable parts of distributed meat are given to the elderly and the daughter-in-law is given a small piece of meat. She will not get offended, because she takes meat according to her own position. "This is Kyrgyz people's democracy!" – he stated. It was so strange for him to accept how in other countries children sue their parents for inequality and he sadly admitted that with globalization Kyrgyz children are losing their good qualities. On the contrary, being one of the activists of giving voice to children, Qvortrup (1990) starts his article with the history of western societies where he mentions the right to be 'heard' as a sign of democracy. Qvortrup's "democracy" contradicts the "democracy" that this middle-aged Kyrgyz man described and the democracy in the former meaning would assume the loss of *yimanduluk* in a local Kyrgyz context.

Some more qualities were added to the meaning of *yimanduuluk* with the influence of Soviet Union and Islam on Kyrgyz people. In Islam, which is becoming strong in Kyrgyzstan, the first and the most important meaning of *yimanduuluk* is to recognize God, be afraid of God and know that God is watching. Islam also focuses a lot on clothes for girls, stating that *yimanduu* girl is the one, who covers her head and body.

During the Soviet time *yimanduu* person was the person who knew how to behave properly in the public. For example taking a place and sitting still and not moving without permission at school, or being quiet in cinemas and waiting for the break, so as not to disturb others during the film were accepted as qualities of a well-mannered person. Several people, who were brought up during the Soviet time mentioned how their parents would send them to another room when guests came and they listened to their parents and did not go out until guests left. Sometimes they even did not see the faces of guests. *Yimanduuluk* during the Soviet time had more connection to discipline. Further I will look at discipline more in details.

Discipline

Yimanduu child is a disciplined child. Kyrgyz people achieve discipline through proverbs as well as with prohibitions and scolding. Kyrgyz people do not stress much on the length of being a child, but the quality of a child matters a lot to them.

Scolding is one of the elements of raising a child and it has positive consequences. Parents scold children in order to keep them disciplined. It is also a way of gaining respect, which is based on a hint of fear in front of parents, otherwise children would "get onto the heads of their parents", "wander" or "become disobedient".

When a child starts to understand what is good and bad, parents start using "prohibitions" in their upbringing, i.e., many "Don'ts"[5]. These prohibitions are not the prohibitions that limit a child from its everyday activity or rights, but prohibitions are on deeds, which a child should learn to avoid in its life. The examples of such prohibitions are: "Don't kick the door when you open"; "Don't push people on your way"; "Don't fetch water in darkness"; "Don't pour dirty water on the street"; "Don't join when elderly people are speaking"; "Don't sit facing your back to people when pouring tea"[6]. These prohibitions regulate not a child's behaviour, but its relationship with and attitude to others. The concern of parents on "What people would say, if their child acts inappropriately", urges them to watch after their children's manner. As one of my informants said, "a well brought up child is mother's happiness" and it is usually mothers and grandmothers from whom children learn many prohibitions and proverbs.

Proverbs and sayings are used regularly in a Kyrgyz people's everyday life for educating purposes. People themselves underline the philosophy of Kyrgyz people to deliver wisdom through few words. From the early age children receive many proverbs about "a good child" *versus* "a bad child", such as "a good child is a hardworking child, a bad child is a spoiled child"; "a good child is obedient, a bad child is shy", which already lays pathways in a child's consciousness of what is expected from a good child. A good "*jigit*" (young man) is the one, "who speaks less and listens more". A child who speaks much and argues with the elderly is a child without *tarbiya*, a child without *yiman*.

Instead, Kyrgyz parents pressure their children to observe and grasp. One of my informants noted that Kyrgyz people were nomads and lived close to nature and depended on nature. Parents tried to sharpen in their children the ability to feel the situation and adapt quickly, otherwise they would not be able to survive. "Watch and learn" tactics is very strong among Kyrgyz people, and these are qualities parents assume will be learned by children. A Kyrgyz child is evaluated not only on its own terms, but also in terms on the people by whom it is raised. The proverb "The apple does not fall far from its stem" is highly believed by Kyrgyz people. There is a similar proverb in Kyrgyz, which is complemented by other sayings, such as "*Ejesin korup singdi osot, agasyn korup ini osot*" (A younger sister grows by watching her elder sister, a younger brother grows by watching his elder brother), "*Enesin korup kyzyn al*" (marry the girl, by looking at her mother).

The last proverb means that one can evaluate his future bride by evaluating her mother. That was the basis for a traditional marriage of Kyrgyz people, which was a negotiated marriage. "*Bel kuda*" (Belly in-laws), "*beshik kuda*" (Cradle in-laws) were already appointed by friends who wished to see each other as in-laws. Even today, when searching for a good spouse, it is usually mentioned how "parents of the bride or groom are good people", which implies that a child is also a good person. A bad child shames its parents. That is why parents pay great attention to raising their children with good qualities and skills. *Tarbiya* is not only good manner and discipline, but also skills, which I will discuss in detail further.

Work as Upbringing

In this article I do not look at the concept of work itself, instead I look at its role in an enculturation process, in shaping a Kyrgyz child. Kyrgyz people think of work as one of the means of upbringing. The more work a child performs, the cleverer a child becomes and the more it learns. First, through work children gain skills, which are needed in their lives. Especially girls are examined by their in-laws. If a girl fails the examination, it is only the girl's mother who is criticized, or on the contrary, praised, if she does well.

Second, parents gain respect through strict upbringing, which is realized through discipline and work. One lady's husband was a strict person, who always made her children work. She was against that and let her children out to play when her husband was at work. Later she started to notice that her children ignored her orders, and they became disciplined in presence of their father. After that she concluded that it is good if children are brought up strictly and she not once mentioned that a good child is the one, who works and helps parents.

Third, work builds good manner in children, otherwise they become egoist and incompetent. One old Kyrgyz man noted that now children are being brought up in a wrong direction and the reason for that is *barchylyk*, which means life in sufficiency. According to him, now there is enough food for children to eat; parents dress them and shoe them, and buy whatever their children demand. Everything is ready for children that they do not work. It was also mentioned by other informants that easy life without work spoils children and makes them lazy and brings up a child, who lacks diligence. The concept of work is tightly connected to the concepts of "*yimanduuluk*" and discipline, all of which are the characteristic of *tarbiya* – good upbringing.

Conclusion

In this chapte, I defined a child and determined its childhood by looking at what a child really is, what status it holds and what role it plays in a particular society. A child cannot be defined on its own – a child is carrying a value, a child is creating a relationship, and a child is holding a meaning. By looking at the concept of "child" through local perceptions on the construction of and upbringing a child, I aimed to show not the "problematic", but a "normal" childhood of Kyrgyz children. I showed that the "normalness" in child work or "muted child" among Kyrgyz people does not underestimate a child, but on the contrary gives a positive impression about the child. I did not touch the issue of agency directly. However, my arguments on local concepts on enculturation showed that agency can be understood and accepted differently in different cultures and by giving voices to children, one can steal "an ideal childhood" of children in that society.

Due to space limitations, I also did not look at exceptional cases such as problematic child, disobedient child, or children that are brought up by grandparents or other relatives, while their parents are working abroad, which is also a common case in Kyrgyzstan. Neither did I touch the influence of globalization in the development of Kyrgyz youth, which is changing the model of a Kyrgyz child.

A Kyrgyz child is determined not by age, but by relationships, attitude, tasks, and expectations. It is not the length, but the quality of childhood, which matters to Kyrgyz people. A child is constructed through constant building, planting, teaching, and moulding not only by its parents, but the whole community. The concepts of *bata*, transmission of qualities, *tarbiya*, *yimanduuluk*, discipline and work are all inseparable from a Kyrgyz child. In the same way it is impossible to look at a Kyrgyz child out of the context of Kyrgyz culture, as children are the bearers and continuers of cultural values, especially in traditional societies. Children in each culture are unique on their own and the study of children in each culture requires separate judgement.

Not only the juxtaposition of child and adult, but also juxtaposition of children of different ages or children within one family could contribute immensely to the study of childhood. James and Prout (1990) talk about childhood as past, future, timeless culture of childhood, where children are juxtaposed to adults and how shift goes from childhood to adulthood. In Kyrgyz culture age is not an indicator of child-adult distinction and there is not a clear division between a child and an adult, because a Kyrgyz child experiences not the shift from childhood to adulthood, but the shift from childhood to personhood. This is what a Kyrgyz childhood is all about.

NOTES

1. For more information see Platenkamp, J. (2010). *Becoming a Lao Person: Rituals of Birth and Socialization in Luang Prabang, Laos*, in *Anthropology of Values*.
2. *Chachala* (a Kyrgyz word) consists of sweets, small fried pieces of bread, biscuits, which are used in rituals to "invite" abundance, goodness, and "sweet" life.
3. *Boorsok* (a Kyrgyz word) – small fried pieces of bread.
4. *Yimanduu* (a Kyrgyz word) is an adjective of the word *yimanduuluk* (noun), mentioned above.
5. My informants noted that they start to use prohibitions with a child, when the child starts to "understand", which is the age of 6 or when a child starts to go to

school. However, I noticed that parents already start using "Don'ts" much earlier than that.

6. One can find more prohibitions in Murzakmetov (2007), who points out prohibitions related to food, clothes, activity and ethics.

REFERENCES

Alderson, P. 1998. "Understanding, wisdom and rights: Assessing children's competence," (pp. 157-172) *In:* D.K. Behera (ed.), *Children and Childhood in Our Contemporary Societies*. Delhi: Kamla-Raj Enterprises.

Alex, G. 2009. *Learning and Embodying Caste, Class and Gender: Patterns of Childhood in Rural Tamil Nadu*. Chennai: National Folklore Support Centre.

Aries, Ph. 1962. *Centuries of Childhood: A Social History of Family Life*. New York: Random House.

Behera, D.K. (ed.). 2007. *Childhoods in South Asia*. New Delhi: Pearson Longman.

Berger, P., R. Hardenberg, E. Kattner, & M. Prager. (eds.). 2010. *The Anthropology of Values: Essays in Honour of Georg Pfeffer*. Delhi: Pearson.

Bueler-Niederberger, D. 1998. "The Separative View – Is There Any Scientific Approach to Children", (pp. 51-66). *In:* D.K. Behera (ed.), *Children and Childhood in Our Contemporary Societies*. Delhi: Kamla-Raj Enterprises.

Chowdhury, A. 2007. "Family Effectiveness in Developing Competencies: A Case of Disadvantages Adolescents in Berhampur," (pp. 306-320). *In:* D.K. Behera (ed.), *Childhoods in South Asia*. New Delhi: Pearson Longman.

Christensen, P. 2000. "Childhood and the Cultural Constitution of Vulnerable Bodies", (pp. 38-59). *In:* A. Prout (ed.), *The Body, Childhood and Society*. New York: St. Martin's Press, Inc.

Gregory, Ch. 2010. "Siblingship as a Value in Middle India", (pp. 3-18). *In:* P. Berger, R. Hardenberg, E. Kattner & M. Prager (eds.), *The Anthropology of Values: Essays in Honour of Georg Pfeffer*. Delhi: Pearson.

James, A. & A. Prout. (eds.). 1990. *Constructing and Reconstructing Childhood: Contemporary Issue in the Sociological Study of Childhood*. Basingstoke: The Falmer Press.

James, A., Ch. Jenks & A. Prout. 1998. *Theorizing Childhood*. Cambridge: Polity Press.

Jenks, Ch. 2005. *Childhood*. 2nd ed. London and New York: Routledge Taylor and Francis Group.

Lancy, F.D. 2008. *The Anthropology of Childhood: Cherubs, Chattel, Changelings*. United Kingdom: Cambridge University Press.

Montgomery, H. 2009. *An Introduction to Childhood: Anthropological Perspectives in Children's Lives*. Oxford: Wiley-Blackwell.

Murzakmetov, A. 2007. *Kyrgyzdardagy balanyn torolushuno jana osushuno bailanyshkan yrym-jyrymdar menen ishenimder (Tushtuk Kyrgyzstandyn materialdary boiuncha)*. Synopsis. Bishkek.

Murzakmetov, A., 2011. "Termele ber archa beshik," *Shookum*, August [online].

Otten, T. 2010. "The Concept of Biba among the Rona of Highland Orissa: Wedding

Rituals to Ensure Health", (pp. 143-161). *In:* P. Berger, R. Hardenberg, E. Kattner & M. Prager (eds.), *The Anthropology of Values: Essays in Honour of Georg Pfeffer*. Delhi: Pearson.

Platenkamp, J. 2010. "Becoming a Lao Person: Rituals of Birth and Socialization in Luang Prabang, Laos", (pp. 180-200). *In:* P. Berger, R. Hardenberg, E. Kattner & M. Prager (eds.), *The Anthropology of Values: Essays in Honour of Georg Pfeffer*. Delhi: Pearson.

Qvortrup , J. 1990. "A Voice for Children in Statistical and Social Accounting: A Plea for Children's Right to be Heard", (pp.78-98). *In*: A. James & A. Prout (eds.), *Constructing and Reconstructing Childhood: Contemporary Issue in the Sociological Study of Childhood*. Basingstoke: The Falmer Press.

Solberg, A. 1990. "Negotiating Childhood: Changing Constructions of Age for Norwegian Children", (pp. 118-137). *In*: A. James & A. Prout (eds.), *Constructing and Reconstructing Childhood: Contemporary Issue in the Sociological Study of Childhood*. Basingstoke: The Falmer Press.

UNICEF. 2011. Situation Assessment of Children in the Kyrgyz Republic. Report. [pdf] UNICEF. [Accessed 25 February, 2012].

Waterson, R. & D.K. Behera. 2011. "Introduction: Extending Ethnographic Research with Children in the Asia-Pacific Region", *The Asia Pacific Journal of Anthropology*, 12 (5): 411-425.

Zelizer, V. 1985. *Pricing the Priceless Child: The Changing Social Value of Children*. New York: Basic Books.

FOUR

BRINGING UP CHILDREN: A Study of Child Rearing Beliefs and Practices among the Khasi of Meghalaya

GEETIKA RANJAN

Introduction

Child rearing is an integral part of socialization of a child. Despite the continuous, fast paced advancement of "life" as such in this globalized world – a world of consumer culture, each culture specific way of bringing up children reiterates the notion that behind the final, manifested adult world lies the whole process of childhood experiences and child rearing – an ensemble of traditional and modern beliefs and practices, all catering to produce a well socialized groomed individual. A cultural reality, child rearing becomes a micro level specific fact when understood against the backdrop of a particular culture. Certain humanistic anthropologists hold that cultural systems are based on inherently different symbol systems and conceptualizations, precluding any possibility of systematic cross-cultural comparison (Edwards and Bloch, 2010: 487) and some psychologists suggest that a "universal" child development cannot be found (Bloch, 1991, 2000 and Lubeck, 1994). There are some key parameters which determine the overall development of the child. Super and Harkness (1986,1999) and Harkness and Super (2010) emphasize on (a) "the physical and social settings and daily routines in which and through which the child lives, learns, grows, and develops; (b) parenting practices, the culturally regulated routines of child care and child training that are used by the child's caregivers; and (c) cultural belief systems, the cognitive models and folk theories, or *parental ethnotheories*, that caregivers hold and bring to their interaction with children"(cited in Edwards and Bloch, 2010 : 488).

Child care, anthropologically speaking, can be understood as the series of arrangements for the caring of children which derive from family lifestyles and external factors such as the economy and the nature of regulation in the larger society (Zimmer, 1979: 1). Anthropological studies have contributed towards the understanding of child rearing in holism. The interlinked trajectory of culture and personality has been well brought out in the ethnographic works of early anthropologists like Margaret Mead (1928a, 1928b) and B. Malinowski (1929) who contributed further to the understanding of childhood. Later, John and Beatrice Whitings' (1975) *Six Culture Studies on Children* adds a fresh chapter to the understanding of the enmeshed existence of psychology and anthropology. Abram Kardiner (1939) postulated the "basic personality structure" shared by the members of a culture. He discusses the role of the primary and secondary institutions of a culture in the formation of the personality of people of a culture and attributes the formation of the "basic personality structure" to the "primary institutions" of a culture. For Kardiner, "A primary institution is one which is older, more stable, and less likely to be interfered with by vicissitudes of climate or economy" (*ibid.* : 471). These institutions are "most directly concerned with disciplining, gratifying, and inhibiting the infant and young child" (Harris, 2001: 436). The early childhood phase nurtured in the primary institutions of feeding, weaning and training of young children play a pivotal role in the development of the "basic personality structure". While explaining the secondary institutions, Kardiner writes that these "satisfy the needs and tensions created by the primary of fixed ones" (*ibid.*, 476) and emphasizes on "taboo systems, religion, rituals, folktales and techniques of thinking" (*ibid.*, 471) as important secondary institutions. It is between the primary and secondary institutions that Kardiner places the "basic personality structure". Thus, the initial years of childhood in a culture form the platform of shared personality traits of its members. Here we shall focus on the beliefs and practices about pregnancy and post delivery phase and nurturing of early childhood. The emphasis shall be on the food habits, childhood games and lullabies. The focus shall be the very early years of a child's life.

The Khasi

Khasi is a tribe in Meghalaya, a State in India's north-east. Mainly inhabiting the Khasi hills area of the State, the community follows the matrilineal system wherein descent and inheritance is traced in female line, from the mother to the daughter. There is a saying among the Khasi, "*long jaid na ka kynthei*" (from the woman sprang the clan) (Gurdon, 1906: 82). The Khasi, excluding the War (a sub-group of the Khasi), practice female ultimogeniture, the youngest daughter known as *Ka Khadduh* inheriting the lion's share of both ancestral and acquired property of the parents (Pakyntein, 172). The other daughters also receive some share of the property. The term *lap Duh* or extinction is applied to a family which has no female issue or heiress. Such a family is known as *Ing lap Duh*. The term *lap Duh* is also applicable to a woman who has no female issue or is a spinster and such a family and woman is looked down upon (*ibid.*). This underscores the importance of a girl child in the Khasi family. Birth of the girl child is coveted in the Khasi family. However, it would be too naïve to rush to conclude that the girls are the preferred offsprings and boys are at the receiving end. Behind the apparent privileged position of the *Ka Khadduh* (the heiress) lies the heavy responsibility of fulfilling all family obligations. The general assumption that matrilineal descent gives women a dominant position collapses under the weight of the reality of their actual condition — the multiple burden they bear and their actual existence under male-centred authority (Das and Bezbaruah, 2011: 2). Impact of Christianity can be seen in practically every sphere of Khasi life. The present study shows that the Khasis have almost done away with many traditions related to the upbringing of children, such as ceremonies and customs related to the birth and naming of children. Gurdon (1906) has explicitly explained the lengthy process of naming the new born child. Yet there has been partial curtailment of many such practices related to child birth and child rearing.

To state that with time and with the growth in consumer culture as well as with the ushering of the era of globalization the customs and traditions related to child rearing have undergone change would be stating the obvious. As Walsh and Kiernan in their study on Ireland state that our concept of children is context-linked and time specific and has evolved greatly over the past hundred years. In the early part of the century, families were invariably large with a modal size of 7-9 children, reducing to 4-6 children in the 1970s (2001: 1). In the earlier part of the twentieth century, many households contained three generations, incorporating grandparents or grandaunts, parents and children. This model provided assistance for mothers in rearing children, as this was often combined with multiple duties both inside and outside the home. The decline of the prevalence of the three generational family impacted on the availability of personnel to aid child rearing and childcare within the home and many commentators remarked the impact of this on the childcare process (*ibid.*, 4). Paucity of time and a globalized culture may have curtailed the elaborate traditional processes of child rearing, yet the intrinsic essence, the culture specific, tradition enriched beliefs and practices are still adhered to in bringing up children.

The present research is based on both primary and secondary data. I collected data through interviews conducted in the Umshing-Mawkynroh area of the city of Shillong. Khasi parents and mostly mothers were interviewed. These mothers work as domestic helps, as vegetable sellers, newspaper vendors and as employees in offices. Languages of communication were Hindi and English. While carrying out the present research, I observed that Khasi women are very industrious and contribute in an important way to the family income apart from trying to fulfil their responsibility as mothers and wives. It was also observed that the respondents informed about the Khasi beliefs and practices, but could not tell about the reason behind the practice. Beliefs and rituals related to child rearing are undoubtedly alive and continuing yet how these came into existence, the rationale behind their function—are questions which did not receive clear answers.

Beliefs and Practices related to Pregnancy

The Khasi believe that the foundation to an individual's complete personality is laid from the time he/she is conceived in the mother's womb. Thus, during pregnancy, a woman, her husband and other relatives should abide by certain rules in order to ensure the protection and well-being of the to-be-born child. Shillong, a hill station witnesses rainfall almost all the whole year. Presence of snakes is common here and killing snakes for safety is a day to day feature. However, husband of a pregnant woman is forbidden to kill a snake during the pregnancy of his wife. The respondents did not mention the prohibition on the killing of any other creature except the snake as the latter is the only organism which poses threat to life and its presence is a regular feature in the vicinity of the home. According to the respondents, the family members of the would-be parents have to abstain from indulging in illicit sexual relationship. The unmarried sisters of the pregnant woman should not have sex as long as their sister is pregnant. Adherence to this taboo is not much emphasized upon in case of the unmarried brothers of the pregnant woman. The women respondents inform that sexual liaisons before marriage are looked down upon and considered *wrong, but they happen.* Similarly, the Khasi believe that the husband of a pregnant woman should not stray and have sex with another woman. It is believed that if a close relative of the pregnant woman (like the unmarried sister and the husband) breaks this taboo, the child will be born dead. However, if the guilty accepts his/her *crime* and repents then the child in the womb shall be safe.

A new born is fed with a solution of luke warm water and sugar apart from mother's milk for 2-3 days after birth. After a week this is supplemented with boiled and mashed rice and mashed banana. When the baby turns 3-4 months old it is given boiled squash (a gourd like vegetable), boiled pumpkin and boiled potato. On the first birthday (*sngikha*), the ritual of the removal of the natal hair is performed known as *Khap shmuh*. The mother's brother (*ma hap)* cuts the hair with scissors and not with a knife as the sharp metal edge may cause injury to the child. On the same day the child is taken to the church. He is dressed in new clothes—baby suit, cap, socks and shoes—all in white colour, for the God's blessing. In the evening, a grand feast is organized to celebrate the first birthday of the child. On this occasion pork, beef, chicken, rice, etc., is prepared. Khasi children are indulged in and well taken care of irrespective of the economic class of the parents. Khasis believe in the evil influence of the evil eye and follow certain practices to protect the small children from the evil eye.

They apply a little lime on the scalp of the child and also make a cross of lime on his/her navel to ward off the evil eye. While applying the lime the mother mildly spits (*thu thu*), a gesture symbolizing casting away the evil.

In the early childhood years, the child lives in the care of the mother and other women in the family. The father is usually out of the house, working. Mother's are also working, either as domestic help or selling goods. Khasi women working as domestic helps in 5-6 houses leave their children behind in the care of their mother or other elderly women in the family. Those who go to sell vegetables, meat and fish, *kwai* (beetle nut) are seen carrying their infants to work. First the baby is wrapped in a cloth (*jainit*). Then the baby is carried on the back on a bigger piece of cloth (*jainkup)* which is hung on the shoulder like a sling with the baby there. The women go about their chores with the child properly and comfortably secured on the back.

Lullabies and Folk Tales

"The education of very small children is entirely in the hands of their mothers and grandmothers. It is carried on through the medium of lullabies. Very simply defined, a lullaby is a type of song sung by mothers and nurses all over the world to coax their babies to sleep. It is in fact a cradle song. The simplest form of a lullaby is humming or a repetition of monotonous and soothing sounds, often accompanied by a gentle rocking of the child in the arms or in its bed or cradle" (War, 2007: 5). The secure touch, the soothing, familiar voice stands incomparable to all the music of the world played through mechanical devices like the cassette player, CDs, etc. However, the present research shows that young mothers (18-25 years) claimed to know very few lullabies and sang only those for their children. However, their mothers or other elder women in the family have a rich stock of lullabies.

Some examples of Khasi lullabies as reported by the respondents:

Thiah khop khop ko hep barit
Thiah khop khop i'a phi ngan bah
Thiah khop khop u tai u myrsiang
Thiah khop khop u la phet sha khlaw
Thiah khop khop ba ngan dung khaw.

English Translation:

Sleep small child
I will tie you on my back
Sleep or the fox will come
Now fox has run away in the jungle
Then I will pound the rice (If you will not sleep
I will not be able to work).

Thiah thiah noh ko hep
Thiah thiah noh mynta
I mei e la kynoi ia phi mynta
Por mynstep phi la khie

Nga shim ia phi ngan rah
Te shuwa ban ngan ai bam
Nga pyu sum shuwa ia phi.

Ynda phi la dep bam
Nga ledup ia phi bau kynoi
Ynda phi lah ioh thiah
Nga buh ia phi ha jing thiah.

English Translation:

Sleep, sleep son
Sleep, sleep now
Mother is rocking you to sleep
In the morning you wake up
I take you and hold you
Before giving you food, I'll bathe you,
When you finish eating
I will hold you and make you sleep
When you have slept, I'll put you in the bed.

An excellent write-up on Khasi lullabies by Daphinda War explores the hard day-to-day realities of life experienced by the Khasi tribal. She illustrates the folk poetics inherent in lullabies. As a mother, she clearly understands the effectiveness of these poems which humans have responded to as a biological reality (Kharmawphalang, 2007: 3). She analyzes a well known lullaby explaining it against the broader backdrop of the culture from which it emerges. This lullaby involves handling of the infant's fingers by the singer.

Ong kani e ja bei
Ong kani nei wan u ioh
Ong kani pan ram pan chah
phet sha khlo
bam da u sla patho.

English Translation:

This one (finger) says give me rice, mother,
This one (finger) says for whom is the rice,

This one (finger) says let's borrow some,
run to the jungles
let's eat pumpkin leaves.

Daphinda War writes that this lullaby "is sung by the mother who takes the infant's fingers one by one, starting with the small finger, going on to the next, and next, as the succeeding lines come, ending with the thumb, and lifting it to the infant's mouth. There are five lines in the lullaby, each meant for one finger of the infant's single hand. The text of the lullaby suggests some kind of food scarcity which is reflected from lines two to five. The reference to pumpkin leaves, which is an item of a poor man's diet, suggests this. Pumpkin leaves grow abundantly in the jungle and when cooked proves to be very wholesome and filling rice and cucurbits. But inversely, the song might reflect that the baby has been fed and the singer thinks it is time for it to go to sleep, which can effectively be induced by making it suck its thumb. Seen in any way, the lullaby is a highly creative one, aided by some action on the part of the singer" (2007: 7).

Khasis have a very rich heritage of folk tales and fables, which continue to be preserved generation after generation and which form the rich content of stories told to small children. A Khasi house, no matter how humble its standards are, is kept very clean. Cleanliness is a characteristic feature of a Khasi household. The smallest and the simplest of Khasi houses will have a clean look, a small garden or at least some flower pots. Cleanliness as a way of life for the Khasis is well exemplified in a well known folk tale which is very popular with children, titled *The Lazy Turtle* by Bijoya Sawain:

The Lazy Turtle

Long, long ago there lived a turtle in a pond in the woods. Besides being most unpleasing in her appearance she was also known for her slothful ways. The only time she exerted herself was in the evening when the reflection of the stars crowded the pond. She would dive into the water and swim around each star, in turn, circling it for hours, exulting in its beauty.

Now, up in the sky, the handsomest of all the stars, *U Lurmangkara,* the Evening Star began to notice the turtle's charming evening ritual. He was flattered to observe so faithful an admirer of him and his kinsmen, the stars in the sky. He thought it would certainly please her to be the consort of the star and a fitting tribute to so loyal an admirer. So, he decided to come down to earth and propose to her, totally unaware, was he, of her way of life.

One evening he descended with all his wealth and in all its finery to marry the turtle. By the time he realized how unattractive and, unbelievably, sloppy she was in her ways and appearance, it was too late to withdraw. So, as befitted a gentleman of his repute and standing he married her. He showered her with all the luxury and affection he could and very gently tried to change her slothful ways. The turtle, however, instead of endeavouring to improve her, blessed as she was with such an exceptional husband, became even worse. Her adoring husband's devotion made her arrogant, stubborn and even lazier and filthier.

U Lurmangkara admonished her several times, but without success. He tried to teach, explain, cajole so that she may change her way of life, but she did not heed his words. Finally, after many months he, tired and repulsed by the slovenly existence which was totally alien to him, left his wife and returned to the sky.

When he was gone, the turtle realized what a grave mistake she had made and what an immense loss his departure was to her. She trudged around, her head uplifted, trying to locate him in the skies, a phenomenon that exists even to this day. She swam around his reflection every evening attempting to lure him back, but to no avail.

So, the Khasis always say that cleanliness is next to only godliness. To ignore this virtue will not only induce ill health but also unsound judgment, misfortune and loss (Sawain, 2010: 271-272).

Childhood Games

With the television boom coming in a big way, globalized representation of entertainment of small children can be garnered from the popularity of cartoon shows on television and other children programmes and concerns have also been raised about the content of children's programmes on television (Agarwal, 1999). Amidst such a scenario, going back to the games played in the yester years could be very welcome for all round development of the child.

It was interesting to observe that some respondents do not have a television set at home. Their children watch television programmes in the houses of other neighbours who are also their relatives.

Case Study

This is the case of a 24 years old Khasi woman Agnis who is the *Ka*

Khadduh (youngest daughter). She lives with her mother, her husband, her unmarried brothers and unmarried sister in her mother's house. She works as a domestic help in six houses. She has two children; a daughter aged seven years and a son, one year old. Her husband sells poultry and does other odd jobs like working as temporary labour. Her two younger brothers are school drop outs and dependents on the family income. The main and regular source of family income is what Agnis earns, i.e., rupees five thousand per month and almost the same amount earned by her unmarried sister who also works as a domestic help. All the earnings are pooled together and spent under the control of the matriarch, Agnis' mother. The family has eleven domesticated animals – pig, fowls, cats and a dog. Agnis sends her daughter to a well known school in Shillong. A catholic school, it is almost eight kilometres from Agnis' home. A Government Central School is very near to Agnis' house. Agnis does not want her daughter to study in the Central School and chooses to send her to the Catholic school despite the latter charging more fee and calling for higher commutation expense. Agnis has a very hectic daily schedule. She drops her daughter to school every day by shared taxi, goes about her work as a domestic help, and picks up her daughter from school. Her one year old son stays in the care of her mother at home. Agnis has not bought a television as she feels that her children will get spoilt by watching too much TV. Moreover, since her elder married sister who lives near the main house, i.e., Agnis' house has a TV and she and her children daily watch the programmes there. Thus the whole extended family of Khasi sisters and their husbands and unmarried brothers meet and spend time with each other almost on a daily basis.

Khasi children play some games which continue to be part of Khasi childhood from generation to generation. One common game is called *Sohthingkoh* in which a big rectangle is drawn on the ground with a stone or chalk. It is further divided into eight rectangles and squares. One player drops a small piece of flat stone which is drifted from first square to the last while skipping on one leg. The player pushes the small stone from one block to the next with one foot, to reach the last block. If in the process the small stone comes on the line between one block and the other then the player is declared "out" *(ao).* If the player successfully reaches the last block, he/she wins and looking up has to say *oudin.* The other very popular games played by Khasi children are *Iareh* and *Mawkyntiang. Iareh* is like hide and seek, in which children hide and one child has to search for them. In *Mawkyntiang* five small round stones are placed on the ground. One is thrown up and before it falls back, the other four have to be picked up and the falling stone is to be caught in the same hand carrying other four stones. Ludo and snake and ladder are other common games played by children. "Every game represents a certain content expressed in a fixed stabilized form. They contain a positive attitude to life, joy and humour. At the same time they provide the children with the possibility to manifest their fantasy, creative abilities, aesthetic feeling as well as promptness and the like." (Vera Misurcov: www.docstoc.com/search/childhood-games)

Conclusion

Bringing up children in this fast paced, techno savvy world of today comes with its own challenges. Among the Khasi, a tribe, children are growing up amidst the influences of traditional Khasi practices, the Church as well as through exposure to other cultures. As in the case of any other society, Khasi system of child rearing cannot be generalized, as different parameters like class, education and occupation of parents, degree of culture contact with other cultures, exposure to mass media give different shapes to the conclusions on child rearing. Some scholars have noted that definitions of an adequate childhood vary considerably depending on family socioeconomic status. However, what does appear as a general picture is the more or less continuation of traditional child rearing practices as well as the necessary inculcation of the globalised culture brought in the confines of the home through TV as well as through the interaction with the non Khasi world. Early childhood care forms the platform over which a well formed personality is structured and traditional beliefs, practices and folk lore continue to have both pronounced and subtle influence on a child's psyche and his/her manifested presence.

REFERENCES

Agarwal, B.C.1999. *Children's Television in India: A Situational Analysis.* New Delhi: Concept Publishing Company.

Bloch, M.N. 1991. "Critical Science and the History of Child Development's Influence on Early Education Research", *Early Education and Development,* 2 (2): 95-108.

Bloch, M.N. 2000. "Governing Teachers, Parents and Children through Child Development Knowledge", *Human Development,* 43: 257-265.

Das, Gitika and Abhijit Kr Bezbaruah. 2011. "Social Transition and Status of Women among the Khasi Tribe of Meghalaya by Survey Method", *Global Research*

Methodology Journal, 2nd issue, Aug-Sept-Oct.

Gurdon, P.R.T. 1906. *The Khasi*. Delhi : Low Price Publications.

Harris, Marvin. 2001. *Rise of Anthropological Theory*. Maryland : Altamira Press.

Kardiner, Abram. 1939. *The Individual and His Society*. New York: Columbia University Press.

Kharmawphalang, Desmond. 2007. Oral Poetry. *Folklife*. November. 1-24.

Lubeck, S. 1994. "The Politics of Developmentally Appropriate Practice: Exploring Issues of Culture, Class, and Curriculum", (pp.17-43.) *In:* B. Mallory & R. New (eds), *Diversity and Developmentally Appropriate Practices: Challenges for Early Childhood Education*. New York: Teachers College Press.

Malinowski, Bronislaw.1929. *The Sexual Life of Savages in North Western Melanesia*. London: Routledge.

Mead, Margaret.1928a. *Coming of Age in Samoa*. New York: William Morrow.

____. 1928b. "Samoan Children at Work and Play", *Natural History*, 28: 626-636.

Misurcov, Vera. www.docstoc.com/search/childhood-games.

Pakyntein, Valentina, 1999. "Gender Preference in Khasi Society", *In:* T.B. Subba (ed.), *Wonder That is Culture*. New Delhi: Mittal Publications.

Raghavan, C.S.; S. Harkness; and C.M. Super. 2010. "Parental Ethnotheories in the Context of Immigration: Asian Indian Immigrant and Euro-American Mothers and Daughters in an American Town", *Journal of Cross Cultural Psychology*, 41 (4): 617-632.

Sawain, Bijoya. 2010. *Khasi Myths, Legends and Folk Tales*. New Delhi: Sanbun Publishers.

Super, C.M., and S. Harkness. 1986. "The Developmental Niche: A Conceptualization at the Interface of Child and Culture", *International Journal of Behavioral Development*, 9: 545-569.

____. 1999. "The Environment as Culture in Developmental Research", (pp. 279-323). *In:* S.L. Friedman & T.D. Wachs (eds.), *Measuring Environment across the Life Span: Emerging Methods and Concepts*. Washington, DC: American Psychological Association.

Walsh and Kiernan. 2004. "When Two are One: The Changing Nature of Early Childhood Care and Education in Ireland," *ESAI Presentation , CECDE, April.*http://www.cecde.ie/english/pdf/conference_papers/When%20Two%20Are%20One.pdf

War, Daphinda. 2007. "Pleasant Dreams", *Folklife*. November.

Whiting, Beatrice B., and John W.M. Whiting.1975. *Children of Six Cultures: A Psycho-Cultural Analysis*. Cambridge, MA: Harvard University Press.

Zimmer, Richard. 1979. "Necessary Directions for Anthropological Research on Child Care in the United States", *Anthropology & Education Quarterly*, 10 (3): 139-165.

SECTION II

INFORMAL AND FORMAL PROCESS OF LEARNING

FIVE

SANTAL CHILDREN AS GUARDIANS AND INTERPRETERS OF INDIGENOUS KNOWLEDGE

MARINE CARRIN

Forty years ago, I was doing fieldwork in a hill village of Keonjhar in the North of Orissa. The village had a small school where I was living in one room which was contiguous to the boys' dormitory on one side, and to the room of the old Hindu teacher on the other. Every morning, the teacher, a sweet Gandhian fellow of the old type, was singing in praise of Ganesha: "Ganapati ! Ganapati" !! and this emotional prayer which sounded like a desperate call to the god, was followed by the children laughing a little. Then they were taking the prayer as a signal to climb on the wall and get down on my bed... Giggling, they were expecting breakfast and promised in return to teach me everything: "we know all the plants and animals, we know how to listen to them, we know how to catch some of them, we know how to protect them". I had decided to take the boys to their words since Santal men were telling me: "learn, life is colourful for those who learn; a way to tease me, as a young scholar trying to understand 'their culture'".

I conversed in Hindi with the children but I wanted to learn Santali at all cost. I had an old flora, written in the twenties by the Jesuits of Ranchi and republished in 1950, where plant names were written in Hindi and Mundari. I decided to make a start. For animals, I had selected some lists in Bodding's Santal dictionary as well as in Hoffman's *Encyclopaedia*

Mundarica. Plants seemed quite easy, I just asked the children everyday to show me such and such specimen which was already described in the flora. Then I inquired about its use and of the myths which were associated with it. Sometimes some elder boys told me: "that matter we don't know but there is a *gorom baba* (grand-father) who knows—we will take you there, *didi*"! ... Later, in fact, the boys brought to my house Bhagwan Hasdak, an old *ojha* (medicine-man) telling him that I had already learnt a lot, and that they could not teach me any more about plants and animals....

Cultural knowledge is not only transferred from one generation to another; it is also generated among children, giving rise to a children's culture which forms part of the base of the knowledge of the young. Yet it is evident that each generation does not start from a blank slate of cultural knowledge. The approach I want to discuss here, by differentiating forms and modalities of knowledge, is to specify elements of innovation among youth, as well as those borrowed from the previous generation. Innovation, here, refers to knowledge and values generated among the peer group of children and youth, but also to borrowings from outside which bypass, or are rejected by, the parents' generation.

Children as Actors

The Santals, who number 10 to 12 millions, consider themselves as a "tribal people" speaking a different language (Austro-asiatic) and sharing a way of life which implies values different from the Hindus. In previous papers (Carrin, 2005, 2007) I have explored how Santal adults perceive children, and how it is to be a child among the Santals, in a world still shaped by tradition but where indigenous knowledge is pervaded by political awareness and modernity.

Adivasi societies in Central India have often developed a policy of resisting global, capital, savage and corrupt industrial exploitation. The Indian State legitimises its current policies for structural adjustment and liberalisation by promising economic growth for all. But this programme seems necessarily to entail for the rural poor the need for a different model of welfare. For activists and development agencies, sustainability has become inseparable from social equity. This ideology has resulted since two decades in activists trying to mobilize tribal groups for sustainable development (Baviskar, 2005). But *adivasi* assertion has taken a different direction towards a kind of minority identity politics. I shall explore claims about the tribal relationship to nature by showing that these claims do not only concern tribal economy, but aim at redefining the role of *adivasis* themselves in rethinking their world. A central question, here, concerns the transmission of knowledge which is, to some extent, still endogenously determined as the elders, as the village chiefs still embody authority and prestige at the local level. However, their agency is limited, unless they participate in modern roles such as engagement in political parties. I have argued previously that traditional knowledge, as mutual understanding, is changing, as are the positions of power and disempowerment. Later on, I discovered that medicine-men (*ojhas*) were the specialists in indigenous knowledge, and I became their disciple (Carrin, 1986, 1997). More recently, doing research on children, I discovered that they have their own ideas about indigenous knowledge[1]. In this chapter, I try to evaluate how Santal children get access to indigenous knowledge, and how they actively filter it, making it to go well beyond what is provided.

Defining Indigenous Knowledge

What is an indigenous theory? When we read G. Prakash seminal essay "Science between the lines" we understand that the study of the Indian archive involves the analysis of colonialism in culture, as "modernity eclipsed little knowledge and empowered an elite that enunciated the discourse of science" (1996: 58). Because indigenous knowledge has been seen to permit its holders to exist in harmony with nature, it is seen as pivotal in discussions of sustainable resource use (Anderson and Grove, 1987; Ghai and Vivian 1992; Sen 1992). Current formulations about Indigenous Knowledge recognize that derogatory characterizations of the knowledge of the poor and the marginalized may be hasty and naïve. The focus on indigenous knowledge and product systems heralds a long overdue move. It represents a shift from the preoccupation with the centralized, technically oriented solutions of the past.

When I came back to the question of children agency, I found that differences in knowledge was no longer controlled by the elders, but they still provided much of the momentum for social interaction. Following Barth (2002), I argue that knowledge can be understood as a relationship, as an understanding of the balances of sharing, and differences in knowledge are crucial in a society where the corpus of knowledge is changing. In this process, we shall see that children participate in generating the criteria which validate this changing knowledge. Indigenous knowledge of forests and natural resources has been an object of research in India for more than two decades. The appeal of local and indigenous knowledge is not its transfer or operationalization, but its local value as a means of cultural persistence and continuity. In a not so distant past most of the "tribes" of India led a relatively independent and self-reliance life in the forest. Such adaptations still exists for some groups, though their forest habitat has undergone tremendous change the last fifty years. The engagement of the tribals or *adivasis* (from *adi* before and *vasi* resident) with the forest has been both criticized and glorified, as shown by A. Prasad (2003) who has developed a critique of the romanticized notions of tribal life, identity and ecology.

Sarna Religion as a Repertoire of Indigenous Knowledge

Most distinctive of Jharkhand and the Northern part of Orissa is the tribal religion, sometimes called *Sarna Dhorom*, a system of belief in ancestors and the deities called *bongas*, shared by the Mundari speaking tribes[2]. Sarna religion, sometimes seen as pantheist, is not marked by formal institutions, but expressed in family worship of the deities and sacrifices to appease them. The *bongas* are represented by stones and trees and dwell in a sacred grove called Sarna by Mundas, Dessauli by Hos, and Jaher by Santals. In the sacred grove, we find the stones of the spirits associated with the village and with the Creation of Myth. The stones embody these *bongas* who protect the village and the crops, and who are worshipped during the festivals of the agrarian cycle.

Returning to the children, I gradually understood that they were aware of the new religious movements against global warming which were spreading among Oraons and Santals. These movements aimed at revitalizing the forest, mostly led by women, who were planting trees and praying to *Jaher Era*, the female guardian deity of the sacred grove. *Jaher Era* possessed the women weekly, an innovation since possession (*rumok*) is usually taboo to women. Men, on the other hand, continued to be members of the *Sarna Dhorom*, "the return to the sacred grove", the religious movement founded by Ragunath Murmu[3], in the seventies. The ecological dimension has been crucial in reshaping indigenous knowledge around the Sarna, the *adivasi* religion centred on the cult of the *bonga* (Carrin, 2002).

Children as Guardians of Indigenous Knowledge

To show the revival of Sarna religion, I shall quote another small event which happened during another span of field-work I carried out in Hazaribagh (Jharkhand) in 2009. I was in a Santal village, Jobradaga, partly encroaching on the forest. This and the neighbouring sixty-five villages harbour a majority of Santals. Most have been deprived of their lands and are presently trying to regain some of them. Formerly, the Santal of that region used to work as casual labourers for the Hindu Mahtos, who harassed Santal women, a situation which resulted in several murder cases. Nowadays, the Santals try, by all means, to avoid working for the Mahtos, who treat them as untouchables, and the communities avoid contact. The Santals often hold the Mahtos responsible when they fail to find niches in the local market, where they have to compete with other communities. Since most of the Santals do not have enough land, men have to take casual work in illegal mines, carrying coal on their bicycles to sell it to the local mafias. Santal women in their turn try to collect minor forest produce in order to manufacture leaf plates, soap, candles and shampoo. These villages have benefited from the work of an NGO during the last twenty years, and the villagers have been involved in various irrigation works and other agricultural tasks, such as trying to cultivate mushrooms or even rear a new breed of pigs.

The village is sandwiched between Naxalite 'visits' and the Mahtos, who try to harass the villagers—not mentioning the forest officers, who sometimes ask the villagers to provide land tenure papers, and accuse them of encroaching on the reserved forest. The political landscape of the village evokes the market of corruption described by Alpa Shah (2011), against which the *NGO run by adivasi* seems a haven of protection, since its decisions are discussed by all the villagers. Two kilometres away, two nuns have organized a free dispensary and are supervising women's handicraft work for different welfare organizations. One of them has studied sociology at the University of Kolkata, and is quite influential in the *adivasi* NGO, whose direction is taken in charge by a committee of highly responsible graduates, as well as traditional village chiefs. But decisions concerning common welfare, such as schooling, are discussed by all the villagers during monthly assemblies.

But Let Us Come Back to the School...

The literacy rate for tribal children is still below that of the general population. The high percentage of school drop outs, from the lowest levels onwards, is due to the non-functioning of schools in tribal areas, the absenteeism of teachers, language problems and cultural oppression. This often results in the rejection of the mother tongue as inferior, but this is not the case in Hazaribagh where the children view *adivasi* identity with pride. The school where I conducted my interviews is a private boarding school founded by the NGO some years ago. The NGO was directed by a Catholic nun from Goa, who had succeeded, through her personal network, in financing irrigation in the village as well as founding the school. This school is attended regularly by thirty-five to forty children who are taught by *adivasi* teachers, partly paid by the villagers, partly volunteers[4]. The future of the school depends on people's ability to finance it but is proudly perceived by the villagers as "their" project, a school where they hope their children may keep their identity—since they are only too conscious that school is often a place where indigeneity is unmade, especially when children are taught by Hindu teachers, often contemptuous of *adivasi* culture.

Talking with the children I tried to elicit their views concerning plants and animals as indigenous knowledge they could acquire in their leisure time, whenever they were grazing goats, or helping their parents. Compared to the curriculum taught in the school this knowledge seems to rest on observation and does not relate to textbooks. This led me to wonder whether boys and girls could experience the learning of biological categories as a cognitive process. To start, I tried to understand how the children were relating to *adivasi* identity and how they viewed Santali or Mundari in relation to Hindi, perceived as the language of the school and the national language. I should add that I conducted my interviews in Santali, which seemed to surprise the children, who were used to speak Hindi in class since their Oraon teacher did not speak Santali. I could shift to Hindi, if necessary, but I was eager to elicit answers in the mother tongue.

Sharing Santali always implies the feeling of a certain closeness, since, in this area, Santals try to avoid *dikus* (non-tribals) by speaking Santali. Through our conversations we discussed language and identity, and more generally I tried to understand how the children experienced the feeling of belonging to a certain community, having its own traditions. I have divided the children in three age groups, 5 to 8, 8 to 11, 11 to 14, and I have completed these interviews by recording individual narratives of youth aged from 14 to 16 in Jharkhand as well as in Bengal and in Orissa. Analyzing children views on identity, I felt that the idea was linked to the notion of ancestors and to the idea that Sidhu and Kanhu, the leaders of Santal rebellion, have transmitted a gift to the present generation to keep them happy. Moreover, say the children: "if we give this knowledge to others from outside it can be lost. But when we die and when our bones are immersed in the river, this knowledge comes with us". In other words, indigenous knowledge (*bidia*) is perceived as a substance which delimitates the ethnic frontier but which should be kept for oneself, in opposition to school knowledge which is called *sarkari bidia* (government knowledge) and is imposed from outside. In villages where the government gives education and bicycles, children say that they take what is given to them. Nevertheless, the children feel that school training differs from education at home. They say: "in our textbooks, nobody describes our kind of life, everything is easy for the children of the textbooks. Their parents do not fear the forest officers or the contractors. Other children in Mumbai or Chennai should read about our lives, since we read about their lives in our textbooks. This knowledge is not fair". As we see, the children do not feel concerned when the textbooks describe the lives of middle class children, since they resent a kind of social exclusion, not being part of the life of the textbooks.

One day, I had the responsibility to take the class since the teachers were busy at a meeting. While we were discussing, as usual, plants and animals, I requested the children to draw some animals for me. They started by aquatic animals which struck me since these species are important in the Santal creation myth, but the children had another idea. Aquatic creatures, such as shrimps, snails, tortoises, frogs, crabs, were in their opinion the most endangered species, since water was becoming polluted. Some boys described how ponds and rivers had been poisoned by aluminium cleansing and I felt that they were aware of the terrible industrial pollution which threatens Jharkhand (Padel, 2010). "Because of pollution (*bisi* poison), they say, the crabs (*katkom*) and the frogs (*rote*) become smaller, and they do not provide the same food… while the plants wither due to global warming and lose "their vitamins". The children called this knowledge "*ato vidya*" (village knowledge), "we just observe plants and animals and we listen to the elders". The children later explained that village knowledge is the visible part of ancestor knowledge since "it is a knowledge which comes through the blood and catches you after your death" said some youth. They also thought that they could improve on it by listening to their grand-parents, who generally teach riddles and tell folk-tales to the younger generations (Carrin, 1985).

Later, I discovered that children and youth, from remote villages, felt that the forest was still providing food in time of scarcity. These youths knew very well that some *adivasi* students with degrees had returned to the village since they did not have the "right connexion" to get a job. It is what happened to Mausi, a young girl who wanted to become a government school teacher and who could not be recruited despite her high marks. As she said, she will follow the volunteer path. One of the first questions which arise regarding village knowledge concerns its transmission and modalities. I knew that grand-parents were transmitting the names of many animal and plants to their grand-children, but I wanted to know how children experience these biological categories. I had already observed that animals and plants were the favourite subjects of the drawings made by the children …

Animal Categories as Seen by the Children

Folk names for fundamental ethnobiological categories have been shown to be governed by nomenclatural properties. As shown by Berlin (2006: 24) two principles are at work in ethnobiological classifications: onomatopoeia and metaphorical descriptions of properties of the organism observed. Another principle may be understood as the sound symbolism which is at work in the classification of birds, for example.

Children become gradually aware of animal and plant categories when they learn riddles from their grandparents. Riddles are taught to eight years old children and involve different levels of difficulty. The premises of the riddles describe the anatomy of a few animals like the shrimp, the crab or the buffalo while the answer alludes to the way the same animal eats or defecates by comparing it with a tool, or another domestic object. Similarly, some riddles describe how flowers are blooming and how paddy and millet is ripening. Through riddles, children discover that biological functions also concern animals and plants, which are seen to be metonyms of humans. Birds, fish and snakes are the wild animals which appear in riddles: tigers and leopards, considered as favourite animals of the *bongas,* are taboo here. Cultivated plants appear frequently in riddles as well as pepper or chilli, but some thorny plants like *soso*, (*Dyospyros tomentosa*, L.) used in exorcism are taboo. Through riddles children interiorize a natural cosmology which conciliates Nature and Culture, since answers to the riddles concern fire and domestic tools as well as animals and plants (Carrin-Bouez, 1985; Carrin, *in press*). Some grand-mothers know animal tales and describe the astuteness of the jackal (*toyo*) (*Canus aureus*, L.) which appears as the trickster of the Santal folk-tales, a character which evokes the cunning Hindu neighbours who employ their parents. Unlike the jackal, the leopard[5] (*tarup*) is conceptualized as the *vahana* of the forest deities (*bir bonga*) though it was eaten in the past (Bodding, 1925: 481). While children develop a first knowledge of animals through listening to riddles and folktales, they soon experience their first encounters with animal and plants when they roam around the village. The knowledge of animal and plants then becomes genderized, since boys develop some skills, using for snares, when they try to catch birds or rodents, while girls follow their mothers to pluck leaves and dig roots in the forest. Of course this sexual division of knowledge is relative since girls, for example, are also fishing in rice-fields with their mothers along with some boys.

How Boys learn about Animals

The Santals eat the flesh of a great variety of birds, and children and youth are fond of catching quails (*gundri*) (*Excalfactoria chinensis,* L.) or even shooting partridge (*askal*) (*Francolinus vulgaris*, L.), when they know how to use a bow. To catch quails[6], boys keep a female bird as a decoy in a cage placed on the ground, while they arrange a number of snares around the cage. They also capture birds to keep in cages as pets, like the blue jay (*toya)* (*Coracias indica*, L.).

When they do not go to school, boys enjoy trapping small mammals and rodents (*hon*) (*Mus Rattus*, L.) that they roast in the fields. They learn where these animals hide, under the embankment of rice fields. But boys and youths also trap bats and rodents whenever they take goats for grazing. To catch a bat (*barduruc*) one boy generally climbs a tree and beats the sleeping animal while his companions wait under the tree. They know different varieties of bats which include the *cutia* bat, the smaller one, and the rat bat (*hon barduruc*), which is bigger than the less common flying fox (*kahu barduruc)* (*Pteropus medius*, L.). Boys are encouraged to find their own food whenever they can, and they generally eat the animals they catch on the spot. To catch rats, children go to a place where they have found that the rats have burrowed. The small animals are hammered with a stone and singed, then cut up. Small rats are also found in the houses, and then they may be eaten by adults too, especially in time of scarcity. They know about five varieties of rats, a small rat with a bare tail called *uric'hon (Gerbillus indicus,* L.), and a very common rat or house rat (*orak hon),* both of which are easy to catch but are smoked out when necessary. They dig them out and kill them. If that cannot be done, they fill the hole with water to drive them out. They divide the meat between themselves and cook it. Similarly, children enjoy catching tortoises (*horo*). Some live in hills, (*buru horo*)[7], while others are found in the water of the rice fields *(tandi horo*) (*Morenia ocellata,* Dum and Bibr). They are named after domestic pots like *tukuc horo*, whose shape resembles to that of an earthen pot. When a youth finds a king tortoise (*raj horo*)[8], he may decide to take it to the village, and even to offer it to the adults. The flesh of the big tortoise is delicious, they say, and evokes the flesh of the *bongas*. Similarly, the newborn child is compared to a tortoise, since his crane allows us to see the pulsation of his heart until the bone becomes harder, an important step for the Santals who oppose the male bone principle to the female flesh (Carrin-Bouez, 1986).

Formerly, the Santals used to eat a large number of animals, including crabs, tortoises, rats, fishes, birds, and some snakes. They have often been stigmatized by their Hindu neighbours for eating "impure food" and consequently they now try to abstain from it. Women and children, however, feel free to eat all kinds of aquatic animals when they are out for fishing. Women proudly tell me that this allows them to leave the meat to their husbands, who need strength to push their bicycle loaded with coal, delivering to some Mafioso who wait for them at certain places. The road is difficult, and sometimes risky, though the police is fully aware of the business and take bribes from the workers to allow them to pass.

When youth engage in hunting later, they learn how to tackle bigger game. Hunting, here, refers to a chain of ritual sequences, and implies a particular ideology since the young hunters are supposed to learn a certain discipline and to control their impulses. At some moments of the hunt, the men are also supposed to release their tensions, and to evoke sexuality as a metaphor for fertility: they joke about sex and how to please their patron Rongo Ruji (Burnt Vagina) who controls the wild game. More globally, youth know that hunting experience makes a man. Though the ritual meaning of the hunt has been obscured in the minds of many Santals, it is still implicit in the rituals which accompany the hunt. The hunt, as a chain of events, encapsulates different symbolic elements which pertain to the social organization, since the annual hunt (*disum sendera)* included a group of villages or *parha*. Hunting rituals also emphasize the dependence of the Santals on their environment, and on the forest.

Hunting, as a sequence of events, also evoke the memory of the ancestors, at a time when the forest was still crucial for subsistence. For boys, it is a great excitement to participate in hunting, though they do not enjoy the autonomy during the hunt that they usually enjoy with their peers. Under the guidance of their elders, however, they learn how to identify the footprints of animals, especially the various kinds of deer. All kinds of deer are called *jel* (meat), since deer was the only meat the Santals had in the past. Youth know where to find the *badar selep jel (Gazella bennetti,* Sykes*),* the ravine deer which is different from the Indian Black Buck or the spotted deer (*Cervus axis*, Erxl.) Youth also enjoy running after a porcupine (*sukri*), a civet cat *'sogot'* (*Viverra zibetha*, L.) or even a *kubra runda*[9], a kind of wild cat. They listen to stories of hunting leopards (*tarup)* but generally they are not permitted to shoot leopards. They also learn that it is necessary not to kill too many animals in order to favour wild life reproduction.

In the literature we find a distinction between village level hunts (*gire sendera*) and hunting at the regional level (*disom sendera*). Despite the fact that most forests are degraded, Santals and other groups still hunt even when access to the forest is not allowed. Today, hunting in reserved forests, or even wild sanctuaries, represent a mode of resistance, and a way to claim one's rights. More recently the Santals have developed another agenda, trying to persuade the forest officers that hunting is a cultural affair, since hunting is associated with singing and telling old narratives. I have observed that in Mayurbhanj and around Ghatsila, hunting has become a performance of tradition, where Santals are seeking to assert it as an argument proving their indigeneity, stressing rather the importance of gathering and singing the old narratives, than to kill animals (Carrin, *forthcoming,c.*).

Fishing

Girls and children are very fond of fishing with their mothers and they generally use small *torodan* or fish traps. This is in the form of a net, which is circular or oval and made like a basket. The lower end is tightly closed and water may run but fish cannot pass. Children are not usually permitted to use poison, like the noxious substances that men obtain from the forest, for example from the roots of *kita* (*Phoenix acaulis,* Roxb). Boys, and even girls, sometimes place a small *torodan* in the water of the rice field and catch small fish like *puthi hako*[10], or *caole bumbuc*. Bigger fish, such as *bumbuc (Lepidocephalchthys guntea Ham.*Buch*)* are considered excellent food and are sometimes hooked by youth, when they get more experience. Boys also catch frogs, but do not always eat them.

Children knowledge of animals is of course limited, since they do not try to develop it in the same way that the *ojha* (healers) do. The latter try to build an extensive knowledge of the properties of plants and animals, and usually know hundreds of species; unlike the healer, who interests himself in the underlying principles which characterize animal and plants, such as the opposition of flower/flesh and bone, children seem more pragmatic in their approach. What is important for them is to integrate this knowledge with everyday practice. Does this mean that children privilege animals they can catch and eat, and thus tend to ignore other animals found in folk tales, or even the animals connected with the tribal deities (*bongas*)? Are animals also good to think for children?

Children's Knowledge of "Supernatural" Animals

To understand how children become familiar with the notion of sacred places or food taboos, I have to rely on my own observations since this knowledge is tacit. When children are about six, they understand that some places are connected with the *bongas,* who are perceived as hidden kin, not as permissive as the grandparents, who may attack them without any reason. In the same vein, children learn that *bongas* may send disease and death, especially to those who do not pay attention to the taboos. These taboos are highly genderized, as girls must avoid certain acts permitted to boys, such as ploughing, fishing, using a small weapon and so on. Similarly, a boy should not husk paddy or take part in transplantation. It is difficult to understand how children learn about death, but they certainly learn that one should avoid calling dead kin by the personal name, since the name must be lost when dead kin become ancestors. When Santals live in a multi-ethnic village with Mundas and Oraons, who have a megalithic culture, children often sit in the burial ground and are conscious that the stones "echo the voices of the dead", as they say. Some boys, who feel they have already got some special gift, like being able to foretell the future, may choose to learn more about the *bongas* and to master indigenous knowledge (*bidia*). They become disciples (*chela*) of an *ojha*. But the process is not easy, says Ramon, a boy of sixteen, who had to overcome the sarcasms of his parents. They wanted him to do computer studies. As he told me, "this kind of boon is not easy, one gets almost ashamed of it, and my father wanted to take me to an healer to exorcize me, he was persuaded that I had been bewitched, and that the idea to help people in becoming a healer was a pure superstition. But I argued that many of us, even with degrees, do not find a job in the city. I have chosen to help my community, I shall not indulge in exorcism (*husit*). I have started to collect plants, labelled with names and uses, and I bring them to the village dispensary where they can be used by people. I shall become a modern village doctor".

The training lasts two years and includes learning about diseases, medicinal plants and ritual techniques such as divination, possession and exorcism. Moreover, the boy learns that a good *ojha* should be partly feminine in order to fight female malevolent deities. The sexual conversion, though symbolical, is experienced as embarrassing nowadays by most of the youth. The prestige of the *ojha* is sometimes at stake in villages where modern medical facilities are found, and several youths have pointed out to me, proudly, that there are no longer any traditional healers in their village. These modern views also imply that indigenous knowledge is depreciated, though the Santals who have a pharmacopoeia of five hundred plant and animal species which has been analysed (and partly found relevant by Ayurvedic doctors), have the reputation of having extensive knowledge of the forest, of herbal medicines, and of magical treatment of diseases. Some youths still decide to become at least part-time healers and learn more systematically about the tribal deities (*bonga*). This knowledge implies that they know how to visualize the *bongas* through dreaming, and that they are able to identify a *bonga* through possession. A Santal *ojha* learns, through invocations (*mantras*) and exorcism formulae (*jharni*)[11], a large amount of informations concerning at least two hundred deities. Some *bongas* are of human origin, as ancestors become *bongas* three generations after their death, when they lose their previous personality. Ancestors (*hapram ko*) may also trouble humans, but they can be appeased with rice-beer libations and sacrifices. The wrath of the ancestors is generally rooted in inheritance conflicts or village disputes, while the anger of *bongas* may not be rooted in any conflict; the *bongas* are supposed to be perverse, and they do not justify their attacks.

Myths relate the origin of some *bongas* to the landscape: everybody knows about *buru bongas*, who live in the hills and are propitiated every year to get rain, but nobody knows why these deities bring calamities. Causality must be questioned through divination and the healer has to find out who is responsible for the attack: an ancestor, a *buru bonga*, a clanic deity, a village deity, or any other *bonga,* roaming in the forest or anywhere else. The list is endless. I have argued elsewhere (Carrin-Bouez, 1986; Carrin *in press*), that knowledge of *bongas* is organized in the form of hierarchical lists, where the malevolent spirits are conceptualized as causing diseases. For example, the *dain bonga*, "*bonga* of the chief witches" and *sima bonga*, the "spirits of boundaries" are included in the more general category of the spirits of the forest, the *bir bonga*, showing that entities related to the wilderness are associated with illness and misfortune (Carrin-Bouez, 1986).When youth engage in learning about *bongas*, they internalize certain techniques. The healer is supposed to be feminine when he, among other disciples, parades clad in a *sari*[12] with his *guru* during the *Dasae daran*, a ritual "wandering" that takes place every year in September (Carrin-Bouez, 1986). The party goes from village to village, and the disciples sing to get closer to their *guru* and to the sun[13], which in the songs is associated with *bidia,* knowledge itself. These songs describe how the *guru* is supposed to dismember and reconstruct his disciple's body in the sky, allowing the disciple's feminine sensitivity to emerge. In this ritual, which involves a healer and his disciples, the youth sing, wandering from one village to another and begging alms from the villagers. While singing, they are supposed to metamorphose themselves in spiders, which weave threads between the earth and the sky. They also take other forms (*rup*) such as the monkey (*harun*), leopard (*tarup*)[14], crocodile (*tayan*) (*Crocodilius palustris,* Less.), deer (*mirgi*), or vulture (*garur)(Leptopilius dubius,* L.) and while possessed they imitate these animals, considered as the *vahan* of the *bongas* who possess the *ojha's* disciples. In everyday life, it also happens that when some leopard comes to the village, it is understood as a sign of the deities.

More generally, older boys slowly learn "tales about Santals who have married *bongas*" and which are presented as real experiences (Carrin, 1996; Andersen, Carrin and Soren, 2011: 319-338). To be seduced by *a bonga* is exciting, though it may be dangerous. Dreaming of the *bonga's* world is seen as living a second emotional life, but has different consequences for boys and girls. The relationship between boys and *bongas* is asymmetrical. But in case of girls, asymmetry is even more striking, when male *bongas* seduce, rape and kill their victims telling them they are punished for some transgression. Thus, only women who become witches are supposed to become familiar with leopards and tigers, which are the vehicles (*vahan*) of some powerful *bongas*. Similarly, girls should avoid to get possessed since possession (*rumok*) is associated with witchcraft (Carrin, 1997).

Girls and Plant Knowledge

While some boys try to learn about medicinal plants, girls follow their mothers in the forest to learn about edible plants and some common medicinal roots and herbs. To gather wild vegetables and leaves is the work of women. The latter do not go alone in the forest, but go together in a body, at a time agreed upon. When entering the forest, they will invoke the *bongas* to protect the small children they have left in the village. Girls know how to pluck leaves and to dig for tubers with a *kointa*, a special digging stick. They also learn which plants should be avoided, since they cause loose bowels. Later they also learn how to cook some vegetables in curry, while others should be roasted.

Girls learn how to identify a large quantity of leaves (*arak*) such as *bhorkond arak* (*Hymenodyctum exelsum*, L.) which are used in curry, *cutur lutur arak*, small leaves in the shape of ears, and *coro mokoc arak* (*Hibiscus sabdariffa*, L.) which are also cooked in curry. They also learn that some leaves may be a little bitter, like, *durup arak* and *andia dhurup arak* (*Leucas Cepahlotes,* Spreng). They pluck the leaves of creepers such as *dimbu arak* (*Ocymum basilicum*, L.). Very common leaves are *hesak arak,* the leaves of the ficus (*Ficus religiosa,* L.) which are eaten in curry, and *janum arak* the leaves of a thorny plant (*Dyospyros tomentosa*, L.) which are considered tasty. Some of these wild plants also have a medicinal use, like the leaves of the ficus which are used to appease cough. Besides knowing about eighty different leaves, girls learn about tubers (*kanda*) which are used as a staple food during scarcity and some wild fruits such as mushrooms[15] (*ot*) which are the only plants bestowed with a soul (*roa*), are important. Girls know at least five varieties of edible mushrooms which are collected during the rainy season, such as *bin ot* (snake mushroom), so called since its shape evokes a snake, *bunum ot,* a mushroom which grows near an anthill, *busup ot,* which grows near dry leaves, and *gundri gopha* (*Pleurotus osteratus,* L.), which is considered as intoxicating but sometimes eaten in small quantity, Girls learn that most mushrooms are identified with their support while a few are named after their shape such as *catom ot,* "mushroom umbrella". Girls' knowledge also includes some resins, like *hesel jer*, an exudation of *Agnossesissus,* or *lopon jel,* an exudation of (*Terminalia belarica,* Gaertn). Grown-up girls learn how to make a flour of these plants, in order to prepare pancakes. On returning from the forest, women and girls at once arrange for the food to be cooked. They give the leaves, the roots, the tubers and the mushrooms to the cooking women who know which ones to boil and prepare in curry and which ones to roast. Girls also learn how to make leaf plates *(patra)* out of sal leaves (*Shorea robusta* Gaertn), in which food is served. The leaves are pinned together with strains of hard straw. These plates are prepared in large number at the beginning of the hot season. Besides the knowledge of wild plants, girls learn how to grow vegetables in gardens and they also assist their mothers in transplanting rice. Girls also understand that they have to feed plants in gardens and they also take care of chicken while boys graze goats, sheep, cows, and buffaloes.

Children knowledge is oriented towards edible categories since they have to develop a kind of autonomy by learning to find their own food. This pragmatic orientation, however, does not imply that boys and girls forget about other animals and plants, since, as we have seen, they learn gradually that some animals are associated with the deities and "are good to think and good to prohibit" as Tambiah (1969) wrote in his influential article.

Do the ancestors still embody the idea of a given environment? We can answer this question with Bird-David: "The gist of this argument was that, compared to the cultivator's sense of an environment that yield us bounty in return for appropriate conduct and labour, the hunters and gatherers' view can be summed up as the "forest is a parent" who unconditionally "provides food for his children" (Bird-David 1999: 190). But she adds, as a corrective to the idea of "the giving environment", that the Nayak of South India have a relational view of the forest world which is "constitutive of coeval agents of all sorts which are enmeshed in sharing relations". The Santals of Hazaribagh region are still attached to the forest, and children and youth actively participate in revitalizing traditional animal and plant categories. This does not mean that the Santal of this region think of themselves as "relic populations" living in "relic forests" without any outside contact. But the political context perhaps invites them to a certain withdrawal since "one cannot succeed in the town when does not have good contacts".

Plants Animals and the Sharing of Emotions

In folk-tales, some animals such as the jackal, the leopard or the elephant are talking with humans, but these animals seem somehow quite distant to the children who enjoy listening to their grand-parents' tales. Animals in folktales are often seen with humour such as the hare which is forgetful, or they may represent moral values such as the mongoose boy, who is very considerate.

To show how plants and animals are linked to emotions, I shall take another example, the love song (*don seren*) that boys and girls sing together. In these songs, like in myths, we note that plants and animals stimulate emotions and the awakening of desire among boys and girls. In these songs, the landscape encapsulates different kinds of plants and animals, which develop their own agency to witness the secret love of the youth. Here is a short example of this kind of love song, which represents a type of knowledge equally shared by boys and girls.

On the mountain, a jackal gets down majestic,
On the hill, a peacock (marak[16]) is hiding under the leaves,
Two boys, two boys are ploughing,
While two girls fetch water in the low valley.
The boys have seen their father who is ploughing on the hill.
The girls have seen their mother who is ploughing a little downwards
We will go to a rice-field in the forest
We will go fishing, my beloved
We will kill the fish
We will wash the fish and we will make love
We have visited many forest
We have crossed an immense forest, and there you took me, my beloved
I am not very old and I should cry
But I am no more a child, and I should say that you boy, and I, girl,
we had our love....

In this poem, several layers of the landscape are associated with diverse characters: parents, animals, plants, boys and girls. The young couple crosses different forest sectors, while birds and deer sometimes look at them. The first feelings are signified through the movement of the animals, which seems ephemeral. The jackal gets down slowly, to signify the intensity of the moment, while the peacock hides, like a shy girl, under the leaves. In other songs, the forests crossed by the young couples become "burnt", a simile which refers to slash and burn cultivation, but which alludes, here, to the ripening of passion. These encounters between boys and girls take place in the forest, but evoke a time when the landscape was still pristine. The beauty of the forest pervades the feelings of the young couple, as if boy and girl have forgotten, for a while, that the moment of intimacy they share is stolen, as the boy has postponed his ploughing duty on the hill, and the girl has deserted the group of women plucking leave.

In other songs, animals and plants become the companions of the young couple and participate to their secret love:

"When the moon rises,
We go along the plantains,
When the sun rises
The red flowers, the hibiscus bend their heads
One day near the river, there were buffaloes,
We were making garlands out of big greenish flowers,
O my beloved we have not noticed that it was past midnight"......

The *don seren* show that boys and girls share a common language, where animals and plants are no longer linked to daily routine but evoke an intimacy which re-enchants daily life. This re-enchanting experience probably explains why boys and girls still feel attracted to the village and to the knowledge of the ancestors. They may have forgotten clan stories, but they still experience a kind of continuity between plants, animals and humans expressed through the poetic parallelism, since different levels of the landscape—the higher/the lower regions oppose each other as boys oppose girls. This continuity is also expressed in sounds and echo-words as the intimacy of a connection between the sounds and the meaning of a word, which allows the speaker to complement the signifier[17]. This synesthetic sound symbolism which has been studied by Sapir (1929) and brilliantly revisited by Berlin (2006) is used as a cognitive device by native speakers when they elaborate folk taxonomies (Carrin, *forthcoming*). The continuity between children's knowledge of animal categories is thus expressed in love songs and we understand that sound meaning associations of movement, size and shape become applicable to the way animals are named. Children's knowledge of animal and plant world is guided by two principles, the place where the plant and animal is found which seems to inform the utilitarian reason, and the metaphorical associations of the animal or plant with feelings where, for example, the leopard signifies the anxious waiting of the lover while the peacock expresses the shyness of the girl.

This continuity is very important for *adivasis* who claim to follow Sarna religion, and who have managed to get it recognized. Sarna religion means the partaking of a sensitivity where humans, plants and animals share in the same cosmology. The recent acknowledgment of Sarna religion by the government under the Temple Protection Act implies that sacred groves now have to be respected, like temples, and they are signalized in Jharkhand by a board. This law intends to protect the sacred groves from the attacks of the Hindu fundamentalists who, this last decade, have been often trying to defile the *adivasi* Sarna.

Indigenous knowledge is also an experience shared by boys and girls, who often deplore that textbooks pay no attention to village knowledge (Carrin, *forthcoming)*. As Hinsi, a young girl of fourteen, told me: "we should write some supplement to our textbooks, and other children from the cities should read about it. And in the same way, they might also give us some idea of their life in the cities". This remark points to the criticisms which have often been addressed to textbooks used in regions where *adivasis* live. The textbooks do not at all relate to the everyday experience of the children, since indigenous knowledge is not taken into consideration, despite some attempts to indigenize the curriculum (Sarangapani, 2003; Carrin *in press*).

When young children in Hazaribagh are drawing wild animals, they stress how the latter have become smaller, due to the degradation of the forest under the threat of climatic change. This concern has probably helped *adivasi* youth who feel they have to engage with the forest environment. The term engagement refers to Ingold—one of the leading scholars in ecological anthropology—who argues for a "dwelling perspective" which situates humans in an active engagement with the surroundings by developing skills, through the performance of particular tasks (2000: 5). Ingold's examples concern hunter-gatherers and pastoralist communities who have a relational understanding of themselves and their life-world. According to Ingold, the land and the people who inhabit it are caught up in the same existential experience and historical ongoing process. The definition of Ingold makes us understand that the sophisticated knowledge of plants does not refer to a mystical bond linking indigenous communities to nature, as environmentalists often think, but rather to a form of knowledge embedded in experience. In such a perspective, enskilment is an ongoing process of learning, though in some circumstances *adivasis* may prioritize other objectives, taking the forest as a resource in a commodification of nature—nature turned resource for capitalistic extraction and market exchange (Karlsson, 2012: 258).

Children's knowledge of animal and plants focuses on the simultaneity of physical experience, category and sociality through language. It constitutes a domain where collective representations articulate with cognitive processes. Its implications for the study of indigenous knowledge at large (including adult knowledge) are important since categorization and belief is unavoidably affected by cultural relativity. Children's knowledge of ethnobiological categories has its implications for the study of subsistence behaviour and it most relevant to understand ecology as a way to inform practice. Children's and youth knowledge of forest resources is genderized, but we have seen how the love songs allow a sharing of the understanding of the landscape, not only as a source of food, but equally as offering an emotional bond which youth associate with their first amorous feelings. This is the moment when youth feel closer to the ancestors whose knowledge they try to re-enact. This is also the moment where youth succeed in mastering the sound symbolism as well as the knowledge of the movement of animals and plants that they project in the landscape. Santal love songs thus make us understand the centrality of the landscape which encapsulates joy and sorrow as well as ephemeral feelings like doubt, fear, anxiety or bliss.

Children do not only reproduce indigenous knowledge since ethno-biological categories are experienced by recognizing the emotive power of linking a creature or a plant and its name in the botanical and zoological lexicons of the language. This emotive power enables youth to play with animals and plants when they appear in riddles and songs which delineate a domain where semantic properties of ethnobiological categories are interpreted by attributing moral qualities to animals and plants. This interpretive function thus contributes to the renewal of indigenous knowledge which makes us understand that children and youth are active agents in the concentration of useful species but when they share feelings with plants and animals they perceive that they are fully engaged into cultural practices which link environment to their experience as knowing subjects.

NOTES

1. This article is part of a larger project where I argue that Santal indigenous knowledge revolves around three dimensions, the emergence of an historical consciousness, the feeling of a shared identity related to language, and to culture and ecological diversity.
2. The linguistic family includes some nineteen austro-asiatic languages, (N. Zide 1966).
3. Ragunath Murmu invented an original alphabet (*ol ciki*) in the thirties which is still acknowledged by the Santals mostly in Orissa, but also in Jharkhand, Bengal and Assam. See Carrin (*in press*).
4. The NGO tries to get foreign donors to sponsor the village school, and has partly succeeded due to the energy of S. Hasdak, the nephew of the Director of the NGO, a young graduate in rural agriculture, who has decided to try to ameliorate the living conditions of the villagers.
5. The Santals distinguish four kinds of leopards: *lar sakam tarup* (the leopard'colour is compared to the leaf of a creeper), *potea tarup*, a small leopard, *sona cita tarup*, the golden big leopard and *ad bagin tarup*, "the half-tiger leopard".
6. The Santals know at least about three varieties of quails : *gadle gundri*, the blue breast quail (*Excalfactoria chinensis,* L.) *ghura gundri* the bastard quail (*Turnix taigoor,* L.) and *Kasi gundri* the little button quail (*Turnixdussumieri,* L.).
7. Identification unknown.
8. Identification unknown.
9. Identification unknown.
10. Identification unknown.
11. *Jharnis* are formulae which are uttered or sung to guarantee the efficacy of certain substances such as medicinal oil or blood. In some cases, *ojhas* recite *jharnis* to expel the poison in case of snake-bite (P.O. Bodding 1925, Carrin *forthcoming* , Chap. V).
12. When the *ojhas* wear a *sari* they fold it on the right shoulder.
13. The content of the songs allude to a shamanistic voyage which is conceptualized as an ascension along gossamer's threads, that the first *guru* has woven as a ladder between sky and earth (Carrin-Bouez, 1977).
14. Identification unknown. Leopards are not only eaten, their whiskers and claws are used as amulets by the healers (*ojhas*).
15. The Santal know about thirty kinds of mushrooms : boys and girls pluck the white anthill mushroom (*bunum*) (*Entoloma macrocarpium*, L.) the straw mushroom (*busup ot*) (*Volvaria terrestrus,* L.) *dak'mandi ot* (the rice gruel mushroom) etc.
16. Boys shoot the peacock (*marak*) (*Pavo cristatus*, L.) which is roasted and eaten.
17. This is also called synesthesia which has been studied by R. Jacobson (1978 :113) as a way of translating a sensation in different sensory codes. Cf. Carrin (*forthcoming*, Chap. 3).

REFERENCES

Andersen, P., M. Carrin and Santosh Soren. 2011. *From Fire-rain to Insurrection Reasserting Ethnic Identity through Narratives*. Delhi: Manohar

Anderson, D. and R. Grove. 1987. (eds.) *Conservation in African People Policies and Practice.* Cambridge: Cambridge University Press.

Barth, F. 2002. "An Anthropology of Knowledge", Sidney W. Mintz Lecture for 2000, *Current Anthropology*, 43 (1): 1-17.

Baviskar, A. 2005. "Tribal Politics and Sustainable Development", *In:* S.N. Pawar *et al.* (eds.), *Environmental Movement in India: Strategies and Practices.* Delhi: Rawat.

Berlin, B. 2006. "The First Congress of Ethnozoological Nomenclature", Special Issue Ethnobiology and the Science of Humankind, *The Journal of the Royal Anthropological Institute, Man,* 23-44.

Bird David Nurit. 1999. "Animism" Revisited: Personhood, Environment, and Relational Epistemology", *Current Anthropology*, 40 (S1), Special Issue *Culture—A Second Chance?* (February, 1999), pp. 67-91.

Bodding, P.O. 1986. *Studies in Santal Medicine and Connected Folklore.* Calcutta: Asiatic Society (1st Edition 1925-1940).

____. 1932-36. *A Santal Dictionary* (5 vols). Oslo: Det Norske Videnskaps Akademi.

Brosius, J.P. "Endangered Forest, Endangered People: Environmentalist Representations of Indigenous Knowledge", *Human Ecology*, 25 (1): 47-69.

Carrin-Bouez, M. 1985. "La proie du vautour: devinettes et pensée symbolique chez les Santal," *L'Homme*, 95, XXV (3): 71-96.

____. M. 1986. *La Fleur et l'Os: symbolisme et rituel chez les Santal*, Cahiers de l'Homme, EHESS, Paris.

____. 1997. *Enfants de la Déesse, dévotion et prêtrise féminine au Bengale,* Editions du CNRS et MSH, Paris.

____. 2002. 'Le retour du bosquet sacré. Réinvention d'une culture Adivasi', (233-264) *In:* M. Carrin and C. Jaffrelot (eds.).

____. 2013. "Jharkhand: Alternative Citizenship in an Adivasi State", *In:* P. Berger and F. Heidemann (eds.), *The Modern Anthropology of India*, London: Routledge.

____. (*in press, a*) "Transmission of knowledge and the Making of Santal Youth", *In:* D. Blanc, M. Carrin and H.Tambs-Lyche (eds.), *Transfer of Knowledge and Children Agency: Reconstructing the Paradigms of Socialization, A Cross-cultural Perspective.* Delhi: Primus.

____. (*in press, b) Le Parler des Dieux : le discours rituel entre l'oral et l'écrit*, Société d'ethnologie,collection *Ecritures* Nanterre.

____. (in *press*, c) " The Santal as an Intellectual", M. Carrin, P. Kanungo and G.Toffin (eds.), *The Politic of Ethnicity in India, Népal and China,* Delhi, Primus.

____. (*forthcoming, a) Adivasi Sensitivity and the Indian Debate on Indigenous Knowledge.*

____. (*forthcoming b*) "Echo-words in Santali and Sound Symbolism", Paper to be presented at the Winter University, Central University Jharkhand, January 2014.

Damodaran, Vinita. 2005. "Indigenous Forest Rights, Discourses and Resistance in Chotanagpur, 1860-2002", (pp. 115-150) *In:* G. Cederlof and K. Sivaramakrishnan (eds.), *Ecological Nationalisms: Nature, Livelihoods, and Identities in South Asia.* Delhi: Permanent Black.

Ingold, T. 2000. *The Perception of the Environment. Essays in Livelihood, Dwelling and Skill.* London & New York: Routledge.

Jakobson, R. 1978. *Six Lectures on Sound and Meaning*, Cambridge Mass; MIT Press.

Karlsson, G.G. and T.B. Subha. 2006. *Indigeneity in India.* London: Kegan Paul.

Kelkar, Govind and Dev Nathan. 1991. *Gender and Tribe: Women, Land and Forests in Jharkhand.* New Delhi: Kali for Women.

Padel, F. and Samarendra Das. 2010. *Out of this Earth East India Adivasis and the Aluminium Cartel (with a foreword by Arundhati Roy)* Delhi: Manohar.

Prasad, Archana. 2003. *Against Ecological Romanticism Verrier Elwin and the Making of an Anti-Modern Tribal Identity*. Delhi: Three Essays.

Prakash, Amit. 2010. *Politics, Development and Identity,* Jharkhand, 1991-2009.

Sarangapani, Padma. 2003. *Constructing School Knowledge an Ethnography of Learning in an Indian Village.* Delhi: Sage.

Sapir, E. 1929. "A Study in Phonetic Symbolism", *Journal of Experimental Psychology,* 12: 225-239.

Sen, G. 1992. *Indigenous Visions: People of India, Attitudes to Environment*, Delhi: Sage.

Shah, A. 2010. In the Shadows of the State Indigenous Politics, *Environmentalism and Insurgency in Jharkhand, India*. Durham and London: Duke University Press.

Tambiah, S. 1969. "Animals are Good to Think and Good to Prohibit", *Ethnology,* 8 (4): 423-459

Xaxa, Virginius. 2005. "Politics of Language, Religion and Identity: Tribes in India", *Economic and Political Weekly*, 40 (13) (Mar. 26 - Apr. 1, 2005), pp. 1363-1370.

Zide, N. (ed.). *Studies in Comparative Austro-Asiatic Linguistic*. The Hague: Mouton.

SIX

THE NAG BACCHA—"CHILDREN OF THE SNAKE"

Possession and Performance in Western Odisha

LIDIA GUZY

Entranced, musically powerful possession rituals and ritual drama performances, loud and amazing in their creative and aesthetic expression, happen frequently in the Bora Sambar region of western Orissa. Ritual plays artistically connect local traditions with Pan-Indian religious and social concepts. During ritual drama plays, human fates and problems are transformed and enacted on a divine level.

The Bora Sambar Region

The *Bora Sambar* region belongs to the Bargarh district, a western part of the Indian State of Orissa, bordering on the province of Chhattisgarh.[1] Surrounded by the mountains of the *Gandhamardan* to the north and south, the Bora Sambar region extends around the town of Padampur (Padmapur), on a plain watered by the river Ong (Ang), "*which rises in the south-west, describes a great semi-circle to the north and then runs eastward in a widening valley*" (O'Malley, 2007: 3). Literally, *Bora Sambar* means "the region of the deer swallowed up by the cobra". The language of the region is Sambalpuri.

Historically, the *Raj Bora Sambar* can first be traced as an autonomous little kingdom or rather chiefdom of the indigenous Binjhal population, bordering on the tributary Princely State of Patna. However, due to the "inaccessible forest tracts" (Sahoo, 2007: 1) which covered large parts of the area and owing to the lack of written sources, a reconstruction of the structure and boundaries of the historical Bora Sambar kingdom remains difficult.

Bora Sambar, according to the Bengal District Gazetteers on Sambalpur of 1909, belonged to the Maharajas of Patna, "*who were the head of a cluster of States known as the Athara Garhjat (the 18 forts)*" (O'Malley, 2007: 21). Bora Sombar presumably was one of the Athara Garhjats, whose chiefs were indigenous Binjhal. Recent research on Princely States in Orissa has shown the important role of indigenous or tribal communities in establishing a regional autonomy of the local sovereigns, which were also called "little kings" (Schnepel, 2002).

Under the British colonial rule, the status of Bora Sambar changed from *Raj* Bora Sambar (Bora Sambar kingdom) to Bora Sambar *zamindari.*[2] With the establishment of the *zamindari* system by the British colonial Empire in the Bengal Permanent Settlement Act in 1793, many indigenous territories were conferred to feudal lords for the purpose of revenue collection (Bijoi, 2007: 15-27; Munda, 2002). During the British Raj (1858-1947), with its feudal Princely States headed by local governors such as Maharaja (great king), Raja (king) or Nawab (governor)[3] as well as holders of land domaines (*zamindar)* for land tenure and tax collection, the Bora Sambar region was the largest among the sixteen *zamindari* of the Sambalpur district[4] (O'Malley, 2007: 21, 164). The traditional relationship between the Bora Sambar chiefs and the Maharaja of Patna remained. During the British Raj it is reported that "the Binjhal zamindar of Borasambar still affixes the *tika* [the royal sign on the forehead of the king] to the Maharaja of Patna at the time of his accession" (*ibid.*, 76).

While the *zamindari* system as such was abolished with the independence of 1947, the independent India adopted the administrative and regional divisions shaped by the *zamindari* system. The Sambalpur Gazetteer of 1971 estimated the expanse of the Bora Sambar *zamindari* at 2,178 square kilometres (841 sq. miles), containing 476 villages (Senapati/Mohanti, 1971: 516). Today, the regional administration is organized on the basis of the former *zamindari* around the sub-divisional headquarters in Padampur.[5] The region is divided into three *tahsil* (administrative divisions whose centre is mostly a city or town): (1) Padampur, (2) Paikmal, (3) Sohela, and into six administrative blocks: (1) Padampur, (2) Paikmal, (3) Jharband, (4) Gaiselet, (5) Bijeipur and (6) Sohela. The Census of India 2001 counted 3,035 households and 15,442 people in the town of Padampur.[6]

Nag bacha—*The Snake Children and their Rituals*

In the Bora Sambar region frequently and especially during the month of *phalguna* (March) *Nag baccha* rituals happen. *Nag baccha* literally means the "snake children". It is a local trance and possession cult combining the veneration of the snake god Nag—a local deity identified with the Pan-Indian Hindu god Shiva—with male peer group and initiation rituals, indigenous theatre, martial arts performance, music and healing traditions. It is mostly performed by young men from villages with mixed communities of Binjhal, Gond, Mali and Telli.

A *nag baccha* group consists of around 25 to 30 young, mostly unmarried men, often of a comparatively fragile and feminine physical appearance. They have joined the group on their own decision and, after having undergone an initiation, are considered "snake children". The group is led by an older *guru*, an experienced master in the disciplines of *nag baccha*. The group members may belong to different communities from one village or from several neighbouring villages. The *nag baccha* group is called by other villages in order to perform healing ceremonies or to bring the blessings of Shiva.

In the months of October (*dusshara*) and December (*maxir*), the *nag baccha puja* is performed on Mondays. Once started, it has to be continued for seven successive Mondays. On the seventh Monday the concluding and most important sequence of the *nag baccha* ritual takes place: the *binu jatra*, the veneration of the snake hole, a possession ritual that finds its climax before the earthen hole of a cobra in the jungle. Before the start of the *binu jatra*, the members of the *nag baccha* group have to fast for one day. It is told that after fasting the *nag baccha* consume *godd*, an allegedly poisonous substance whose ingredients are kept secret. The taking in of *godd* has various functions. It is a crucial part of the initiation into the *nag baccha* group. Furthermore, it is said to be a counter-poison against snakebites, that when taken in, also bestows healing powers on its consumer. Having digested *godd*, the *nag baccha* are held to have the power to heal snake bites and dog bites, but also mute and deafness, barrenness and sufferings induced by the so called bad eyes (*peten korab dusti*), the local term for the envious malevolence of others, and *dondei,* a term generally designating afflictions ascribed to external forces or influences, often translated by locals with the English term witchcraft. With the consumption of *godd*, which is distributed to them by their *guru*, the young men are also held to gain the knowledge of certain *mantras*, secret verses or short sayings to which healing power is attributed. In fact, the *mantras* are taught to the *nag baccha* by their *guru*. Through *godd*, the young men become initiated as religious specialists, healers as well as members of a male peer group.

After *godd* has been consumed, a further preparation for the *binu jatra* takes place: To the sound of the *sulapar* – the sixteen holy rhythms of the trance ritual – performed by the *ganda baja* village orchestra, the *boil biha,* the "spiritual marriage" of the *nag baccha* comes about. In a state of trance, induced by the music of the *ganda baja* each *nag baccha* "marries" his favourite god or goddess, which means that from now on he is considered a medium of the spirit of this deity. In Adivasi Middle India, spiritual marriages are a common symbolic idiom of exchange and communication with the divine realm and of a ritual specialisation.[7] In contrast to the state of *boil* in the context of goddess spirit possession rituals, *boil biha,* the spiritual marriage in *nag baccha,* is not conceived as the establishing of an identity between the medium and the deity that possesses him. It is supposed that the *nag baccha* does not entirely become the god or goddess he embodies, but that he acts as a medium for the deity's spirit (*boil asibe nag baccha pila upore*) while retaining his status as therapeutic specialist, who maintains his separate personal identity.

When the *ganda baja* village orchestra begins to play the holy sixteen rhythms of *sulapar*, the group of the *nag baccha*, surrounded by the villagers, sets out towards the jungle, where the hiding place of the cobra lies. The rhythms of *ganda baja* drive forward the entranced bodies of the *nag baccha* and direct the ritual crowd from the village towards the forest. The musicians guide the divine spirits by their music. On the musicians "*boil will never come—they are too strong*", a villager explains. The spiritually "untouchable" musicians thus lead the procession.

During the procession, *boil*, the spirit of their respective spiritual spouse, possesses the *nag baccha* men. Villagers, searching cure and advice for their sufferings and ailments, now approach the snake children who, in their trance, are considered oracles and mediums of the divine spirits. But not only do sufferers that seek help approach the *nag baccha*. Also aggrieved and disappointed believers use the *nag baccha* as mediums to address their frustrations and aggressions to deities that did not fulfil their wishes, despite donations they made or severe ritual austerities they underwent. "*Why have you not heard my plead*?" shouts an angry man, "*How much do you want to take from me? I will not give you any more sacrifice! You are a cheater*"*!* In an alienated, rhythmically interrupted and spasmodically hiccup, a *nag baccha* answers his reproaches: "*Too much doubt in you, too much doubt. Don't look backwards; believe my mantra. I will help!*" The ritual disputation seems to relieve the accuser, and he calms down while the whole procession proceeds on its way deeper into the jungle. At times, the trance of the *nag baccha* men becomes wild and aggressive. They perform uncontrolled movements, often directed against themselves. In this situation, it is the task of the *nag baccha* guru, to take care that the possessed snake children do not hurt themselves during their ecstasy.

At some place on their way to the jungle, the *ganda baja* musicians, who lead the procession, stop. The marching crowd also comes to a halt. Now, a performance of the *nag baccha* unfolds which is part theatre, part display of acrobatics and martial arts and part healing séance. This performance is called *devata khel* (god's play). In the *devata khel* each of the *nag baccha* represents the god or goddess he is held to have embraced in spiritual marriage. In a wild mimicry and pantomime the snake children embody their divine parts. The way in which the entranced *nag baccha* move and behave indicates the personality of the specific spirit (*boil*) which possesses them. On the basis of his gestures and movements, the gods and goddesses represented are immediately recognised by the audience. The divine spirits (*boil*) coming upon the *nag baccha* are said to be those of the following gods:

(1) The god Shiva, traditionally symbolised as the aniconic or phallic or *lingam* or snake; (2) his wife Parvati; (3) the Bengali goddess Kali; (4) Ganesh, the elephant shaped god of luck and prosperity; (5) Saraswati, the goddess of education and wisdom; (6) the monkey god Hanuman, the popular and famous supporter of Ram, widely known from the *Ramayana* epoch; as well as (7) Bhairu Dev, the forceful manifestation of Shiva, famous as Bhairava in Nepal and Kashmir – all these deities are widely venerated Pan-Indian divinities of the Hindu pantheon. In contrast (8) Samley, a regional goddess of the Sambalpur district and town; (9) the village goddess Gram Devi; (10) the bloodthirsty goddess Chandi Devi; (11) the snake mother goddess Naga Mata; (12) the fire goddess Agni Kumari; (13) the gods Thakur Dei; (14) Nepur Dei and (15) Bura Raja represent local deities of the Bora Sambar region.

The *guru* of the *nag baccha* group who, contrarily to the other performers, seems very much controlled in his way of acting, mostly represents the spirit of Shiva. Shiva plays the part of a presenter or narrator: he announces which god shall be represented next in the performance.

Hanuman, the monkey god, is embodied by an athletic young person, who starts acting in an idiosyncratic way: he climbs upon trees, where he greedily devours mango fruits, plays tricks at his fellow performers and scares the audience. The performer of Agni Kumari can be recognised by the spectators as he dances wildly and may jump through a fire which is lightened for the goddess. Parvati, Shiva's wife, can be identified because she always remains by Shiva's side. The performer embodying Kali's spirit symbolizes the goddess by sticking out his tongue. Bhairo is depicted in his persistent efforts to help and assist the other performers. The goddess Chandi introduces herself by uttering her own name.

The performer of Ganesh can be identified by the audience, as he feasts on coconuts and advances in circular movements. The goddess Saraswati is characterized by her beautiful dance. The performers possessed by Gram Devi's and Bura Raja's spirit roam around the altar of the respective goddesses. Samley's and Thakur Dei's spirits announce their identities right away. The performer "married" to Nepur Dei's spirit tries to engage the other *nag baccha* in play and jest; and the performer embodying Naga Mata's spirit dances with snakelike movements.

The *nag baccha* performance is interwoven with elements of acrobatics and martial arts. With their bodies, the participants spontaneously form human pyramid structures up to four metres height. They also engage in mock duels, imitating fights while acrobatically avoiding any real bodily collision.[8]

During their performance the snake children are considered as divine oracles and healers. While the *nag baccha* performers are jumping, narrating, dancing or fighting in a state of trance, they are again and again approached by participants of the procession. The *nag baccha* feign to bite those approaching them, in order to suck out their inner poison (*onti*). The symbolical bite is held to be efficient against both mental and physical suffering.

The medical technique of sucking out the poison is in fact the common indigenous remedy for snake bites, which are a frequent accident in the region. The often life threatening snake bites are treated by immediately sucking the poison from the body of the victim, followed by the application of a local antidote made from plants and roots. The *nag baccha* also act as the local medical specialists for the cure of snake bites in everyday life.

Godd, the allegedly poisonous substance consumed by the *nag baccha,* is a cultural symbol of danger but also the symbol of a medical and social antidote. In medical terms, *godd* is the counter poison against snake bites; in social terms, it represents the values of courage and body control. After having consumed *godd*, the *nag baccha* are considered "poisonous" by those around them. It is believed that babies up to the age of six months may die when they come into touch with the sweat of the *nag baccha*. In case a suppliant is accidentally bitten by a "snake child" in the symbolic healing procedure of sucking the poison out during the *nag baccha* performance, it is believed, that he is condemned to die soon. The ritual healing during *nag baccha* is thus conceived to be of a highly dangerous character for the help-seekers.

The atmosphere between the audience and participants of the procession is at once joy and fearful. The audience laughs at the theatrical stunts performed by the embodied deities of *nag baccha*. However, the lookers-on are filled with respect and fear when faced with the assumed spiritual and manifest physical powers of the snake children.

The male *nag baccha* group which uses the cultural idiom of trance mediumship symbolises on the one hand the transcendent power of a divine play surpassing human control. On the other hand, on a human and social level, *nag baccha* symbolizes the handling of danger through courage, specialised knowledge and body control, expressed by disciplined athletic and inventive body techniques, such as martial arts, drama performance and acrobatic movement. The initiated *nag baccha* performers also symbolise the ambivalence of power, which is potentially both: curative and deadly, as the healing ritual always contains a risk for the suppliant. The help-seekers are obliged to give themselves over to the ritually and socially constructed authority of the *nag baccha*; otherwise they put their life at risk. In this manner a dangerous sacredness of the healing process and of the healer himself is established, an unquestioned divine hierarchy between the healer and the patient.

The *binu jatra* ritual reaches its climax with an animal sacrifice in front of the earthen hole of the cobra. Situated under a big tree it reminds of an oversized mole hole. The rhythms of the *ganda baja* village orchestra speed up and escalate. The proximity to the perilous residence of the cobra raises the tension and fear of the crowd. "*Will the cobra come out*?" I think to myself. A musician laughs: "*Our rhythms are strong*", he says, as if anticipating my doubts. He seems self-confident and at ease with the situation.

A male goat is sacrificed to the local goddess Chandi by the *junkar*, the ritual executor of the village in front of the cobra-hole. The temporary

Photo 6.1 and 6.2: Entranced *Nag Baccha*, Village Munda Palli 2006, L.G.

Photo 6.1

Photo 6.2

Photo 6.3 and 6.4: *Nag Baccha* while Treating a Patient, Munda Palli 2006, L.G.

Photo 6.3

Photo 6.4

Photo 6.5: A *Nag Baccha* while Enquiring the Divine Sphere, Munda Palli 2006, L.G.

Photo 6.5

Photo 6.6 and 6.7: *Nag Baccha* at *Binu Jatra*, 2006, L.G.

Photo 6.6

Photo 6.7

Photo 6.8: *Ganda Baja* during *Binu Jatra*, L.G.

Photo 6.8

altar for the sacrificial act consists only of a stone placed in front of the opening in the ground where the cobra hides. The throat of the sacrificial animal is cut in order to let the blood slowly flow to the earth and into the cobra hole. With the flow of the blood a communication with the divine sphere is established: "*Goddess Chandi likes the blood* ", says one villager. The sacrificial donation of a goat may be the fulfilment of a vow (*monosik*) made by the donator – a thank-offering for the granting of a supplication by the goddess. Or it may be a donation intended to enforce a plea made to the goddess. The sacrifice during *binu jatra* thus follows the universal sacrificial logic of *do ut des* (von der Leeuw, 1920-1921: 241-253).

After the sacrifice, the *nag baccha* and the spectators return to their village in order to prepare the meat of the goat for a common meal. The head of the animal is kept by the *nag baccha guru*, whereas the meat is cooked and distributed between the donator – who may be an individual or a family – and the other villagers.

A Ritual for Chandi

The goddess Chandi, to whom the final offering and thus the climax of the ritual *nag baccha* performance is dedicated, according to explanations by villagers, incarnates the pan-Indian goddess Parvati, the wife of Shiva. In this role she is also referred to as Shivani. In the identification between Chandi and Parvati, a shrewd distribution of roles between pan-Indian and local deities and a carefully arranged interplay between the respective values they represent becomes visible. 'Officially', the bloody offering which crowns the *binu jatra* ritual is not donated to the pan-Indian god Shiva, who is customarily honoured with vegetarian or floral donations, but to the local bloodthirsty female goddess Chandi. In this way, the responsibility for the powerful but bloody and thus, in regard to mainstream Hindu religiosity, problematic sacrifice is attributed to the local goddess. But by identifying Chandi with Parvati, Shiva's wife in the pan-Indian pantheon, her spouse may indirectly profit from the potent bloody offering made according to local traditions.

Locals underline that "*neither humans nor gods ever act in isolation but always in relation to each other*". The divine couple Shiva and Parvati represents the pan-Indian and local ideal model of a relation between family lines, communities and individuals through the cultural institution of marriage (*biha*). In the ritual of *nag baccha* the divine couple also manifests symbolically the interrelatedness of different religious and social traditions: Shiva stands for the pan-Indian Hindu tradition, where vegetarian sacrifices – coconuts and flowers – are preferred; the goddess Chandi represents the tradition of bloody animal sacrifice, regarded as especially efficient in Adivasi societies. By identifying the local goddess Parvati as the wife of the Hindu god Shiva, both traditions are shrewdly harmonized through the establishment of a matrimonial bond.

Becoming a *Nag Baccha*

"How does one become a nag baccha"? I asked several *gurus* and members of *nag baccha* groups. All agreed that "*the idea and certainty to be elected to join a nag baccha group emerges through a dream*". In a dream (*sapna*) the god Nag discloses his identity and calls the young man to serve him. The young person then starts to look for a *nag baccha guru* and group in the surrounding villages. It is only after examining his motives to become a *nag baccha* that the *guru* starts to teach him, to give him knowledge – *sikhya deba*. The term *sikhya deba* refers to the initiation, the teaching and the training of the art of *nag baccha*. Central elements are the knowledge of the secret *mantras*, the technique of treating snake bites by sucking out the poison as well as the preparation of herbal medicine, and a set of rules for an ascetic life conduct (*nyam*). The consumption of the allegedly poisonous *godd* initiates the *nag baccha* as ritual specialists and healers.

The *mantras* are secret verses or short sayings which are taught to the *nag baccha* adepts by their *guru*. Every *mantra* is supposed to heal a particular ailment. They are uttered in a low voice or whisper by the *nag baccha* toward the patients approaching them during the *binu jatra* or other healing performances.

Apart from the great *nag baccha* performances, healing procedures are enacted regularly during the ritual for god Nag. Every Monday (*somwaro*), the day dedicated to the worship of Nag/Shiva, *boil* comes upon the snake children at the altar of the *nag baccha* (*nag baccha gudi/ kutti*). Framed by the ritual music of *ganda baja,* the ecstatically moving *nag baccha* then heal snake bites or mental sufferings, which are conceptualised as poisonous substances in the patient's body, by symbolically biting him and sucking the poison out. The art of sucking out the poison is said to rest upon long training and the spiritual advice of the *guru*. After the symbolical biting and sucking, the patient has to consume a medicine based on local roots and plants (*jori buti*). The ritual is then brought to a close with recitations of *mantras*.

Ascetic Rules of Nag baccha

Each "snake child" is required to follow a set of strict rules of life conduct (*nyam*), which includes the following restrictions:

(1) The *nag baccha* do not take any medicine from an urban doctor.
(2) During the days of ritual performances the *nag baccha* have to abstain from meat.
(3) *Nag baccha* have to restrain from fruits categorised as heating up (*kudru*), as for example the mango fruit.
(4) *Nag baccha* have to abstain from long vegetables (*purdha*).
(5) They are not allowed to take popcorn rice (*murhi*) from any other than their own household.
(6) They are not allowed to accept cooked rice from others.
(7) Before a *nag baccha* can perform a *binu puja*, he has to fast on the 7 preceding Mondays.
(8) A *nag baccha* is not allowed to sleep in any kind of bed, but has to sleep on the ground.
(9) A snake child has to consult his patient with an empty stomach; after the consultation and healing ritual the *nag baccha* must wash extensively.

These restrictions indicate important elements of the conceptions related to *nag baccha.* The interdiction to approach an urban doctor signifies a rejection of the urban medical systems and consequently a general rejection of the use of Western medicine. It can be understood as a challenge to medical authorities that indicates a strong self-consciousness and a firm belief in the effectiveness of the *nag baccha's* own practice of therapy. The temporary abstinence from meat in a society which values the meat of goats or fishes as delicacies, points to the common ritual idiom of temporary ascetic practice and vegetarianism connected to ritual specialisation, which is often found in Middle Indian Adivasi societies.[9] Abstinence from meat is considered instrumental to gain perceptive clarity and in consequence ritual effectiveness. The idea of pursuing psycho-physical self-control through dietary restrictions is also expressed in the subsequent prescriptions. The idea of abstaining from fruits which are considered to "heat-up" the human body as well as "phallic" vegetables is directed at curbing of erotic sensuality. The prohibition of eating popcorn rice prepared by others hints to general notions of the capacity of food to transport "impurity". In the South Asian idiom of "purity and impurity" food transactions are generally conceived as dangerous. Food is not 'dead' or static. It has the capacity to take upon itself and thus to transport the dynamic substances of the "purity" or "impurity" of the food donor or cook, which in consequence affect the person digesting it. Particularly in cooked form, food is susceptible to the fluidum of "impurity". Uncooked food, therefore, can be more easily shared. *Murhi* – the popcorn rice—is commonly considered in Orissa as resistant to the transfer of impurity. However, the *nag baccha* even resist from accepting *murhi* from any other than their own household. In this way, they underline their own extraordinary rigour in observing ritual cleanliness and purity rules. The principle of commensalism within one's own household, community or caste is held to be basic to maintain protection from impurity and represents a fundament of the Hindu caste hierarchy[10] as well as a basic social structure of the communal logic of Adivasi societies.[11] The idea of food purity is also underlined in the *nag baccha*'s rule of receiving patients with an empty stomach and to wash themselves after the therapy. In this way, a potential transfer of digested food substances from the *nag baccha* to the patient shall be avoided. The patient can thus be sure to address his ailments and sorrows to a truly pure – and thus effective—healer. The complete inner purity of the *nag baccha* is also held to heighten his capacity to absorb the psycho-social "dirt", the psychological suffering, of the patient. That he has taken this "dirt" upon him and inside himself is the reason, why the *nag baccha* has to wash himself extensively after his therapeutic procedure.

The asceticism of the *nag baccha* is on the one hand based on the creation of purity and ritual cleanliness, on the other hand on the overcoming of fear, indicated by the rejection to use beds, which is highly dangerous due to the widespread peril of snakes that, moving on the ground, enter human dwellings especially in the night time. The *nag baccha* tradition is a practice of male peer groups to develop the values of purity, courage and psycho-physical power in order to control "inner impurity", namely sexual and in a wider sense sensual impulses and fear as well as external danger. In overcoming their own frailty, fear and bodily inconveniences the *nag baccha* are supposed to transcend the problems of others.

Conclusion

The trance mediumship cult of *nag baccha* is an example of a possession cult, as they are vastly spread in cultures of orality. *Boil* in *nag baccha* seems on the one hand to represent a specific state of empowerment, giving the performers extraordinary forces to exert an influence on those surrounding them, an influence that rises to the capability to heal psychological or physical disorders and alleged or real poisoning. On the other hand, it is a highly exclusive category as *boil* is not supposed to come upon everyone, but only upon "*nyam loko*", the initiated, knowledgeable and devoted religious specialists. *Boil* in *nag baccha* seems thus to represent a distinctive state of social and religious power of its young male performers. But this state reveals itself as highly ambivalent: male and female, authoritative and healing, precarious and always potentially dangerous both for those attending the performance as for the performers themselves.

In *nag baccha* rituals the idea of evil and its handling is expressed in the cultural idiom of poison and antidote – *godd* and its handling during the creative trance state of *boil*. Evil, in the local context, seems to represent a dangerous sphere of the totally other, imagined as the sacred and represented by the dangerous cobra snake. This kind of evil is not "evil" in a moral sense, but a perilous otherness. In the local mythology the cobra is sacred as this reptile has an enormous digestive power (it can devour cows) and—like all snakes—it lives as well under the earth as well as above the surface.[12] The cobras' persistent transfer from a subterranean "underworld" where the dead are supposed to live and the sphere of the humans above makes this reptile both dangerous and holy.

The dialogical encounters between the entranced *nag baccha* and the disappointed believers in the course of the *binu jatra* may be seen as a kind of practical theodicy, a performative justification of the embodied divine in the face of individual suffering and frustration. The *nag baccha* tradition is a local practice to deal with suffering, and thus an example of a local healing tradition, based on ritual music, trance-mediumship and the factual and symbolic removal of the individual psycho-social suffering as well as the real poison of snake bites. In this context it is significant to note that a certain vulnerability and receptiveness seems prerequisite for acting as a *nag baccha*. Compared to the musicians, at whom "*boil will not come*" for they are spiritually "*untouchable*" and thus strong, the snake children are young, unmarried, often feminine and sensitive men who due to their socio-psychological fragility are held to be especially receptive towards the divine. This vulnerability and psychological receptiveness becomes the basis for the ritual effectiveness of the snake children: touched by their spiritual spouses (*boil biha*) they transform their vulnerability and frailty into power and the capacity to heal others. The performance of *nag baccha* turns out to be double-sided: On the one hand it celebrates the value of trance, in terms of a rejection of human control as a sign of divine presence. On the other hand the value of the control of the body is celebrated through ascetic rules and athletic exercises. Another notable feature of double-sidedness or ambivalence in the *nag baccha* performance is the simultaneity and intermingling of tension, fear, danger and a forceful presence of the divine with humoristic elements and outright comedy. The presence of joyful and humorous elements in the performance of the *nag bacha* constructs dynamics of tension and relaxation that are likely to contribute to the psychological and physical relief the patients experience during the ritual play.

NOTES

1. The Bargarh district, one of the most western districts of Orissa, was established on April 1, 1993. To the north, it borders on the State of Chhatisgarh, to the east on the district of Sambalpur; to the south lies the district of Bolangir and Subarnapur and to the west the district of Nawapara. The Bargarh district can be divided into 3 natural partitions, (1) Bargarh Plain, (2) Bora Sambar, (3) Ambabhona and Lakhanpur (see http://orissadiary.com/orissa_profile/district/Baragarh.asp, retrieved on 12.02.2010).
2. *Zamindari* is the historical term for a land tenure and patronage system introduced in rural India by the Mughal dynasty (1526-1858) and adopted by the British colonial rule in the course of its politics of Princely States and distribution of land domains. The *zamindari* system was based on the collection of taxes by landholders (*zamindar*) possessing proprietary rights in the collection of revenues but not in the land itself. The *zamindar* acted as an intermediary between the government and the inferior revenue farmers. The term *zamindar* generally denoted a person who had landholdings, proprietary rights and tax collection responsibilities, ranging from autonomous or semi-independent chieftains to peasant-proprietors.
3. For the history of the Princely States see Ramusack, 2004; Coplan, 2002; Kulke, 2005.
4. At this time the Barghar district, to which Bora Sambar belongs today, was a subdivision of the Sambalpur district (O'Malley, 2007: 200).
5. The area consists of 17 revenue inspection circles and includes 8 police stations: (1) Bijeipur, (2) Sohela, (3) Melchamunda, (4) Gaiselet, (5) Padampur, (6) Paikmal, (7) Jahrband, (8) Buren.

6. http://www.censusindia.gov.in Population_Finder\View_Village_Population.aspx?pcaid=2030&category=N.A.C.
7. As described by Vitebsky (1993) for Soara shamanism and by Otten (2010: 33-51) for the ritual healing specialists of the Rona of southern Orissa. "Spiritual marriages" are also a common notion among the Alekh gurumai, the female ritual specialist of the new proselytising ascetic religion Mahima Dharma in Koraput (Guzy, 2002).
8. The mock duels of the nag baccha performance are a variety of the regional martial arts performance *bari khel*, where artificial duels avoiding bodily contact are fought with wooden sticks.
9. Such as for example the Desya of Koraput (Berger 2001; Guzy 2002, Otten 2008).
10. On the connection between food, eating, commensalism, connubialism and caste hierarchy, see Dumont (1986:168-195); on food substances, impurity and caste, see Marriott (1968: 133-172); on food as a potential bearer of pollutants, see also Douglas (1966: 33-35, 127).
11. An impressive example of commensality of food as a central value for an Adivasi society, is given in Peter Berger's ethnography of the Gadaba of South Orissa (2007: 28-46).
12. In the Bora Sambar region, as all over India, snakes are generally worshipped as divine manifestations.

REFERENCES

Berger, Peter. 2001. "The Gadaba and the 'Non-ST' Desia of Koraput, Orissa. Some Observations on their Interrelations", (pp. 57-90). *In:* Georg Pfeffer and Deepak K. Behera (eds.), *Contemporary Society: Tribal Studies*. Vol. 5. New Delhi: Concept Publishing Company Pvt. Ltd.

Berger, Peter. 2007. *Füttern, Speisen und Verschlingen. Ritual und Gesellschaft im Hochland von Orissa, India*. Indus Ethnologische Südasien-Studien, Band 11. Berlin: Lit Verlag.

Bijoi, C.R. 2007. "Adivasis of India. A History of Discrimination, Conflict and Resistance", (pp.15-27). *In:* Aditi Chanchani, Mamata Dash, Rosemary Viswanath, Sinduja Ananthkrishnan, Vidhya Ragan (eds.), *This is our Homeland. A Collection of Essays on the Betrayal of Adivasi Rights in India*. Bangalore: Equations.

Douglas, Mary. 1966. *Collected Works. Purity and Danger. An Analysis of Pollution and Taboo*. London: Routledge.

Guzy, Lidia. 2002. *Baba-s und Alekh-s – Askese und Ekstase einer Religion im Werden. Vergleichende Untersuchungen der asketischen Tradition Mahima Dharma in Orissa/östliches Indien*. Berlin: Weissensee Verlag (Dissertation).

Leeuw, Gerardus von der. 1920-1921. Die do-ut-des-Formel in der Opfertheorie. In *Archiv für Religionswissenschaft*, 241-253.

Marriott, McKim. 1968. "Caste Ranking and Food Transactions. A Matrix Analysis," (pp.133-172) *In:* Milton Singer and Bernhard Cohn (eds.), *Structure and Change in Indian Society*. Cambridge: Cambridge University Press.

Munda, Ram Dayal. 2002. India's Protection and Promotion of Tribal Rights: Obligations under ILO Convention on Indigenous and Tribal Peoples, 1957 (No.

107). (Paper presented at Indigenous Rights in the Commonwealth Project South and South Asia Regional Expert Meeting, 11th-13th March 2002).

O'Malley. L.S.S. 2007 (1909). *Bengal District Gazetteers Sambalpur*. New Delhi: Logos Press.

Otten, Tina. 2008. "People of the Hills: How Rona Deal with Social Change", (93-118) *In:* Marine Carrin (ed.), *People of the Jangal: Reformulating Identities and Adaptations in Crisis*. Kopenhagen: Curzon Press.

Otten, Tina. 2010. "The Concept of Biba among the Rona of Highland Orissa. Wedding Rituals to Ensure Health", (pp. 33-51). *In:* Peter Berger, Roland Hardenberg, Ellen Kattner und Michael Prager (eds.), *The Anthropology of Values: Essays in Honour of Georg Pfeffer*. Delhi: Longman.

Sahoo, Bhakta Puran. 2007. "Borasambar: A Peep into its origin and Early History", In *Bora Sambar Cup 2007 Souvenir*. Padampur: No Publisher.

Schnepel, Burkhard. 2002. *The Jungle Kings, Ethnohistorical Aspects of Politics and Ritual in Orissa*. New Delhi: Manohar Publications.

Senapati, N. and B. Mahanti. 1971. *Orissa District Gazetteers, Sambalpur*. Cuttack: Orissa Government Press.

Vitebsky, Piers. 1993. *Dialogues with the Dead*. New Delhi: Cambridge University Press.

SEVEN

FORMAL SCHOOLING AND INDIAN TRIBAL CHILDREN

CHRISTINE FINNAN

Schooling in a Global Context

Today, almost all nations encourage or require universal primary education as a means of increasing national economic productivity and encouraging individual social mobility (Boli & Ramirez, 1992; Drèze & Sen, 2002; Froerer & Portisch, 2012; McNeely, 1995). It is taken for granted that universal schooling is a basic human right that will pull nations and individuals out of poverty. The call for universal education assumes either the advisability or inevitability that all children, despite cultural differences and geographic location, should learn a state-specified body of skills and knowledge (especially, literacy and numeracy) to function in a global world. The global reach of this belief has led to a surface level uniformity across all school systems (Anderson-Levitt, 2003). Countries such as Japan and South Korea are held up as examples of how investment in human capital through provision of universal education and health care make countries more globally competitive (Sen, 2013). Examined at the macro level, there is little question about the value of universal education, especially basic literacy and numeracy, for nations' economic growth and individuals' ability to move into the mainstream of their society.

This chapter does not intend to refute the argument supporting provision of universal education; evidence is striking that basic literacy and numeracy, especially for women, lead to better health and economic outcomes for impoverished populations (Drèze & Sen, 2002). Rather, this chapter sets out to contextualize the discussion of universal education, examining how formal schools change and are changed by local cultural and economic practices, how they affect language loss of vulnerable indigenous people, and whether the promise of formal schooling is realized for many of the world's poorest, most geographically isolated people. To better understand why the promise of universal education has not been uniformly realized, we need to look locally and deeply and consider the social and cultural context of placing schools into societies that hold different traditions and assumptions (Anderson-Levitt, 2003). We also need to consider whether universal education develops or liberates people, prepares them for active involvement in democratic decision-making (Drèze & Sen, 2002) or serves as a vehicle for state domination, inculcating docility and conformity into the poor (Pollock & Levinson, 2011).

Here, it is focused primarily on formal schooling of Indian tribal children, builds on research conducted within two subfields of anthropology: anthropology of childhood and anthropology of education. This research provides anthropological insights into how children learn outside of formal schools, the interplay between the institution of the school and community social and cultural traditions, and the potential mismatch between cultural expectations guiding most schools and those held by minority populations. This chapterbegins with a brief summary of key theories and findings drawing from international anthropological studies of childhood, learning, and education. These findings shape the examination of issues surrounding formal schooling in India, especially that provided to tribal children.

Anthropologists Examine Learning in Childhood

A critical body of anthropological research on childhood focuses on how children learn to be fully functional members of society within the ecology of their natural, social, and cultural environment. Much of the research takes place in societies without formal schools or with children as they engage in activities outside of schools. Most of these studies conclude that children learn without being formally taught; they learn "organically" through observation, play, chores and being present to the daily life of their community (for example see, Gaskins & Paradise, 2010; Lancy & Grove, 2010, 2011; Rogoff, 1990; Spindler, 2000; Wenger, 2008), and as they learn collectively within "communities of practice" (Lave & Wenger,

1991). This body of literature also emphasizes the active role children take in their own learning; they learn because they need and want to, not because they are told they must. Typically around the ages of five to seven, children are rewarded for exhibiting "sense" and are given increased responsibilities, recognizing that they have learned sufficient cultural knowledge to contribute to the community (Lancy & Grove, 2011; Rogoff, Sellers, Pirrotta, Fox & White, 2008). Ironically, formal schooling usually starts at this age, removing children from opportunities to take responsibility and placing them in the role of passive recipients of knowledge.

Outside of schools, formal instruction is rare, sometimes occurring during formal apprenticeships, although most apprenticeships primarily rely on observation rather than direct instruction (Lancy & Grove, 2010). Ceremonies held as part of rites of passage may also involve formal instruction transmitting religious or spiritual knowledge to initiate as their transition to adulthood is recognized (Kruger & Tomasello, 1996; Spindler & Spindler, 2000). Stories, legends, and myths carry important cultural lessons, but they are typically told for adult enjoyment and edification; children may be allowed to listen quietly but they are rarely the targeted recipients of the message (Basso, 2000; Spindler, 2000).

Anthropologists Examine Education and Schools

Another critical body of anthropological research focuses on schools[1] and the formal educational process. One strand of this research examines the mutual adaptation of communities and schools as formal schools are introduced into relatively homogeneous, isolated local communities. In most cases, the school systems were created in the image of school systems of colonizers or missionaries and have little connection to local concepts and practices of what and how children learn. The research illustrates a mutual adaptation process; the introduction of formal schools changes cultural expectations, the social order, and what is considered important knowledge within the community, while simultaneously school practices, curriculum, and expectations change to be consistent with local social and cultural expectations. For example, in Sierra Leone practices that look like cheating and grade buying to outsiders, requests for "blessings", are actually adaptations of cultural beliefs that knowledge is a valuable commodity that should be paid for (Bledsoe, 1992). In more recent research in Sierra Leone, Bolten (n.d.) found that students in rural communities value schooling not for what they learn or for possible social mobility, but rather to be known as "students" rather than lower status "youths". Rival (2000) reports similar findings from the Ecuadorian Amazon. In this case, missionary schools disrupt the social order and subsistence patterns of the indigenous people, but result in little literacy and hygiene learning. Families leave the jungle to live near the school compound for material goods, not for the curriculum and possibility of social and economic mobility. Additional research points to the false promise formal schooling holds for social and economic advancement. A vignette from Sierra Leone is illustrative; a teacher asked the class what a great scholar is, and a student responded, "an overeducated person" (Bolten n.d.). These students saw few examples of people from their village advancing through formal schooling, yet they continued to attend school.

These studies exemplify a large body of anthropological research that problematizes the assumption of world culture theorists that schools and school systems are becoming more common over time. Across the world, systems are put into place that provide a common shell for schooling (e.g., age-graded classrooms, compulsory attendance until a specified age, common focus on literacy, numeracy, and teacher-centred instruction, and frequently co-education); as nations jockey for position in international comparisons, this shell becomes increasingly similar. However, as Anderson-Levitt (2005, 2003) concludes, a common set of models and policy debates exist across the world, but at the local level, the lived experience of schooling varies greatly. This variation is the result of many factors including local cultural and political influence on schools, lack of true commitment by the national elite to equitable educational attainment, and mismatches between centralized curriculum and designated medium of instruction and local knowledge and languages.

Another strand of anthropology and education research focuses on why schools repeatedly fail children of racial, ethnic, and linguistic minority groups. For too many of these children, the promise of education is not met, affecting not only their aspirations but also their sense of self. Research indicates that children take multiple paths as they cross borders between school and home/community/peer expectations; some assimilate to dominant expectations; some are able to function well in multiple settings; some see themselves as failures at school, and others actively rebel (Carter, 2006; Phelan, Davidson & Yu, 1998). One explanation for active opposition to school is that students assume that promises of social and economic advancement through education are false; they would rather actively oppose the system than be disappointed by it (Fordham, 1988; McLeod, 2009; Ogbu, 1978). Another explanation for chronic underachievement is that children of ethnic and racial minority groups and lower social classes have not acquired the cultural capital expected by school systems. They do not learn mainstream expectations for how to interact with adults, when to advocate for themselves, and what to expect from their education in their homes (Bourdieu & Passeron, 1977; Lareau, 2003; Reed-Danahay, 2000). Another explanation for achievement disparities focuses on language in the classroom and how children are affected by mismatches between how they communicate at home and expectations for language use in school (Heath, 1983; Cazden, 2001). This is especially problematic when children come to school not knowing the language of instruction and when they assume that their mother tongue is inferior to the dominant language (Mónzo & Rueda, 2009). All of this research shares a focus on schools as structured to support and perpetuate the dominant social and cultural order.

In summary, an anthropological perspective provides needed nuance and context to calls for universal schooling. It provides examples of how children learn when formal schools are not there to define what "learning" means; it illustrates how both the local community and the concept and process of schooling are changed when formal schools are introduced to a community, and it describes how children negotiate different social and cultural expectations of the school and their local community. By deepening the focus at the local level, anthropological research tests the unquestioned acceptance of the individual and societal benefits of formal schooling. As Anderson-Levitt (2003, 2005) describes, despite a common shell (e.g., teacher-centred instruction, age-grading, focus on literacy and numeracy) schools differ greatly because of local assumptions about how, what, and why we learn. Anthropological research across many cultures illustrates the mutual adaptation that occurs when school systems are introduced into local contexts; not only is the indigenous culture changed, but the essence of "school" changes to become something quite different from what central planners designed. This body of research also demonstrates the cultural gaps that exist between the assumptions underlying most school systems and the cultural assumptions many children bring to school. As children navigate these different cultural assumptions and expectations they may choose to assimilate to dominant assumptions, actively oppose such assimilation, find a productive balance between expectations, or see themselves as failures. This research provides a broader context in which to analyze Indian tribal children's experience with formal schooling.

Formal Schooling in Tribal India

Commitments to Universal Education in India

In order to increase national economic productivity and to address historic inequities based on ethnicity, caste, class, and gender, India has implemented universal free and compulsory education for children aged between 6 to 14 years. Across India, the belief in the power of education to lift people out of poverty is widespread. As Drèze and Sen write in describing education in India, "The value of basic education as a tool of social affirmation appears to be well seized by the people. In fact, a common finding of village studies and household surveys is that education is widely perceived by members of socially or economically disadvantaged groups as the most promising means of upward mobility for their children" (2002, 144). India's commitment to free compulsory education is enshrined in Article 45 of the Constitution and is continuously reconfirmed through subsequent legislation (Drèze & Sen, 2002), most recently through the Right of Children to Free and Compulsory Education Act of 2009 (RTE) (Singh & Nagpal, 2010). Given high illiteracy levels and educational inequity, this commitment has been slow to be realized for many reasons, including the poor quality of education provided to many children. Drèze and Sen point out that universal education will not occur until "the actual education is of high enough quality to make it worth attending school" (2002, 184).

Drèze and Sen's statement above gets at the crux of the problem with Indian education. Although schooling has been compulsory for over 60 years, "India has 22 per cent of the world's population, but 46 per cent of the world's illiterates" (Kingdon, 2007, 168); too many children are either not attending school or not gaining basic literacy skills while in school. Poor school quality (especially facilities, teaching, textbooks and other resources) leads to poor student learning. Problems are especially acute in rural areas and among India's poorest children. For example, in a recent study of student learning in 160 rural schools, researchers found that:

- Children are learning at rates far below what textbooks expect.
- Home languages are not used in instruction even though language greatly impacts student learning.
- Child-friendly practices known to be effective are rarely used.
- Teachers have limited ability or desire to teach for student understanding (Bhattacharjea, Wadhwa & Banerji, 2011).

Legislation such as RTE is designed to address such problems, but legislation alone is unlikely to overcome a long history of social and economic inequity, lack of commitment to government schools by all who can afford private schooling, limited educational resources, and poor teacher quality. Privatization of education in India is of special interest because it blurs the responsibility for educating all children and assumes money buys quality. Interestingly, RTE recognizes the vicious cycle that exists in relation to private schools, requiring that all private schools set aside 25 per cent of their seats to "enroll children from weaker sections and disadvantaged communities" and that no seats in this quota can be left vacant (Singh & Nagpal, 2010, 123). This stipulation in the RTE recognizes the powerful draw of private schools for many families, even those with few resources (Kingdon, 2007; LaDousa, 2007; Tooley, 2009). This stipulation likely underestimates the difficulty of overcoming class, caste, gender, and religious barriers through legislation and the ingenuity of private schools to bypass mandates that will be unpopular with their existing clientele.

A number of problems prevent Indian government schools from achieving the goal of universal literacy and numeracy through compulsory education. First, it has been difficult to arrive at a workable policy on the medium of instruction. Although multilingualism is the norm in India, agreeing on the medium of instruction has been difficult (Mohanty, 2006; LaDousa, 2010). Despite official policy that schools teach three languages (in Hindi speaking States: Hindi, English, and a regional language; in all other States: the regional language, English and Hindi), most children are taught either in the regional language or English. As Mohanty writes, "On the whole, the three-language formula and other policy formulations have mostly remained political and ideological statements far removed from the actual practices, which were quite diverse" (2006, 275). Government schools tend to teach in the regional language through Class 4 and introduce another language, usually English after that. Most private schools boast that they provide instruction only in English. As English fluency is equated with economic and social advancement (LaDousa,

2010), many low-income parents sacrifice to send their children to lower-cost English medium schools of marginal quality (Mohanty, 2006). This reliance on English marginalizes all Indian languages stigmatizing those who do not speak fluent English (LaDousa, 2010; Mohanty, 2006). Children, whose mother tongue is not the regional language or English, are seriously disadvantaged, having to learn the regional language before understanding lessons (Mohanty, 2006; Pattanayak, 1990).

Second, the quality of school facilities and curriculum is often subpar. Despite recent facilities upgrades and clear specifications in RTE about minimal facilities expectations, too many school facilities are lacking basic amenities. As Singh and Nagal write, "According to a survey, of the 1.29 million government and private schools covered, over 60 per cent do not have electricity, almost 50 per cent do not have boundary walls to ensure the safety of students and 46.4 per cent do not have toilets for girls" (2010, 124). Textbooks are available in most schools, but they are often too difficult and irrelevant to children's life experiences (Bhattacharjea, Wadhwa, & Banerji, 2011).

Third, there is serious concern with teacher quality. Government school teachers are required to complete Class 12 and undergo training offered through a district training facility; once hired, they are government employees and their jobs are relatively secure for life. Schools, especially those in remote areas, increasingly rely on para-teachers who work on a contract basis, receive lower salaries, and have little pedagogical training (Govinda & Josephine, 2004). Regular teachers are criticized for high absenteeism and for not teaching when they do come to work (Govinda & Bandyopadhyay, 2011). During teacher training, they receive training in content and pedagogy and are made aware of child-friendly instructional practices, but classroom observations indicate that few teachers use these child-friendly practices. Most instruction is conducted through lecture, recitation and seatwork (Bhattacharjea, Wadhwa, & Banerji, 2011) with children passive recipients of teacher knowledge. Teachers are often unsympathetic to children and families of poor, lower caste or tribal children and are accused of physically and verbally abusing children (Balagopalan & Subrahmanian, 2003; Vavavi, 2003). In defence of teachers, Govinda and Bandyopadhyay write that, "There is also a growing criticism that teachers are often not given the conditions to ensure teaching and even less, learning. Teachers who are themselves products of the poor education system, are often seen as obstacles to educational change rather than as a key human resource" (2011, 32).

Fourth, serious inequities exist within the educational system. Despite legislation and efforts of advocacy groups, girls and children of lower castes, tribal groups, and religious minorities too often receive subpar education, if they educated at all. The following section will detail these issues as they relate to tribal children.

Schools and Education of Indian Tribal Children

Tribal groups in India were once isolated, living in relatively closed communities in which they enjoyed cultural autonomy and economic independence in India's inland forests and jungles. In 2001 they constituted 8.2 per cent of the Indian population; most (82%) living in eight States (Sedwal & Kamet, 2011). At one time they spoke at least 400 languages, but the number of extant languages is declining rapidly (Nambissan, 1994). Formal schooling of tribal children expanded rapidly in the 1980s and 1990s (Froerer, 2012); prior to their introduction, tribal children learned as described above, by observation, play, and imitation. Most were illiterate and many adults today remain illiterate.

Since the days of British colonial rule, tribal people have lost much of their autonomy and independence. Their lives have been negatively affected by urban encroachment, environmental degradation, and loss of land to dams and mining (Behera, 2007, 2013; Roy, 2011; Sedwal & Kamat, 2011). Decades of government and corporate corruption, police brutality, and false promises of adequate schools and other social services have made the promises of Naxalite or Maoist groups increasingly attractive to those who hope to stay in the forest. The unrest caused by clashes between government forces (police and military) and the Naxalites has further disrupted the lives of tribal groups (Dash, 2006; Roy, 2011). Marginalized by this social and environmental degradation, many tribal groups today suffer from malnutrition and related health issues, illiteracy, and disruption of traditional spiritual, political, language, and subsistence systems. The situation for those who flee the forest in hopes of finding work in urban areas is not much better. Marginalized in ways similar to members of lower castes, and poorly equipped for urban life and occupations, most tribal migrants to towns and cities live in squalid conditions in city slums or on the streets (Nath, 2007; Roy, 2011).

Were schools truly the avenue for social mobility, they would be equipping tribal children to take advantage of the promise of India's modernization and role in a globalized economy. However, this has not happened, in part because of the poor quality of schools in tribal communities and their lack of relevance to tribal life. Access to schools is not a problem for most tribal children. States are required to provide primary schools (Class 1-5) within walking distance for most students (Sedwal & Kamet, 2011; Singh & Nagpal, 2010). In more remote areas the primary school may be a one room, one teacher school, combining Class 1-5. Upper primary and secondary schools are concentrated in larger settlements, and tribal students either have to travel long distances on poorly maintained roads or board with people near school. Parents are reluctant to allow their children, especially girls, to travel so far (Froerer, 2012). The Central Government offers incentives (e.g., mid-day meals, a free uniform, free textbooks, and attendance scholarships for girls) to encourage tribal student attendance; these incentives have positively affected attendance rates (Sedwal & Kamer, 2011). Although access to schools has improved, the quality of education is hampered by the language of curriculum and instruction and also by the lack of effective teachers, especially by teachers' perceptions of tribal children as learners.

The language used in curriculum and instruction is important for at least three reasons. First, unsurprisingly, children struggle to learn lessons if they do not speak or understand the language of instruction. Most tribal children come to school speaking one of 400 tribal languages and may not have had much exposure to the regional language prior to starting school. Given that government schools teach in the regional language in primary schools, this hampers children's ability to learn lessons until they gain sufficient fluency in the regional language. Most textbooks are in regional languages, Hindi or English, and many use examples in stories and problems that are appropriate to middle class urban India, but not for rural, and especially tribal India (Bhattacherjea, Wadhwa & Banerji, 2011; Mohanty, 2006).

Second, because language and identity are so closely linked, ignoring children's mother tongue, especially in the early grades can have deleterious effects. Mother tongues are known to provide "social and emotional identity to individuals, express the essence of their cultures, and give them a sense of rootedness" (Nambissan, 1994, 2751). Pattanayak carries this idea further and writes that being concerned only about losing access to content knowledge is a "positive suppression of human talent. It deprives individuals and society of free choices, curbs creativity and innovativeness and restricts participation or potential participation in multiple spheres of human interaction, thus imposing limits on freedom" (1987, 8 in Nambissan 1994, 2752).

Third, language policies further marginalize vulnerable people by relegating their mother tongues to the private sphere of home and community and elevating state or international languages to power venues such as schools (Mohanty, 2006). In this process, they compartmentalize their language and culture as inferior to that of more dominant languages. The Bodo, living in Assam, are one of the only tribal groups to successfully assert their language rights. After four decades of agitation for Bodo-medium schools, their language and culture are taught with positive effects (Mohanty, 2006). Unfortunately, most other tribes passively accept the official belief that their children benefit from instruction in a dominant language. As Mohanty writes, "They seem to have accepted their marginalized status by a clear dissociation between the perceived instrumental and integrative functions of languages" (2006, 271).

Language of instruction is not the only deterrent to tribal student learning. Most teachers who work in schools serving tribal children are not members of the tribal groups, have little understanding of tribal cultures, and typically do not seek to teach in such remote schools. Many grudgingly take these posts, hoping to quickly transition to an urban post or one closer to their homes. The para-teacher programme described above is used extensively in small tribal schools. In these schools the para-teacher may have completed only Class 8, and they are often the only teacher in the school, instructing all children Class 1-5. There are numerous issues with the para-teacher concept (see Govinda & Josephine, 2004) but for tribal schools, they are a mixed blessing. On the one hand, para-teachers are required to be local residents so they should understand the local culture and language; on the other hand, they are poorly prepared to teach and then are given the difficult task of teaching across a large age-span (Govinda & Josephine, 2004).

Except for the few tribal people who teach in tribal schools, most teachers are not sensitive to the culture, language, and special needs of tribal children; in fact, many explicitly degrade and disparage tribal children. For example, Sedwal & Kamer (2011) provide examples of teachers expressing negative beliefs about the "uneducability" of children of lower castes and tribal groups. They recount how children are afraid to talk about the verbal abuse, physical punishment, and avoidance of touching meted out by upper caste teachers in school. Krishna Kumar, in his influential book *Social Character of Learning* (1989) describes how a secondary school teacher's actions teach an ambitious tribal student how to be "backward" by degrading the student's responses to questions. Balagopalan (2003) found multiple examples of overt discrimination in schools. Teachers were quick to describe students as "slow" and "unclean" and to label their parents as "drunks". Those who teach tribal migrants in cities "consider the children inferior, both mentally and culturally" (Nath, 2007, 269). Given that teachers are held accountable for student learning without taking into account poverty, family illiteracy, and cultural and language differences, it is not surprising that they pass the blame for poor academic performance to students and their families (Balagopalan & Subrahmanian, 2003). In addition, without explicitly addressing societal inequities and social and cultural diversity in teacher training, teachers are unlikely to rise above societal prejudices (Govinda, 2011).

Views on the benefits of formal schooling have changed over time within tribal communities. Until the 1980s few tribal children received any formal schooling, so many of today's children are first-generation literate. Given a more traditional worldview, lack of exposure to formal schooling, and limited experience of the benefits of life in a global society, tribal adults could easily discourage schooling as a foreign intrusion. However, Froerer (2012) found in her research in Chhattisgarh that adults want their children to complete Class 1-5 and become "schooled people" so, that they can write their names and the name of their village, engage in financial transactions with merchants without being cheated, and avoid being taken advantage of in other transactions with the wider world. They even think that primary education makes their daughters more marriageable (Froerer, 2012). They do not, however, see the value of upper primary or secondary education. To parents advanced schooling is "an expensive and time-consuming means to an end that was not achievable by people like themselves, who lacked the connections and economic resources to translate school certificates into meaningful employment" (350). This view of advanced schooling as out of reach to "people like them" illustrates tribal parents' astute understanding of Indian society by recognizing, and possibly accepting, their inferior role in the larger Indian society (Balagopalan, 2003). Froerer found that adults were very pragmatic about their daughters' futures, "For girls, acquiring domestic skills (managing the household, assisting with agricultural work and animal husbandry) that would enable them to contribute to the immediate needs of their own families was perhaps the most important activity around which their lives revolved—and around which their future would largely be determined" (2012, 346-47).

In some cases, tribal children have high expectations for continued education while those who are beaten down by the experience are eager to leave school. Much like the children described by Anderson-Levitt (2005) who pleaded to enter school, the tribal girls Froerer interviewed wanted to go to school and avoid the isolation and drudgery of their domestic life. They aspired to complete secondary school and "become someone". For them continued education meant postponing marriage and possibly leaving the tribal village or returning to the village to serve as a health care worker or teacher. Where girls hoped to postpone marriage through schooling, parents worried that too much education would make their daughters unmarriageable, unable to perform domestic duties expected of a wife and daughter-in-law. In most cases, girls did not fulfil their ambitions to continue in school. For many other tribal children who suffer from abuse from teachers and peers, the dream of achievement through schooling is fleeting. Nath (2007) and Sedwal & Kamet (2011) describe the dehumanizing effect of school; they describe school as a place where tribal children learn to see themselves as inferior and incapable of learning.

Conclusions

The intersection of school-based education and Indian tribal children provides an ideal case to examine the feasibility and local reality of universal, compulsory education as a vehicle for social and economic mobility. Given the history of discrimination against tribal people and their vulnerable position in a modernizing India, their children are, on the one hand, those who can benefit most from formal schooling, while, on the other hand, they have the most to lose if the promises of school completion are false.

As described at the beginning of this chapter, anthropological research provides a rich and vivid picture of how learning occurs without or outside of formal schools. With the spread of universal compulsory schooling to tribal villages in India, it is clear that traditional ways of learning in these communities have already been altered. Although children continue to learn domestic and agricultural skills at home and in the community, their perspective on the value of traditional work has been altered. As Sedwal and Kamat (2011) write, when children attend school, they learn to see the mental work done in school as superior to the physical work done in the village. This is also reflected in their vision of "becoming someone", implying that traditional paths are for "nobodies" (Froerer, 2012).

The introduction of formal schools into or near tribal villages has resulted in a mutual adaptation of school expectations and processes and the village social, cultural and economic dynamics in ways similar to those described earlier (e.g., Bledsoe, 1992; Bolten n.d.; Rival, 2007). Froerer's ethnographic study points to how formal schools have changed traditional views of important knowledge. Although adults continue to value traditional domestic and subsistence work, they now also value basic literacy as a tool for interacting more effectively with the outside world. Consistent with other findings (e.g., Bolten n.d.), tribal adults' belief that children can become "overeducated" affects the educational process in tribal communities; few children continue their education beyond Class 5. Similar to Rival's conclusion that formal schooling leaves Ecuadorian children unprepared for life in the wider world and within the jungle, Vavavi (2003) and Balagopalan (2003) reach the same conclusion for Indian tribal children. Not only are they not competitive for jobs requiring school completion, but they no longer value traditional work. Consistent with research compiled by Anderson-Levitt (2003; 2005), the shell of universal schooling (e.g., age-grading, compulsory attendance, co-educational attendance, teacher-centred instruction) is evident in tribal village schools, but local variations reflect tribal social, cultural, and economic patterns.

Research on tribal children's schooling experience contributes to the vast anthropological literature on the discriminatory treatment of historically marginalized children in schools. Research conducted in village schools and among tribal migrants to urban centres documents that they too often enter a rather hostile learning environment. Although tribal children are included in classrooms, they are often assumed to be unable to learn and are viewed as dirty and undeductable by teachers and non-tribal peers. Their learning is hampered in part by the fact that many of them are first-generation school learners (Govinda, 2011) but also by the language of instruction used in most schools and by the quality of teachers assigned to schools in tribal areas or urban slums. The lack of knowledge of and respect for tribal cultures and languages negatively affects children's confidence and willingness to learn school lessons.

Recommendations

Although it is tempting to romanticize cultures as they were before they were buffeted by encroachments from the outside, one characteristic of all cultures is that they change and adapt, and that cultural clocks cannot be rewound. We will never return to a time when tribal people lived in relative isolation and their children learned to become productive members of the community without formal schooling. This being the case, below are some recommendations to improve tribal children's school experience.

Improve Teacher Quality

India is not alone in struggling to place good teachers in all schools. Teacher quality has a profound effect on student learning, and the effect is more pronounced for children growing up in poverty and for those who bring cultural and linguistic diversity to school. First generation learners are especially vulnerable. Ideally, high quality teachers, not para-teachers, would come from tribal communities, but this is unlikely until school quality improves so that tribal students can pass Class 12 examination and enter teacher training. In addition, tribal communities need evidence that continued education pays off so that they will encourage their children to become teachers. The best way to accomplish these goals is to improve teacher training. Effective teacher training should balance pedagogical content knowledge and knowledge about children and their communities (Finnan, 2009). Teachers need to know their content and effective ways to teach it, but they also need to know about child development and the social, cultural, and linguistic influences on their learning. Of critical importance is making teachers aware of their own cultural biases; without understanding themselves as culture bearers, they are likely to judge children different from themselves as deficient (Spindler & Spindler 1994). All teachers need awareness of tribal cultures, even those teaching in urban areas because they are likely to teach a diverse group of children including migrant tribal children.

Improve Quality and Relevance of Curriculum and Instruction

Across India there is a call for more relevant curriculum and child friendly instruction. Relevant curriculum draws on children's home and community experiences to teach more universal lessons. This is especially true for tribal children who live in isolated, remote areas. Most importantly, teachers need to involve students in their own learning and make connections to their lives. Even if textbooks and other curricular materials are more generic, all subjects, reading, mathematics, science and social studies can be made relevant to tribal children's lives with a little creativity and a great deal of awareness of their lived experience. Given that many tribal children are either first-generation school attendees or come from homes with little formal schooling, their families are unlikely to help them make connections between school learning and home learning. The challenge in teaching tribal children is to make learning relevant to their lives while also teaching key skills needed for social and economic mobility.

Diversify the Language of Instruction

Multilingualism is the norm in India, and it is critical that children learn at least the regional language if not English. However, total immersion into an unknown language limits children's ability to keep up with lessons and devalues their mother tongue and their sense of self. Since many tribal children come to school without knowing the regional language, they are more likely to succeed in school, and see it as place that values them, if they are taught in their mother tongue, at least during the first years. Given that few non-tribal teachers speak tribal languages, they may need to partner with a tribal para-teacher who can provide the language bridge for students.

Create Partnerships between Schools and Tribal Leaders and Parents

Given their history of broken promises, tribal groups have good reason to be wary and skeptical of governmental institutions. It is heartening that tribal parents see the value of sending their children to primary school to gain a degree of literacy and numeracy, but they will continue to question the utility of continued schooling until communication between school officials and the community improves. Recent efforts to establish community councils and parent-teacher groups (Govinda, 2011) are a step in the right direction. With more open communication, both sides will better understand and value different perspectives on schooling. As parents become more comfortable at school, they may seek out adult literacy opportunities that will not only help them, but will also benefit their children.

Combat Poverty and Social Inequity at a State and National Level

Poverty and social inequity are not unique to India. Many people in the United States, like in India, believe that schools can undo centuries of inequity, discrimination, and social stratification. Across the world, poverty and inequity adversely affect student learning (Ladd, 2011). Until we seriously ask how children who are inadequately housed, clothed, and fed can achieve the dream of social and economic mobility through education, we perpetuate a system of false promises.

NOTE

1. Bradley Levinson makes an important distinction between education and schooling. He sees education as "humanity's unique methods of *acquiring, transmitting,* and *producing* knowledge for interpreting and acting upon the world" [italics in original] (2000, 2) and schooling as an institutionalized learning environment separate from where the learning will be applied.

REFERENCES

Anderson-Levitt, K. M. 2003. "A World Culture of Schooling"? (pp.1-26). *In:* K.M. Anderson-Levitt, (ed.), *Local Meanings, Global Schooling: Anthropology and World Culture Theory.* New York: Palgrave Macmillan.

____. 2005. "The Schoolyard Gate: Schooling and Childhood in Global Perspective", *Journal of Social History, 38*, 987-1006.

Balagopalan, S. 2003. "Neither Suited for the Home nor for the Fields: Inclusion, Formal Schooling and the *Adivasi* Child," *IDS Bulletin, 34*: 55-62.

Balagopalan, S. & R. Subrahmanian. 2003. "*Dalit* and *Adivasi* Children in Schools: Some Preliminary Research Themes and Findings", *IDS Bulletin, 34*: 43-53.

Basso, K.H. 2000. "Stalking with Stories", (pp. 41-52) *In:* B.A.U. Levinson (ed.), *Schooling the Symbolic Animal: Social and Cultural Dimensions of Education.* Lanham, MD: Rowman & Littlefield Publishers.

Behera, D.K. 2007. "The Impact of Drought on the Indigenous Children: The Case of Kalahandi District in Orissa", (pp. 274-290) *In:* D.K. Behera, (ed.), *Childhoods in South Asia.* New Delhi: Longman.

____. 2013. "Dam, Development and the Exclusion of the Indigenous People: A Case from Odisha", (pp. 167-188) *In:* U. Skoda, K.B. Nielsen & M. Qvortrup (eds.), *Navigating Social Exclusion and Inclusion in India: Structures, Agents, Practices.* London: Anthem.

Bhattacharjea, S. W. Wadhwa & R. Banerji. 2011 *Inside Primary Schools: A Study of Teaching and Learning in Rural India.* Mumbai: Pratham Mumbai Education Initiative.

Bledsoe, C. 1992. "The Cultural Transformation of Western Education in Sierra Leone", *Africa, 62*: 182-202.

Bolten, C. (n.d.) "A Great Scholar is an Overeducated Person: Misrecognition and Education in Sierra Leone". Unpublished manuscript.

Boli, J. & F.O. Ramirez. 1992. "Compulsory Schooling in the Western Cultural Context", (pp. 25-38) *In:* R.F. Arnove, P.G. Altbach & G.P. Kelly, (eds.), *Emergent Issues in Education: Comparative Perspectives.* Albany NY: State University of New York Press.

Bourdieu, P. & J.C. Passeron. 1977. *Reproduction in Education, Society and Culture.* Trans. R. Nice. London: Sage.

Carter, P.L. 2006. "Straddling Boundaries: Identity, Culture, and School", *Sociology of Education, 79* (4): 304-328.

Cazden, C.B. 2001. *Classroom Discourse: The Language of Teaching and Learning.* Portsmouth, NH: Heinemann.

Dash, S.P. 2006. *Naxal Movement and State Power: With Special Reference of Orissa.* New Delhi: Sarup & Sons.

Drèze, J & A. Sen. 2002. *India: Development and Participation.* New York: Oxford University Press.

Finnan, C. 2009. *The Upper Elementary Years: Ensuring Success in Grades 3-6.* Thousand Oaks, CA: Corwin Press.

Fordham, S. 1988. "Racelessness as a Factor in Black Students' School Success: Pragmatic Strategy or Pyrrhic Victory"? *Harvard Educational Review,* 58 (1): 54-84.

Froerer, P. 2012. "Learning, Livelihoods, and Social Mobility: Valuing Girls' Education in Central India", *Anthropology and Education Quarterly,* 43: 344-357.

Froerer, P. & A. Portisch 2012. "Introduction to the Special Issue: Learning, Livelihoods, and Social Mobility", *Anthropology and Education Quarterly,* 43: 332-343.

Gaskins, S. & R. Paradise. 2010. "Learning through Observation in Daily Life", (pp. 85-118) *In:* D.F. Lancy, J. Bock, & S. Gaskins (eds.), *The Anthropology of Learning in Childhood.* Lanham, MD: Altimira.

Govinda, R. 2011. "Issues and Priorities for Action and Research", (pp. 404-419) *In:* R. Govinda (ed.), *Who Goes to School? Exploring Exclusion in Indian Education.* New Delhi: Oxford University Press.

Govinda, R. & Bandyopadhyay, M. 2011. "Access to Elementary Education in India", (pp. 1-86) *In:* Govinda, R. (ed.), *Who Goes to School? Exploring Exclusion in Indian Education.* New Delhi: Oxford University Press.

Govinda, R. & Y. Josephine. 2004. "Para-teachers in India: A Review", UNESCO International Institute of Educational Planning. Retrieved from http://www.unesco.org/iiep/eng/research/basic/PDF/teachers5.pdf

Heath, S.B. 1983. *Ways with Words: Life and Work in Communities and Classrooms.* Cambridge: Cambridge University Press.

Kingdon, G. G. 2007. "The Progress of School Education in India", *Oxford Review of Economic Policy, 23*, 168-195.

Kruger, A.C. & M. Tomasello. 1996. "Cultural Learning and Learning Culture," (pp. 369-85) *In:* Olson, D., & N. Torrance (eds.), *Handbook of Education and Human Development: New Models of Learning, Teaching, and Schooling.* New York: Oxford, Blackwell.

Kumar, K. 1989. *Social Character of Learning.* New Delhi: Sage Publications.

Ladd, H.F. 2011. *Education and Poverty: Confronting the Evidence.* Working Papers Series SAN11-01. Durham, NC: Duke Sanford School of Public Policy. Retrieved June 4, 2012 from http://sanford.duke.edu/research/papers/SAN11-01.pdf

LaDousa, C. 2007. "Liberalisation, Privatization, Modernization, and Schooling in India: An Interview with Krishna Kumar", *Globalisation, Societies and Education, 5*: 137-152.

LaDousa, C. 2010. "On Mother and Other Tongues: Sociolinguistics, Schools, and Language Ideology in Northern India", *Language Sciences,* 32: 602-614.

Lancy, D.F. & M. A. Grove. 2010. "The Role of Adults in Children's Learning", (pp. 145-180) *In:* D.F. Lancy, J. Bock, & S. Gaskins (eds.), *The Anthropology of Learning in Childhood.* Lanham, MD: Altimira.

Lancy, D.F. & M. A. Grove. 2011. "Getting Noticed: Middle Childhood in Cross-Cultural Perspective", *Human Nature,* 22: 281-302. Doi 10.1007/s12110-011-9117-5.

Lareau, A. 2003. *Unequal Childhoods: Class, Race and Family Life.* Berkeley, CA: University of California Press.

Lave, J. & E. Wenger. 1991. *Situated Learning: Legitimate Peripheral Participation.* Cambridge: Cambridge University Press.

Levinson, B.A.U. 2000. "Introduction: Whither the Symbolic Animal? Society, Culture, and Education at the Millennium", (pp. 1-11) *In:* Levinson, B.A.U. (ed.), *Schooling the Symbolic Animal: Social and Cultural Dimensions of Education.* Lanham, MD: Rowman & Littlefield Publishers, Inc.

McLeod, J. 2009. *Ain't No Makin' It: Aspirations and Attainment in a Low-Income Neighborhood.* Boulder, CO: Westview Press.

McNeely, C.L. 1995. *Constructing the Nation-State: International Organization and Prescriptive Action.* Westport, CT: Greenwood.

Mohanty, A. K. 2006. "Multilingualism of the Unequals and Predicaments of Education in India: Mother Tongue or Other Tongue", (pp. 262-283) *In:* O. García, T. Skutnabb-Kangas & M.E. Torres-Guzmán (eds.), *Imagining Multilingual Schools: Languages in Education and Globalization.* Bristol, UK: Multilingual Matters.

Monzó, L.D. & R. Rueda. 2009. "Passing for English Fluent: Latino Immigrant Children Masking Language Proficiency", *Anthropology and Education Quarterly,* 40 (1): 20-40.

Nambissan, G.B. 1994. "Language and Schooling of Tribal Children: Issues Related to Medium of Instruction", *Economic and Political Weekly,* 29: 2747-2754.

Nath, N. 2007. "Stories of Struggle for Survival: Slum Children's Lives and Voices", (pp. 261-273). *In:* D.K. Behera, (ed.), *Childhoods in South Asia.* New Delhi: Longman.

Ogbu, J.U. 1978. *Minority Education and Caste: The American System in Cross-Cultural Perspective.* New York: Academic Press.

Pattanayak, D.P. 1990. "Introduction". (pp. v-xii) *In:* Pattanayak, D.P. (ed.), *Multilingualism in India.* Bristol, PA: Multilingual Matters.

Phelan, P., A.L. Davidson & H.C. Yu. 1998. *Adolescents' Worlds: Negotiating Family, Peers, and School.* New York: Teachers College Press.

Pollock, M. & B.A.U. Levinson. 2011. "Introduction", (pp. 1-8) *In:* B.A.U. Levinson & M. Pollock (eds.), *A Companion to the Anthropology of Education.* Malden, MA: Blackwell Publishing.

Reed-Danahay, D. 2000. "Habitus and Cultural Identity: Home/School Relationships in Rural France," (pp.223-236). *In:* B.A.U. Levinson (ed.), *Schooling and the Symbolic Animal: Social and Cultural Dimensions of Education.* Lanham, MD: Rowman & Littlefield, Publishers.

Rival, L. 2000. "Formal Schooling and the Production of Modern Citizens in the Ecuadorian Amazon", (pp. 108-122) *In:* B.A.U. Levinson, (ed.), *Schooling and the Symbolic Animal: Social and Cultural Dimensions of Education.* Lanham, MD: Rowman & Littlefield, Publishers.

Rogoff, B. 1990. *Apprenticeship in Thinking: Cognitive Development in Social Context.* New York: Oxford University Press.

Rogoff, B., M.J. Sellers, S. Pirrotta, N. Fox & S.H. White. 2008. "Age and Responsibility", (pp. 251-263) *In:* R.A. LeVine and R.S. New (eds.), *Anthropology and Child Development: A Cross-Cultural Reader.* Malden, MA: Blackwell Publishing.

Roy, A. 2011. *Walking With the Comrades.* New York: Penguin.

Sedwal, M. & Kamet, S. 2011 "Education and Social Equity in Elementary Education", (pp. 87-122) *In:* R. Govinda (ed.), *Who Goes to School? Exploring Exclusion in Indian Education.* New Delhi: Oxford University Press.

Sen, A. 2013, June 19. "Why India Trails China," *The New York Times.* Retrieved from http://www.nytimes.com

Singh, S. & C. Nagpal. 2010. "The Right of Children to Free and Compulsory Education Act of 2009", *World Affairs,* 14: 118-134.

Spindler, G. 2000. "The Transmission of Culture", (pp. 141-176) *In:* G.D. Spindler (ed.), *Fifty Years of Anthropology and Education: 1950-2000.* Mahwah, NJ: Lawrence Erlbaum Associates.

Spindler, G. & L. Spindler. 1994. *Pathways to Cultural Awareness: Cultural Therapy with Teachers and Students* (eds.), Thousand Oaks, CA: Corwin Press.

____. 2000. "There are no Dropouts among the Arunta and Hutterites," (pp.181-189). *In:* G.D. Spindler (ed.), *Fifty Years of Anthropology and Education: 1950-2000.* Mahwah, NJ: Lawrence Erlbaum Associates.

Tooley, J. 2009. *The Beautiful Tree: A Personal Journey into How the World's Poorest People are Educating Themselves.* Washington, DC: CATO Institute.

Vavavi, A.R. 2003. "Schooling for a New Society? The Social and Political Bases of Education Deprivation in India", *IDS Bulletin 34*: 72-80.

Wenger, M. 2008. "Children's Work, Play, and Relationships among the Giriama of Kenya", (pp. 289-306) *In:* R.A. LeVine & R.S. New (eds.), *Anthropology and Child Development: A Cross-Cultural Reader.* Malden, MA: Blackwell Publishing.

EIGHT

SOCIAL EXCLUSION OF TRIBAL CHILDREN FROM SCHOOLING IN ANDHRA PRADESH

V. SUBRAMANYAM

Introduction

Children are considered as one of the excluded groups in almost all societies including tribal society. They are experiencing the problem of exclusion in certain contexts and situations in their daily life at home, community, peer group, society, schools and other public or private institutions. It is a well-known fact that children are the future contributors for societal and human world development; otherwise they are considered as "mirror of the future". According to Carol Ballamy (1996) "children—their needs, rights, well-being and contribution to society—belong at the very centre of development, if the world is evolved into a more peaceful, productive and equitable place". Even today, worldwide in general, children continue to be subjected, wholesale to violence, abuse, deprivation and neglect which are considered as factors for social exclusion[1] of children in any human society or group which is no exception to children of tribal communities.

In general children have no voice to express their views boldly before their parents and elders, moreover, they are submissive and expected to uphold the decisions of their parents and other elderly kin members of their family. Children are among the most disempowered groups in society. They have little power or influence over the social processes and they can seldom protect themselves from abuse. Customary law considers children as property of their respective families and gives them no individual rights. The widespread acceptance of highly exploitative labour practices and the practice of genital mutilation of girls are among the most extreme examples of the vulnerability of children. Certain children are excluded from school for both economic and social reasons. This obviously results in child labour. For poor families the need to get additional income takes precedence over education. Children not only work, but are often forced into the most risky forms of employment. Child prostitution is reported in many underdeveloped and developing countries. In rural and tribal areas especially in the drought prone areas bonded child labour is still found (Subramanyam, 2010).

The cultural practice of early child care, enculturation[2] and education reflects largely on the personality development of a child. It is based on the assumption that child development has a particular structure, consisting of a series of predetermined stages which lead towards the eventual achievement of logical competence. Childhood is a social phenomenon (Qvortrup, 1993). In general children are included in the social and cultural processes of the society at large. Usually, the family has additional responsibilities for children. Children are also contributing to the production as well as the reproduction of society itself, biologically, organizationally and culturally. They, therefore, have a legitimate and indisputable claim on relevant and adequate resources within all spheres of social and cultural life. Children and childhood must incorporate into the centre of social, economic and political aspects of the society. This should not be interpreted as a plea for legitimating children as labour in the conventional sense. But it is an argument for the recognition of school labour, which cannot be separated from labour in society at large, as these activities are integrally interwoven with processes in the labour market.

The earlier anthropological studies on "children and childhood" clearly point out that child rearing and socialization practices are patterned in very dissimilar ways in different cultures. For the protection and growth of children, they are encouraged to go to school and protect themselves from participating in work. Therefore, children outside the context of the home, children idling on street corners and children absent from school, are believed to be 'at risk' or in some way deviant. The practice of child labour prevents them from schooling. Children over the age of five and under fourteen who are orphaned or found living in idleness would be bound into agricultural service or craft: so that these children may be bred up to labour; principle of work culture is implanted in them at an early age and laziness is discouraged. The male children aged between 6 and 14 years usually keep on watching their cattle in many remote societies, whereas the female children in the same age group take care of their younger siblings and attend to other domestic chores.

Cultural interpretations of 'childhood' and 'adulthood' have been studied by anthropologists. However, it is also useful to understand the mechanism and forms of social exclusion of children in different cultures. Children everywhere are by definition in a subordinate structural relation to adults. In certain cultures, childhood ends by custom at puberty or marriage, in others it stops at the completion of compulsory schooling and entry into work. The transition from childhood to adulthood is more visible in some traditional cultures. Chronological age is entirely irrelevant, birth dates are a matter of insignificance and ignored altogether. Large majority of the tribal parents do not know the schooling age for children and they do not record the birth dates of their children. They consider that attainment of menarche by girl child and mustache and pubic hair by male child as an indication to their adulthood. In many East African societies, membership of an age set based on broad generational criteria is more important than individual chronology. The distinction between 'childhood' and 'adulthood' is denoted not by arrival at a particular age threshold but by group participation in rites of passage. The means by which adults assert their authority over children varies from culture to culture. It is a matter of long tradition in several societies that children are treated as the property of their parents and commoditized in exchange of gifts and favours between neighbours and kin. There is a practice of delivering up daughters as brides or domestic helpers in Ashaninca in the low land Peruvian rain forest and the Akha and Lahu in the hills of Burma and Thailand. Likewise in Srilanka, the recorded laws of both the Sinhala and Tamil communities refer to the parental right to sell or surrender children in time of need as payment against a loan or as a gift to an official as a mark of respect (Goonesekere, 1993).

Children are seen as the central part of the family's purpose. They are mechanisms for the proper upbringing of children and their incorrect behaviour using appropriate punishments (including regular beating) to enforce discipline. Children were seen as inherently sinful and in need of guidance. Since nineteenth century much concern to 'save' children from labour and exploitation. The idea of childhood as a special phase was even more strongly reinforced by the development of compulsory state schooling. This came late in the day in Britain as compared with continental rivals like Germany and at first was not taken very seriously in parts of the country which saw child labour as essential. However, as the century progressed it was the need for the child to attend school, which ended the worst form of child labour (Hendrick, 1997). The idea of child centredness as a key focus for policy development had firmly taken root, paving the way for twentieth century which is described by many commentators as "the century of the child".

The development and gradual extension of compulsory schooling (along with the corresponding decline in child labour) changed children from being an economic asset to be valued as part of family strategy for survival. Children were being seen as a liability something into which the parents had to pour resources in the hope of receiving emotional and expressive rewards (affection, pride, etc.) rather than financial returns (Anderson, 1972).

Schooling also creates a period of ambiguous status for children. The period of compulsory schooling is a time when children are not physically dependent (breast feeding, nappy changing, etc.) on adults, yet they are not adults themselves. From nursery school to their late teens they occupy a kind of limbo status with confused signals about rights and responsibilities offered at every turn. What is implicit in the provision of schooling though is the fact that this is a time when they are in need of protection, nurturing and guidance. Further, it is clear that since twentieth century the welfare of children is not just a family responsibility. Children are seen as increasingly the responsibility of the state, which intervenes in their education, health, diet and upbringing in ways designed to improve the national well-being by developing its future citizens.

Distinctions within the childhood are also causing exclusion of the girl-child to schooling in many caste and tribal societies. Systematic gender bias in the family and school, the formal institutions of childhood, results in major gender disparities in survival and welfare in some nations. Physical disability is another causative factor for exclusion of disabled children to schooling. Poverty in many societies results in increasing the number of disabled children. Lagerwall and Tiroler (1995) convincingly described "the relationship between poverty and incidence/prevalence of disability within a given population group. Poor people tend to become disabled because of their living conditions. This makes them even poorer. They do not eat enough food or well balanced food, they live in unhealthy houses, and they have dangerous jobs and are more exposed to violence. If people are disabled, there is greater likelihood that they are poor and *vice versa*".

Anthropology and Education

Cultural anthropologists have also paid much attention on the issues of education and illiteracy among aboriginals and contributed some literature to the educational research. "Anthropology and education" refers to anthropological research in classrooms, homes and neighbourhoods (Spindler, 2000). Some of the most interesting research has been done in classrooms, where anthropologists observe interactions among teachers, students, parents, and visitors. Jules Henry's classic account of the American Elementary School classroom (1955) shows how students learn to confirm to and compete with their peers. Anthropologists also follow students from classrooms into their homes and neighbourhoods, viewing children as total cultural creatures, whose enculturation and attitudes toward education belong to a context that includes family and peers.

In most of the tribal pockets of India, majority of the tribes have their own dialects, multilingual student groups attend the schools. The teacher plays a vital role in dealing with the students in classroom situation in teaching. In a diverse, multicultural population, teacher should be sensitive to and knowledge about linguistic and cultural differences. Children need to be protected so that their ethnic or linguistic background is not used against them. That is what happens when a social variation is regarded as a learning disability. In most of the multi-tribal village schools, children face the problem of linguistic discrimination in classroom. Even today, in large majority of the tribal schools at primary level the medium of instruction is the regional language, 'Telugu'. Only a few multilingual teaching schools were established in tribal areas of Andhra Pradesh. Tribal children are excluded from school education because of teaching in regional language. An anthropological cultural orientation to the teachers is definitely helpful to tackle this problem amicably.

Cultural anthropologists take education process not only as knowledge building process but also as cultural transmission. Education is an intrinsic aspect of culture of any given community, more so with tribal communities. Anthropologists are of the opinion that teachers and students need cultural understanding of the society as it helps to facilitate the accommodation of cultural differences in modern classroom setting.

They also stress the importance of studying simple societies and their educational systems, which are so useful in understanding of education and educational process in complex societies. Some of the pioneer anthropologists like Herskovits (1943), Haimerdorf (1944), Mead (1953) and Spindler (1955) have contributed to the engagements between anthropology and education and out of their works emerged a special branch of anthropology of education. Some of the concepts like culture, socialization or enculturation, innovation, diffusion which are of special relevance to education particularly the education of ethnic minority learners and aboriginal groups.

Scheduled tribes in India are a residual category of the British classification which has been carried over into India's independence. Tribes are defined by assorted criteria of language, location and are at different developmental stages. Social scientists, particularly, sociologists and social (cultural) anthropologists suggest that tribal communities need formal education and awareness to take part in all the developmental programmes designed by the Indian government, without proper preparation, their involvement in partial and development in various aspects shall be dwarfed.

The first contribution to the study of educational problems of scheduled tribes in India was made as early as 1944 by Furer Haimendorf who suggested educational schemes specifically for the Gonds of Adilabad district in Andhra Pradesh State. The scheme was drawn up against the background of the culture and environment of the Raj Gonds. The scheme paid rich dividends for the tribes of that area and even now forms the basis of educational planning for the tribes all over the country. This was the first time he pointed out that an educational programme for tribes has to be in consonance with their habitat, economy and culture in a given area.

The educational process in tribal societies closely linked with the socio-cultural milieu wherein a high illiteracy rate is normally recorded. It can be attributed that there exists a "culture of silence" and the "legitimization of exploitation", leading to exclusion of tribal from the mainstream society. To do away the social exclusion of the tribes through inculcating education as a primary social mobility in terms of equity is essential. The present educational discourses aiming at inclusive education of tribal children have not been successful to achieve their objectives.

Based on the above background in this chapter an attempt is made to explain the mechanism, forms of exclusion and inclusion of tribal children in their society broadly and in specifically their schooling. This chapter is prepared on the basis of field observations in some of the schools in eleven tribal mandals of Visakha agency area as part of major research project, carried out during 2008-2010 with the financial support of University Grants Commission, New Delhi. The educational status of tribes in Andhra Pradesh State and Visakhapatnam district is presented in this chapter, based on the secondary data of Tribal Cultural Research and Training Institute, Hyderabad. Tribal Welfare Department of Andhra Pradesh, Hyderabad, and Integrated Tribal Development Agency, Paderu, Visakhapatnam district. The analysis is mostly descriptive and comprises of explanations from an anthropological perspective. It also discusses anthropologists' contribution to education and usefulness of anthropological methods for education research especially among aboriginal groups with linguistic diversity and multiple cultural complexities.

Background of the Tribes in the Study Area

The State of Andhra Pradesh represents 35 tribes with a population of 50.24 lakhs which constitutes 6.59 per cent to total population. In Andhra Pradesh State, the district Visakhapatnam consists of 16 tribes with the population of 5,57,572, which constitutes 14.55 per cent to total population of the district. More than 90 per cent of tribal population in the district Visakhapatnam is distributed in eleven tribal *mandals*, namely, Aruku Valley, Ananthagiri, Dumbriguda, Gangaraju Madugula, Paderu, Hukumpeta, Pedabayalu, Munchingput, Chintapalle, Gudem Kothaveedhi, and Koyyuru. About 56.4 per cent of the geographical area in the district is covered with thick forest growth of numerous trees and dales where the tribals inhabit centuries together. The tribes found to live in the Visakha agency area[3] are: (1) Bagata, (2) Valmiki, (3) Kotiya, (4) Rena or Rona, (5) Reddi Dora, (6) Konda Dora, (7) Nooka/Mooka Dora, (8) Manne Dora, (9) Agency Goudu, (10) Konda Kammara, (11) Konda Kapu, (12) Mali, (13) Dulia/Mulia, (14) Khond, (15) Gadaba, and (16) Porja. Among these tribes, Gadaba, Khond and Porja are considered as most vulnerable groups and at pre-agricultural stage of economy. Large majority of the children in vulnerable tribes have no access to school education, and a very low literacy rate is recorded among these tribes.

The economy of the tribes is agro-forest based, and subsistence in character. The Agency Goudus are traditional pastoralists and Konda

Kammaras are the artisans who made iron and wooden implements. At present these two tribes are also not completely depending on their hereditary callings and practicing shifting cultivation in addition to non-timber forest produce collection alike that of other tribes in this region. Large majority of the tribal people are confined to their cultural traditions and practices. Many tribes have their own dialects, however, majority of them speak the regional language 'Telugu'. Around 60 per cent of the tribal population stand at below poverty line. Poverty, food insecurity, indebtedness, illiteracy and ill health are the major socio-economic problems to large number of tribal people. Very high incidences of malnutrition, maternal, infant and child mortality rates are recorded in Visakha agency area. The tribals are still exploited by the non-tribal money lenders and traders due to their innocence, ignorance and illiteracy. Education plays a vital role for the upliftment of tribal and releases them from the clutches of exploitation by external agencies including the non-tribal money lenders and traders.

Tribes due to their geographical isolation have remained excluded from the mainstream population. Poverty and non-participation of these groups in many development programmes (including education), coupled with administrative bottlenecks have also contributed to the slow development over the years. The snail's pace development in many tribal areas is mostly due to lack of access to agricultural land, control over forest wealth, apathy towards formal education, health services, protected drinking water and other infrastructural facilities like electricity, roads, postal and modern needs. Spatial discrimination prevails in between the aboriginals and the mainstream population.

Exclusion is understood in terms of their location as most of the tribal settlements are small and scattered homesteads, not well-connected with the mandal and district headquarters. Self-imposed isolation to maintain their identity and segregation are of much concern to the tribal communities, which inhabit in hills, forests, deserts, and few in islands. Some of the features of caste system are found among these groups, penetrated through culture contact with the neighbouring caste communities (Subramanyam and Rama Mohan, 2010).

Educational Status of Tribes

In general very low literacy rate was recorded among tribals at both national and Andhra Pradesh State levels. The literacy rate among scheduled tribes at National level was 47.10 per cent whereas at Andhra Pradesh State levels, it was 37.03 per cent as per 2001 census. In regard to growth of literacy among scheduled tribes from 1971 to 2001, at national level during 1971 was 11.29 per cent whereas in 2001, it was 47.10 per cent at Andhra Pradesh State level during 1971 it was 5.34 per cent and it was 37.03 per cent in 2001. When we compare the literacy rate among STs at both national and State (AP) levels, with that of general population, there is no remarkable growth of literacy among *adivasis*. The literacy rate among tribal population in Visakhapatnam district was 34.34 per cent as per 2001 Census. The tribal male literacy rate in the district was 45.98 per cent, whereas tribal female literacy rate was 22.67 per cent. As per 2001 Census, the literacy rate of total STs increased to 47.10 per cent as against 65.38 per cent among general population. The difference between the literacy rate of total STs and general population was 18.28 per cent. The literacy rate of S.T. males increased to 59.17 per cent as against 75.85 per cent among overall males and the difference was 16.68 per cent. In the case of female literacy rate it was 37.76 per cent of S.T females as against 54.16 per cent of overall females and the difference was 19.40 per cent. The female literacy rate in A.P. is only 25.50 per cent. It is interesting to note that about 74.50 per cent of tribal females in A.P. are illiterates. Understandingly, female literacy rates at all points of time are lower than those of males. This is true irrespective of whether one considers STs or general population. The disparity in literacy rate between overall population and S.T. population is higher among females than among males. The study result of educational status among scheduled tribes in Eastern Ghats of Andhra Pradesh during the year 2006 also coincides and shows similar trend. About 63 per cent of tribal respondents (both sexes) in the sample of 257 were illiterates. Even among the literates, majority of them had only primary level of education.

The concern of tribal education is mainly, with the Tribal Welfare Department of State and routed through the Integrated Tribal Development Agencies (ITDAs) in all the Sub-Plan areas of Fifth Schedule. Table 8.1 shows the tribal welfare educational institutions in Andhra Pradesh.

From Table 8.1 it is noted that the A.P. Tribal Welfare Department has established 10,881 educational institutions in different tribal pockets of Andhra Pradesh State. Out of the total, 506 hostels are meant for providing boarding and lodging facilities to the tribal students, another 538 are Ashram/Residential type of schools, providing schooling, boarding and lodging services to tribal students. It is interesting to note

Table 8.1: Educational Institutions in the Tribal Areas of Andhra Pradesh.

Sl. No.	*Institutions*	*No. of Institutions in accordance with Sex*		*Total*
		Boys	*Girls*	
1.	Hostels	387	119	506
2.	Ashram Schools (T.W.)			
	(a) Primary Schools	-	-	163
	(b) Upper Primary Schools	-	-	202
	(c) High Schools	-	-	139
	Total (2)			504
3.	Maabadi/Alternative Schools	-	-	5441
4.	Residential Schools (Gurukulams):			
	(a) Schools of Excellence	3	-	3
	(b) General	10	09	19
	(c) PTGs	07	01	08
	(d) English Medium Residential Schools	04	-	04
	Total (4)	24	10	34
5.	Upgraded Junior College:			
	(a) General	19	10	29
	(b) PTGs	03	01	04
	(c) Ekalavya	02	03	05
	Total (5)	24	14	38
6.	(a) Independent Junior Colleges	04	-	04
	(b) Ekalavya	01	-	01
	(c) College of Excellence	03	-	03
	Total (6)	08	-	08
7	Mini Gurukulams	-	41	41
8	Government Primary Schools (T.W.-G.V.V.K.S.)	-	-	4317
	Total	853	278	10881

Source: D.T.W., A.P, Hyderabad.

that only 278 institutions are exclusively meant for girls, whereas 853 institutions are meant exclusively for the boys, the rest of the institutions are providing co-education for both the boys and girls. In addition to these, around 286 schools complexes were established in that area by the Tribal Welfare Department, out of which about 55 school complexes exist in Visakha agency area. The total enrolment of tribal students in all management schools from class-I to class-X during 2004-2005 was 12, 70, 37, 68, out of the total students enrollment, 53,96,977 were boys and 63,33,791 were girls. It is evident that the enrollment of girls into the schools increased in number during the period. Table 8.2 shows the growth rate of schools enrollment in Andhra Pradesh state.

Table 8.2: Enrollment of Tribal Students in Schools.

Period	*Enrollment*		*% of Growth among Scheduled Tribes*
	General Population	*Scheduled Tribe Population*	
1981	71.60	3.26	196.36
1991	106.35	6.39	96.01
2001	129.82	10.29	61.13

Source: D.T.W., A.P., Hyderabad.

From Table 8.2 it is noted that the highest enrollment growth was found in the year 1981, followed by 1991 and 2001. Overall there is an increasing trend in school enrollment of tribal children. The dropout rate of scheduled tribe students from class I-V is 49.82 per cent in Visakhapatnam district whereas in A.P. State it is around 49.73 per cent. In the case of the dropout rate from class I-V it is 64.98 per cent at Visakhapatnam district level, whereas it is around 74.7 per cent at A.P. State level.

Table 8.3 shows district-wise number of government primary schools for scheduled tribes children and their strength during the period 2006-2007. From Table 8.3 it is noticed that about 3,153 government primary schools were established and functioning in the scheduled areas of Srikakulam, Vizianagaram, Visakhapatnam, East Godavari, West Godavari, Guntur, Prakasam, Nellore, Chittoor, Adilabad, Warangal, Khammam and Kurnool districts in Andhra Pradesh. The total students' strength in all the schools was 94,355. The highest number of 919 schools was established in Adilabad district, followed by 617 schools in Visakhapatnam district, 382 schools in Khammam district, 349 schools in Vizianagaram district, 221 schools in Srikakulam district, 220 schools in East Godavari district, 183 schools in Warangal district and 115 schools in Kurnool district. The concentration of tribal population is more in the aforementioned districts, when compared to the remaining districts like West Godavari, Nellore, Prakasam, Guntur and Chittoor districts in which the number of government primary schools is not more than 63 schools. The highest student strength is also corresponding to more frequency number of schools existed in the eight scheduled districts as mentioned above.

Table 8.3: District-wise Number of Government Schools and Number of Students Studying.

Sl. No.	*Name of the District*	*No. of Government Primary Schools established*	*% to Total*	*No. of Students*	*% to Total*
1.	Srikakulam	221	7.01	4324	4.58
2.	Vizianagaram	349	11.07	7864	8.33
3.	Visakhapatnam	617	19.57	24820	26.30
4.	East Godavari	220	6.98	3015	3.20
5.	West Godavari	63	2.00	668	0.71
6.	Guntur	10	0.32	340	0.36
7.	Prakasam	22	0.70	868	0.92
8.	Nellore	50	1.59	685	0.73
9.	Chittoor	02	0.06	185	0.20
10.	Adilabad	919	29.15	29543	31.31
11.	Warangal	183	5.80	7137	7.56
12.	Khammam	382	12.12	12721	13.48
13.	Kurnool	115	3.65	2185	2.32
Total		3153	100.00	94355	100.00

Table 8.4 shows district-wise number of *Ashram* schools and hostels that were established by the Government of Andhra Pradesh. Totally 599 *Ashram* schools and 441 hostels were started in all the 23 districts of Andhra Pradesh. The number of schools and hostels varies from one district to another district. Highest number of 113 *Ashram* schools exist in Adilabad district whereas highest number of hostels are found in Khammam district.

Table 8.4: District-wise Number of Ashram Schools and Hostels.

Sl. No.	*Name of the District*	*No. of Ashram Schools*	*% to Total Ashram Schools*	*No. of Hostels*	*% of Total Hostels*
1.	Srikakulam	41	6.84	9	2.04
2.	Vizianagaram	55	9.18	17	3.85
3.	Visakhapatnam	102	17.03	13	2.95
4.	East Godavari	58	9.68	19	4.31
5.	West Godavari	33	5.51	18	4.08
6.	Khammam	74	12.35	45	10.20
7.	Warangal	39	6.51	40	9.07
8.	Adilabad	113	18.86	11	2.49
9.	Nellore	01	0.17	24	5.44
10.	Krishana	01	0.17	19	4.31
11.	Prakasam	16	2.67	22	4.99
12.	Chittoor	01	0.17	16	3.63
13.	Ananthapuram	01	0.17	17	3.85
14.	Kurnool	09	1.50	10	2.27
15.	Rangareddi	04	0.67	12	2.72
16.	Medak	04	0.67	16	3.63
17.	Karimnagar	11	1.84	15	3.40
18.	Nizamabad	03	0.50	13	2.95
19.	Nalgonda	11	11.84	36	8.16
20.	Mahaboobnagar	14	2.33	20	4.54
21.	Guntoor	08	1.34	32	7.26
22.	Hyderbad	-	-	07	1.59
23.	Kadapa	-	-	10	2.27
Total		599	100.00	441	100.00

Source: D.T.W., A.P., Hyderabad.

Table 8.5 shows the tribal welfare educational institutions in Integrated Tribal Development Agency (ITDA), Paderu, where the study was carried out. From the table it is noticed that all the 108 educational institutions are under the control of Tribal Welfare Department, and attached to ITDA, Paderu. Around 36,290 school children were provided

Table 8.5: Tribal Welfare Educational Institutions in ITDA, Paderu.

S.No.	*Type of Schools*	*Number*
1.	High Schools	51
2.	Upper Primary Schools	08
3.	Primary Schools	44
4.	S.T. Hostels	15
5.	Number of Hostels/Boarders	118/36290

Source: ITDA, Paderu, Visakhapatnam.

with boarding facilities. The data obtained from ITDA, Paderu, indicates that around 1300 lakhs rupees are spent every year to maintain all the educational institutions.

Several inclusive policies have been adopted by the Central and State governments to improve literacy rate among disadvantaged groups. Certain educational acts have been included in the Constitution specifically for scheduled tribe children. The Indian States' commitment to the education of S.T. children is contained in Article 15(4), 45 and 46 of the Constitution of India, and implicit in the recent constitutional amendment on right to education[4] over the successive Plan periods, the national as well as the State governments have made considerable effort to address the educational and socio-historical disadvantage faced by the scheduled tribes, primarily through expanding physical access to schooling for S.T. children by relaxing norms for establishing schools in tribal habitations and encouraging enrollment by meeting some of the costs of schooling. Special schemes pertaining to schools education of SC/ST children currently include (1) Free supply of textbooks and stationery at all stages of school education; (2) Free uniforms to children in government approved hostels and *Ashram* schools and in some States also for children in regular schools; (3) Free education at all levels; (4) Pre-Matric stipends and scholarships to students at Middle and/or High Schools stage; (5) Girls and boys hostels for SC/ST; and (6) *Ashram* schools for tribal children started with the intention of overcoming the difficulties of provisions in remote regions.

In regard to elementary education, Andhra Pradesh Government has undertaken several measures to reach out to tribal communities, such as the Girijan Vidya Vikas Kendras with standards I and II in areas where vulnerable communities reside, *Mandal* level elementary schools, special residential schools, called *Ashram* schools mainly in tribal areas, the alternative schools, etc., and monitoring systems such as the school complex system. There have also been some special programmes such as bridge courses and back to school initiatives for dropouts.

Inclusive education strategy of the government definitely provides the equal opportunities to almost all the children, irrespective of caste, class, creed, religion, and gender in order to avail educational facilities of the government. This strategy is definitely helping the children belonging to the most vulnerable deprived and marginalized communities of Indian society for their inclusion in the ongoing educational development process. However, the literacy level among tribal population has not improved significantly even though certain National Education Policies have been formulated and implemented. Some of the salient features of National Policy on Education (1986), Sarva Siksha Abhiyan (SSA) and Right to Education Act, as mentioned below:

According to National Policy on Education (NPE, 1986) "education has to produce self-assured, more productive, more capable and more thinking type of citizens. It is not the innovative mind that is to be developed, but it is creature mind that is to be developed". Education is to develop self-assurance and capacity, to think independently on the part of the individual. The productive capacity of the individual has to be developed.

The National Policy on Education (NPE) 1986, as modified in 1992, emphasizes three aspects in relation to elementary education such as (1) Universal access and enrollment; (2) Universal retention of children up to 14 years of age; and (3) A substantial improvement in the quality of education to enable all children to achieve essential levels of learning. The policy emphasizes that education must play a positive and interventionist role in correcting social and regional imbalance, empowering women, and in securing a rightful place for the disadvantaged and the minorities. Government is firmly committed in providing education for all, the priority areas being free and compulsory elementary education, covering children with special needs, eradication of illiteracy, education for women equality, and special focus on the education of scheduled castes, scheduled tribes and minorities.

Sarva Siksha Abhiyan (SSA) is an extension of DPEP. It is an effort for Universalization of Elementary Education (UEE) by community ownership of school system. The objectives of Sarva Siksha Abhiyan (SSA) are: (1) All children in school, education guarantee centre, alternative school, back to school camp by 2003; (2) All children complete five years of primary schooling by 2007; (3) All children complete eight years elementary schooling by 2010; (4) Focus on elementary education of satisfactory quality with emphasis on education for life; and (5) Bridge all gender and social category gaps at primary stage by 2007 and at elementary level by 2012 and universal retention by 2010.

Sarva Siksha Abhiyan implemented in partnership with the States, addresses the need of 209 million children in the age group of 6-14 years. It covers 9.72 lakh existing primary and upper primary schools and 36.95 lakh teachers. National Programme for Education of girls at elementary level (NPEGEL) is an important component of SSA. Another important component of SSA is the education guarantee scheme and alternative and innovative education, which is specially designed to provide, access to elementary education to children schoolless habitations and out of school children. It supports flexible strategies for out of school children through bridge courses, residential camps, drop-in-centres summer camps, remedial coaching, etc. It helped to provide elementary education to 85.67 lakh children in 2004-2005. Centrally sponsored mid-day meal scheme is also in operation under Sarva Siksha Abhiyan programme. Kasturba Gandhi Balika Vidyalaya (KGBV) was launched in August 2004 to set up 750 residential schools at elementary level for girls belonging predominantly to the SC, ST, OBC and minorities in Economically Backward Blocks (EBBS). Another important feature of SSA is to increase the number of senior secondary schools.

After reviewing the education situation at national level again the Right to Education Act was passed in 2009 by the Central Government and it came into effect from April 2010. The main objective of this act is to provide free and compulsory education to children in the age group of 6-14 years. The important aspect of this education act is that the right of children to free and compulsory education till completion of primary education in a neighbourhood school. It classifies that "compulsory education" means obligation of the appropriate government to provide free elementary education and ensure compulsory admission, attendance and completion of elementary education to every child in the age group 6-14 years. 'Free' means that no child shall be liable to pay any kind of fee or charges or expenses which may prevent him or her from pursuing and completing elementary education. Even after two years of its enforcement, the situation of primary education in tribal areas has not improved much due to lack of proper infrastructural facilities in many schools. In large number of schools, the older tribal children are out of school especially in the habitats of most vulnerable tribes who still live in the remote and interior forests of inaccessible areas. The tribal children are literally excluded from schooling in such areas primarily due to geographical and ecological barriers; and secondly, because of economic backwardness. The other reasons like parents' illiteracy, teacher absenteeism, medium of instructions, content, school timings, holidays, proper school building, proper supervision, pre-school education; many single classroom schools, low enrollment, high dropout rate, untrained teachers, etc. are very common in the tribal areas of Andhra Pradesh in specific and other tribal areas in general.

Access to Education

Empirical evidences clearly denotes that large majority of the tribal children do not have access to formal education, even though, the government has taken several initiations since India's independence to fulfil the educational needs of the *adivasis* across the country. The question of access has been a major concern in the field of education right from the days of the Constituent Assembly which made a provision in the Constitution by promising free and compulsory education for all children under 14 years of age. At the policy level too, the fact that a wider access to education is essential for development as well as for the effective functioning of democracy has been recognized. But there has been a big gap between intent and attainment, and this chasm is beginning to be bridged slowly. A wide range of factors affecting educational access of tribal children are poverty, cultural practices, teacher quality, linguistic diversity, medium of instruction, geographical and ecological conditions in which they inhabit. Govinda (2010) explained the problem of access to education in its varied dimensions, makes two things clear, one that there are still a large number of children with little or no access to schooling; and two, that such children have their concentration in certain specific segments of society. Tribals are one such segment where majority of the children are out of school.

The reporter of *Hindu* daily newspaper dated on 12th November, 2011, clearly brought out that "even sixty four years after independence, basic education remains a dream for millions of children". One year after the Right to Education Act was implemented, 81 lakh children are out of school in Andhra Pradesh State. Majority of these children belong to the marginalized, deprived and vulnerable communities including the tribal communities. The study conducted by Child Line on the issue of access to education in Visakhapatnam city also reveals the same kind of situation. As per Dalton the centre co-coordinator of Child Line:

> "*it is estimated that there are 150-200 million street children across the world. India is home to the largest number and it is said to touch 18 million. In most of the countries especially the African continent*[5] *the main cause for the children to make the streets their home is war or internal strife. But in India the main reason is broken families*".

Dalton points out that most children who are found at the railway station or bus shelters are orphans, run away from abusive parents. But quite a few of them are trafficked children (*Hindu*, 12, 2011). Generally, the street children are out of school akin to poor tribal children. Poverty is the major cause for non-availing of school facility by the tribal children. More than 60 per cent of the vulnerable tribal population stands at below poverty line in India, and they are not in a position to avail the education facility.

Exclusion of the Girl-child from School Education

In many tribal societies the girl-child is discriminated and excluded from school education for several reasons. We agree that all children have needs, but because she is female, the girl-child is particularly vulnerable to discrimination, exploitation and neglect. Research studies on this issue in many countries of the world indicate that the girl-child is discriminated against from the earliest stage of life through her childhood and into adulthood. Girls are often treated as inferior and are socialized to put them last. Existing discrimination against the girl-child in her access to nutrition and physical and mental health services endangers her current and future health. Early marriage and early motherhood among aboriginals can severely curtail educational and employment activities and are likely to have a long-term adverse impact on them and their children's quality of life. Severe malnutrition among tribal girl children excludes them from schooling and increases their morbidity and mortality rate.

"Gender discrimination can undermine education access and the tribal girls are more likely to be excluded from school. Even in societies where girls attend in number roughly equal to boys, gender stereotyping in texts and materials used in school, and the neglect of female pupils by teachers are widespread and entrenched problems. In the United States, for example, girls are systematically steered away from mathematics, science and technology, subjects that tend to lead to well-paid jobs" (King, 1990).

The Fourth World Conference on women held during 1994, generated momentum to have the rights of the girl-child recognized as a specific theme for the platform for action. The main issues of contention during negotiations included child marriage, sexual exploitation, female genital mutilation, education, parental rights and responsibilities. Delegates of the conference agreed to the following:

- That child marriage is detrimental to the healthy development of a young girl and should be made illegal;
- That female genital mutilation is an act of violence (this is the first time there has been agreement on female genital mutilation at the international level); and
- That governments and non-governmental organizations (NGOs) develop formal and informal educational programmes that support and enable girls to acquire knowledge, develop self-esteem and take responsibility for their own lives.

The platform for action includes a commitment to eliminate all barriers that impede the schooling of married and/or pregnant girls and young women and recommends the provision of affordable and physically accessible child care facilities to help achieve this.

With respect to parental responsibilities the platform reads: "taking into account the rights of the child to access information, privacy, confidentiality, respect and informed consent as well as the responsibilities and duties of parents and legal guardians to provide in a manner consistent with the evolving capacities of the child, appropriate direction and guidance in the exercise by the child of the rights recognized in the convention on the right of the child and in conformity with the convention on the Elimination of Discrimination against women. In all actions concerning children, the best interests of the child shall be a primary consideration".

The Vision of Girls

The vision for a future, of the girl-child will be free from today's problems. In future, every girl and young woman will have access to education and free of discrimination. A future, where all women, young and old, will have full access to health care, related information and complete control of their bodies. In future where women and men shall share equally in the sense of ownership of the achievements of their countries. Also, a future where women can actively participate in determining a new world order free from armed conflict and guided by the principles upheld in the culture of peace. A future where a commitment to the preservation of our natural environment shall be reflected in all our international, national and local development plans. In future, work done by women shall be recognized as an indispensable contribution to the world's economic growth.

It is observed that many disabled tribal children are excluded from school education. Due to extreme poverty, environmental dangers, hazards, housing, poor hygiene, lack of social support and rehabilitation facilities, proper health care, etc. most of the children in tribal societies are invariably encountered with the problem of physical disability. Generally, the disabled are also more likely to be handicapped. Disabled children frequently suffer from social isolation and powerlessness. Many are deprived of access to school and other services even when their siblings attend. Neglect not only impedes physical and cognitive development but also damages the emotional and social confidence of child, intensifying its dependence on the family and its isolation from the world outside. A significant proportion of tribal children with disabilities die of malnutrition or disease as a result of neglect. Some others are abandoned in maternity hospitals, pediatric wards or thrown in streams or in the bushes of forests[6].

Forms of Exclusion faced by Tribal Children in Schooling

The tribal children face some of the exclusionary practices in schools. Usually, the non-tribal teachers who are working in the tribal areas consider them less knowledgeable and incapable of learning, down looks their cultural practices with ego centric bias. These teachers are hesitant to interact very closely with the tribal pupil in the class room situation due to their uncleanliness and inability to keep up with academic work.

Derogatory references to their communities, name and cultural practices make them feel excluded from classroom processes and school activities.

The teachers lack proper understanding of their diverse background. Primary focus is often on integrating them into mainstream cultural and educational domains often resulting in devaluing of tribal culture and heritage. The tribal children with poor family background feel inferior in classroom and often dropout. Those that persist do so at the cost of losing their own sense of identity and cultural background.

Stereotyping of tribal culture in syllabi and textbooks, lack of recognition of tribal system of knowledge and role models, etc. also develop a feeling of exclusion in tribal children from school education system. Geographical isolation and segregation of tribal population are other causes for tribal children inaccessibility to education. Medium of instruction in regional language, content of textbooks and syllabi ignore students' own knowledge and experience and focus mostly on the dominant language and culture. Not understanding the standard school language as well as courses content, the children are unable to cope with their studies and end up repeating grades and eventually dropping out from schools. The "three language formula" in schools that has been the cornerstone of the language policy in India is not uniformly implemented across the country. This policy is not applicable and suitable to many tribal areas of India as students with multiple linguistic backgrounds are found in a single classroom.

Certain multilingual teaching schools were established in the tribal areas of Andhra Pradesh by the State Tribal Welfare Department. In addition to this, teaching in mother tongue or language was introduced at first and second standard levels in some schools. Even then, the school enrollment is very low and very high dropout rate is recorded in several tribal schools. Education in the medium of tribal language in initial years is also very difficult because many tribal dialects have no script, tribal language may not even be generally recognized as constituting a legitimate language, there may be a shortage of educational materials in the tribal language, there may be a lack of appropriate trained teachers, there may be resistance to schooling in the mother tongue by students, parents and teachers. If there are several mother tongues background students represented in one class, it multiplies the problem even further.

Many experts on tribal education opined that mother tongue is the best medium of instruction at class 1 and class 2 levels of primary education. The tribal development departments have tried to address this problem by establishing residential or *ashram* schools for tribal children, but there is a need, not just for many more residential schools, but also for improved quality in these schools. The residential or ashram schools need to be strengthened with consolidated approach; all the problems of tribal education need to be examined in holistic perspective including recruitment of teachers of similar social and cultural backgrounds and provision of curriculum and textbooks that do not demotivate tribal children.

The following aspects are to be taken into consideration for inclusion of tribal children in school education system of tribal areas in India:

- Teaching in the mother tongue by recruiting the teachers who possess skill in teaching tribal students in their own language;
- Development of educational materials in local languages using resources available within the community;
- Establishing regional/State resource centres in tribal-dominated states for providing training, academic and other technical support for development of pedagogic tools and education materials catering to multilingual situation;
- Training of teachers in multi lingual education;
- Sensitization of teachers to tribal cultures and practices;
- Incorporation of local knowledge in the curriculum and textbooks;
- Creating spaces for cultural mingling within schools so as to recognize tribal cultures and practices and obliterate feelings of inferiority and alienation among tribal children; and
- Involvement of community members in school activities to reduce social distance between the school and the community.

Concluding Remarks

The tribals are basically excluded from mainstream society due to geographical isolation and segregation. They are classified as one of the excluded human groups living in most economic backward condition. More than 60 per cent of the vulnerable tribal population stands at below poverty line. Around 53 per cent of tribal people at national level are illiterates, whereas at Andhra Pradesh State level about 63 per cent of them are illiterates. The literacy rate among tribal women is still very low both at national and State levels. Still large majority of the tribal children have no access to formal education. Low enrollment and high dropout are recorded in many tribal communities of India. The illiteracy of the tribal parents at family level is considered as one of the major causative factors for low enrollment and high dropout rate in many tribal pockets of India. In Andhra Pradesh State, majority of the children belonging to the most vulnerable tribes like Chenchu, Kolam, Thoti, Konda Reddi, Khond, Gadaba, Porja and Savara have no access to formal education and are excluded from school education system due to poverty, ecological and geographical constraints. The inclusive education policies of national and State governments are neither benefiting the vulnerable tribes nor enhancing the literacy rate and quality of education specifically in the tribal areas.

The recent Right to Education Act is more appropriate and relevant for enhancing literacy rate and quality education in tribal areas, if it is to be implemented whole heartedly by the concerned tribal welfare department of the State. Special focus on tribal education is still needed from Central and State Governments to achieve the estimated literacy target in tribal areas of India. Free and compulsory pre-school education has to be provided to all the tribal children who are in the age group of 3-5 years, in addition to the nutritional programme of Integrated Child Development Scheme (ICDS). Adult education programme needs to be reintroduced or revived in the tribal areas in order to improve the literacy rate among adults, youth and elderly tribal population, which in turn will increase the school enrollment, retention and reduce the dropout. All welfare and economic programmes need to be linked with the literacy programmes of tribals. Still more numbers of *ashram*/residential type of schools are needed to fulfil the objective of inclusive education policy specifically in tribal areas. Proper infrastructural facilities need to be provided in each and every tribal school with a view to enhance literacy rate and provide quality education to tribal students. Different management schools in the tribal areas should be brought under a single management and administration in order to avoid educational disparities. Periodical evaluation of educational programmes and proper monitoring of school education are very essential to tackle the problem of illiteracy and education development among tribals. Special attention is still needed to address the gender bias and discrimination in school education as well as to improve the literacy rate among tribal women. Anthropological holistic or integrated approach is much useful to understand the processes of exclusion and inclusion of tribal children in school education system and also to provide amicable solutions for various problems associated with tribal education in India. Dormitory system of education is much suitable to many tribal communities, which should be promoted in order to achieve the education development goal in the tribal areas of India.

NOTES

1. According to Amartya Sen (1997) "Social exclusion emphasizes the role of relational features in deprivation".
2. Enculturation is the cultural process through which a growing child learns to conform to his or her own cultural traditions.
3. Visakha agency area is the part of Eastern Ghats in Andhra Pradesh State- Eastern Ghats is considered as the abode for tribal population, where nine Integrated Tribal Development Agencies are located to look after the welfare and development of tribes.
4. Article 15(4) underscores the State's basic commitment to positive discrimination in favour of the socially and educationally backward classes and/or the SC and ST Article 45 declares the State endeavour to provide free and compulsory education for all children until they complete the age of 14 years. Article 46 expresses the specific aim to promote with special care to the educational and economic interests of SC/ST (focus paper NCF 2005).
5. It represents highest number of tribal population in the world. India has second largest tribal population, next to Africa.
6. It is noted that in recent times number of abandoned tribal children becoming more even in the tribal areas of Visakhapatnam district. Such kind of situation has not prevailed earlier in the tribal societies.

REFERENCES

Anderson, M. 1972. *Family Structure in Nineteenth Century*. Lancashire, Cambridge: Cambridge University Press.

Carol, Bellamy. 1996. "Preface, Children Mirror of Future, Development," *Journal of the Society for International Development*, 1: 8.

Haimendorf C V, Furer. 1944. "Aboriginal Education in Hyderabad," *Indian Journal of Social Work*, 5 (2).

Gunasekare, S.W.E. 1993. *Child Labour in Sri Lanka: Learning from the Past*. Geneva, ILO Child Labour Collection.

Government of India. 1964-66. *Report of the Education Committee* (D.S. Kothari Committee).

Hendrick, H. 1997. *Children, Childhood and English Society 1880-1990*. Cambridge: Cambridge University Press.

Henry, J. 1955. "Docility or Giving Teacher What She Wants," *Journal of Social Issues*, 2: 33-41.

Herskovits, M.J. 1943. "Education and Cultural Dynamics," *American Journal of Sociology*, XL (XII): 109-121.

King, E. 1990. *Educating Girls and Women*. Washington D.C: World Bank.

Lagerwall, T. and G. Tiroler. 1955. *Poverty and Disability*. Stockholm: Swedish International Development Authority.

Mead, Margaret. 1953. *Cultural Patterns and Technological Change*. Paris: UNESCO.

Qvortrup, J. 1993. *Childhood as a Social Phenomenon, Lessons from an International Project*, Vienna: European Centre for Social Welfare, Policy and Research.

Sen, Amartya. 1997. *On Economic Inequality* (2nd Edition). Oxford: Clarendon Press.

Spindler, George D. 1955. *Education and Anthropology*. Stanford, California: Stanford University Press.

____. 2000. *Fifty Years of Anthropology and Education*, 1950-2000. Mahwah, NJ: Erlbaum Associates.

Subramanyam, V. 2010. "Social Exclusion and Inclusive Policy: An Overview," (pp.29-36) In: V. Subramanyam and K. Sekhar (eds.), *Social Exclusion, Integration and Inclusive Policies*. Jaipur: Rawat.

Subramanyam V. and K.R. Rama Mohan. 2010. "Exclusion and Inclusive Policies for Scheduled Tribes: The Case of Sub-plan Area of Visakhapatnam District of Andhra Pradesh, South India," *Journal of Social Sciences*, VIII (1): 16-27.

SECTION III

PLAY AND LEISURE TIME ACTIVITIES

NINE

CRICKET AND KABADI: Peer Play and Child Subjectivity in Munda Villages of Odisha

ZAZIE BOWEN

In tribally dominated areas such as Mayurbhanj of Odisha State and international projects of rural development emphasize schooling as never before, increasingly structuring the lives of children, many of whom remain active in the agro-forestry economies of their families and villages. Squeezed between their school work and other work, children still prioritize unsupervised play with their peers in the village. The different expressions of their peer play provide a special mode of interaction with spatial and social contexts that has important ramifications for children's subjectivities and represents a domain in which adults are not overwhelmingly in control. Drawing upon ethnographic fieldwork with school aged children in rural villages of Western Mayurbhanj, Odisha in 2008, this chapter examines the unsupervised peer play of Santal and Ho school students and how it shapes their subjectivity.

The chapter is informed by Ortner's (Ortner, 2005) articulation of subjectivity as "the ensemble of modes of perception, affect, thought and desire that animate acting subjects" and her insistence that subjectivity also involves "the cultural and social transformations that shape, organize and provoke those modes of affect" (Ortner, 2005: 31). She pointed to an analytical approach that moves back and forth between examinations of cultural processes and the inner states of acting subjects (Ortner, 2005). There are entanglements between the cultural fields of children's play and other village level cultural fields: religion, politics, social set-ups, economic expressions, in which we may discover aspects of children's subjectivities at work.

Discussions on child subjectivity frequently set up a binary between childhood as unfinished *subject-in-process* and adulthood as "finished" subjectivity (Kennedy, 2002). Cognitive development and socialization literatures typically reflect this paradigm. Recent critiques, however, problematize the over-focus on presumed static adult paradigms as the templates for socialization and the under-recognition of young people's roles in transforming the social context each generation (James and Prout, 1990; James, Jenks *et al.,* 1998; James, 2007). They also investigate how bias in favour of adult subjectivity in diverse social analyses may marginalize the perspectives and experiences of the very old and the young, just as gender-blind characterizations marginalize female subjectivities and social roles (Hardman, 1973). Kennedy offers a post-modern dismantling of the binary by calling for a perspective that considers "the child in the adult and the adult in the child". He suggests further that scholars consider the ways that being a *subject-in-process* represents a lifelong state perpetually nurtured by the kind of playfulness typically attributed to children testing unchartered social, imaginal and geo-spatial territories (Kennedy, 2002). This view casts an optimistic light on both play and the subject-in-process and underscores the significance of play studies.

How are subjectivities expressed and shaped in play for young people in Munda (Santal and Ho) villages? All children begin life as open negotiators and are introduced to a culturally and historically mediated model of the internal and external relations of the self (Kennedy, 2002). They learn what thoughts and feelings are appropriate to express or suppress, what telepathic knowledge of the Other to pay attention to, trust, admit to and ignore or dismiss. Their interactions with significant others make up a self-concept, as if seen by the Other, that is both clear and obscure, confirmed and contradicted in interactions with others and the surrounding constructions of and about the spatial environment (Kennedy, 2002). Munda children's sense-making is part of a plural, emergent dialogical self that is shaped by a set of historical, cultural, political and economic circumstances and which shapes their inter-subjectivity. From about five years of age peer play becomes an important mode through which subjective and inter-subjective sense-making occurs as each young person develops their inter-corporeal relations with their spatial world and with family, age-mate peers, village community, school community and wider communities.

Methodologies

In 2008, I resided with Santal, Ho and scheduled caste families in remote-rural far north Odisha near the border of Jharkhand throughout much of an annual seasonal cycle and participated in the daily and seasonal routines of the families of the area whose occupations mainly involved rice cultivation and forestry. In the course of learning about school-aged children's peer play in rural villages I spent much time in the company of children in the fields and main village street (an important play site) of several villages, and in other sites where children would play, hang out and roam around, such as the ghats at village ponds and river banks, under key village shade trees in the *akara* (tribal village meeting ground), the Ho graveyards, the large granite outcrops near the base of hills and in areas of jungle and post-harvest rice fields. While much of this study was carried out after school (between four to six p.m.), I also spent many days in a number of village schools, interviewing students, teachers and principals and visiting classes. Following Morrow's lead in eliciting narratives from school students (Morrow, 2004), I recruited sixty students from a single primary and high school to write a seven-day personal journal of their activities. Students from the same school also wrote essays reflecting on topics such as "My play and work" and "Me, My Family and My Village" as part of their participation in this study. The collection of student essays and journals, originally written in Odiya and later translated into English by Mayurbhanj college students, form part of the analytical data drawn on in this chapter along with my own ethnographic field-notes. This play ethnography is restricted to elementary school-aged children from five to fourteen years old. While there are many children within this age group who dropped out of school or never attended, most of the children with whom I was in regular contact in 2008 were school students. By and large then, this chapter explores the peer play lives of Santal and Ho elementary students in their rural villages.

Munda Identity in Mayurbhanj: Locating the Study

Santal and Ho peoples (both part of the Munda Austro-Asiatic linguistic group) constitute between seventy to eighty per cent of the population in the villages of Jamda Block, in western Mayurbhanj District, Odisha. They share some notable affinities in annual festival cycles, social organization and language structure. Most Mayurbhanj Santal and Ho people are readily able to understand each other. Two key local informants narrated to me that over a century ago, Ho and Santal peoples (entering mainly from Singhbhum) began settling in the then densely jungled area between Chaibasa (Singbhum, Jharkhand) and Rairangpur (Mayurbhanj, Odisha). They began to dominate over their sparsely populated predecessors, many of whom relocated to neighbouring Keonjhar District. Over many decades the Ho and Santal peoples founded increasing number of villages in what was later named "Jamda Block" and cleared surrounding forests, establishing the paddy fields that dominate the plains landscapes today. The now intensively cultivated plains are surrounded by forested hills with granite peaks and diverse flora and fauna. Fuel-wood collection in the forests is a secondary economic activity for many households. Engagement with the forests through hunting, herd grazing and foraging for medicinal, edible and other forest products remains a central part of cultural identity for both Ho and Santals.

As the demographic and political majority in Jamda Block, Santal and Ho cultural and political identity is pervasively expressed in *Sarna* and tribal political organization. *Sarna* is a pan-tribal religious movement centred on the sacred grove (*jaher*) and associated daily, annual and life-cycle sacred performances and festivals dedicated to communication with spirit entities (*bonga*) that permeate the entire geo-physical, ancestral and subtle-realm landscapes[1]. The revitalisation of *Sarna* is a significant part of recent Mayurbhanj political reassertions of sovereignty associated with the Jharkhand movement (Carrin, 2012). Santal and Ho children become aware of the presence of *bonga* within their households and in the village from their earliest days and negotiate their presence in their lives. They are also alert to the location of the village sacred grove, which is off limits to them, except on specified occasions. Political identity of Santal and Ho is also well expressed in Jamda *via* tribal village governance structures that involve a village chief (*Manjhi*), deputy chief (*Paranik*), messenger (*Godet*), guardian of village morals and youth (*Yog Manjhi*), priest (Naiki/*Dewari*), priest's assistant (*Kudam* Naiki) (Hembrom, 1996). Children soon learn that the Manjhi is the ultimate authority in settling disputes, dealing with marriages, divorces and judicial matters (theft, property disputes, misconduct, violent crime, breaches of social norms and accusations of witchcraft) priests and their assistants enact and oversee village and panchayat level judicial, social and ritual processes). Village committees comprised of elders and male representatives from all village households play an important role in all negotiations and settlements, with decisions finalised *via* a (male representative) democracy. Children observe such socio-political processes taking place within their village, even though they, as with women, have no direct role in them.

Local expressions of Santal and Ho identity and organization are also in constant interaction and negotiation with the identity paradigms of local Hindu caste and scheduled caste communities and with State-initiated social, economic and political projects through such instruments as the rural Block Development Office, the *Integrated Child Development Scheme* and schools. The Santal and Ho sovereign structures run parallel to the constitutional and electoral system of Panchayat Raj which produces local leadership roles for elected representatives who may or may not be Santal or Ho alongside the traditional Santal or Ho village chief and chiefly and priest structures. While the role of the Santal and Ho headman is still pivotal in Jamda villages, various issues arise from this situation of dual Panchayati Raj (Pradhan, 2011).

Most villages are organized into hamlets (*sahi*). Some *sahis* are occupied by non-Santal and Ho peoples who were originally patronized by the land-owning, rice cultivating Santal and Ho households and received residential security and annual ritual payments after *Makar Samkranti* (the post-harvest winter solstice festival) in exchange for their occupational caste services such as blacksmith, iron work, pot making, cloth weaving, carpentry, dairy husbandry, midwifery and other ritual services. These symbiotic *jajmani* exchanges still perpetuate a local economy that is self-sufficient in many respects.

However, historical and contemporary tribal communities and their symbiotic relations with scheduled caste Hindu peoples interface with wider social and economic processes provoking a stream of political, economic and cultural mutual responses and counter responses. For example, cheap availability of factory cloth and clothing has made the occupations of many Jamda weavers obsolete. In the last generation members of one extended weaver family with whom I was closely acquainted have turned to a range of occupations including: rice cultivation and forestry along side their Santal and Ho neighbours; teaching and other government service jobs such as police, postal and Block development office work; trade/small business; seasonal migration for mining, factory work or other urban occupations such as higher studies and security guard work. Santal and Ho households too, although possessing village and agricultural land tenure now commonly have family members who migrate between the village and elsewhere for work and study. This is increasingly precipitated by both intensified climatic unpredictability (droughts and untimely rains) and economic transformations associated with the radical impact of neo-liberalisation.

Locating Children and Childhood in Mayurbhanj

Santal and Ho children occupy critical positions amidst rural transformations. On one hand they remain important economic actors in the family production units –in production routines that deeply intertwine economic and cultural values. On the other hand school-going children are expected to fulfil full-time student obligations including attending school, tuition classes and carrying out homework study tasks. Not to speak of the time involved in getting to school and attending to the required grooming appropriate for school. These dual work-loads (Nieuwenhuys, 1994; Pramanik, 2007) place children in unique as well as volatile cultural and economic positions. The personal diaries examined in this study reveal how young people negotiate multiple expectations. Yashwant[2] for example, recorded in his journal:

> *When I got up at four am I went to my garden. I plant vegetables and prepare beds for sowing sa'g seeds. ...When I return home I take bath and then sit for study. Between seven and nine am I go for tuition with my friends. Tuition is important for me. When I come home I get ready for school.*

He also discloses, "My mother works very hard. I don't go to school everyday. My mother is old. I help her in her work". On a Saturday his journal shows the diversity of his activities:

> *From five until seven am I ploughed our rice field. From nine until twelve I went to school. From twelve until three I played and did long jump. From three o'clock until six o'clock p.m. I was serving rice beer and wine to the customers in our wine shop.*

Bearing in mind the diverse workloads that young people negotiate, it is worth considering children's volition to play. In Jamda this volition is undeterred by children's multiple workloads and time with peers often becomes a way young people make sense of their responses to macro and micro forces that shape their lives and in turn provide ways that they as peers may shape their context.

> *I was playing cricket. My friend hit the ball over the boundary for six and the ball was lost. We were on 50s. We tried to find it but failed. It was evening and darkening. Then we all returned home. I washed my hands and feet. I sat for study. My father came and scolded me for I am spending time without doing anything. I told him that I like to play.* (Yashwant Marndi)[3].

This was a diary excerpt from a student who participated in a seven-day personal journal exercise, part of the research methodology I employed in the 2008 rural childhood and play ethnography. His remark to his father, who had scolded him for too much play with his friends, reflected a common assertion by young people to safeguard their own peer play in whatever unstructured moments they could find. Similarly, when I mildly suggested my Mayurbhanj adoptive-kin nephew that he should give play a rest due to his malaria fever the night before, he replied, "Auntie, if I don't play everyday, I don't feel mind-fresh". After school the village streets and surrounding fields would be enlivened with different groups of children playing games and this social environment, buzzing with excitement and fervour was intensely attractive for young people. The seven-day journals written by numerous elementary school students and oral narratives of others revealed a pattern in young people's daily routines. Many of them reported that they 'hang out' to play with friends after school between the hours of 4.00 p.m. until 6.00 p.m. Many of the same children reported waking up in the hours between midnight and dawn to study and carry out their home work tasks by kerosene lamp[4]. This suggested to me that students either believed this was a quiet time to study, or that they preferred to sacrifice their sleep time rather than study and complete homework straight after school, thereby missing out on the time when so many of their peers would be playing and hanging out together in and around the village in unsupervised peer gatherings. In brief, despite multiple obligations that structure young people's daily lives, most school going children within the villages prioritized play with their friends, even if they had to make sacrifices for this. This fervour for peer play is partially related to the spatiality of rural villages, for when I spoke with young people in the township of the Jamda Block headquarters, play time was increasingly reported as a solitary, indoor pursuit, especially amongst girls and taken up more by television watching.

The Play Concept in Mayurbhanj

During the course of fieldwork in Mayurbhanj I encountered negligible commentary about *what play is* as a concept—such commentaries are universally rare beyond the domain of play scholars (Groos, 1901; Piaget, 1951; Berlyne, 1960; Vygotsky, 1966 (first published 1933); Bateson, 1972; Hardman, 1973; Turner, 1982; Eisen, 1988; Factor, 1988; Spariosu, 1989; Lancy, 1996; Sutton Smith, 1997)—however certain things stood out in enactments of play by both children and adults that revealed a conceptual approach. For instance the boundaries between sacred acts and playfulness were frequently blurred. Sacred performances directed to spirits and deities invoked playfulness and children's play referenced sacred performances. Most festivals and tribal circle-dances involved elements of obligatory playfulness, mimetic cross-dressing, joking, playful antics and trickster figures. Children are both active in the play antics associated with sacred performances and also produce playful meta narratives with their peers about sacred performances. Once I overheard a group of young people (about seven to thirteen years old) in a neighbour's compound laughing uncontrollably as they enacted a role-play drama about the mimetic activities of a sacred performance. On several occasions I observed small children sitting in the shade of trees, soberly enacting make-believe dramas and role-playing village ritual performers or spirit mediums. The connection between playfulness and sacred/divine states suggests a particular subjective attitude toward and experience of divinity that is open and playfully unpredictable.

Geertz's work on deep play and subjectivity in relation to the Balinese cock-fights poignantly illustrates how this instance of Balinese gambling play reveals deeper conceptualizations about subjectivities within an interpretable social order (Geertz, 1973). In Mayurbhanj Santal and Ho communities too, play enacts relations between individual subjects and the social and economic orders at the inter- and intra-village levels among young people as the following example shows:

> *In my village we perform dramas with other people and during them I play the Casio and we sometimes enter drama competitions in different villages and we get prizes.* ("Play and Recreation", Jamda Student Essay Collection, 2008)

While translating the above essay, my interpreter, Shri Gurucharan Hansda explained to me:

> *The prize offered at these drama competitions is usually a goat and when there are enough goats collected in one village as prizes, the village community (as decided by the chief) organises a special festival in the village, called Pray Jom (Santali)–Jom means to eat and every household in that village will invite their relatives (from near and distant villages). This means, say Tarana village won prizes in several villages, then they will appoint certain families to care for the prize goats and when there are enough prize goats amassed from winning various sports and drama competitions they will hold the Pray Jom. For this they need about 25-30 goats, which may take three to five years to collect. And they will eat the cooked meat in an outdoor field like a picnic and the occasion is arranged any time between harvest and sowing, i.e., January to April* (Hansda 2008).

Thus, competitions in Mayurbhanj reflect wider village and inter-village relations, thereby shaping the subjectivities of players in specific ways that reaffirm their identifications with their village community and with inter-village networks. Recent regimes of competition in which school-going children participate which imbibe in them a sense of district, State and national relationships, shaping their subjective identities in different directions, illustrated in the following student essay on play.

> *In world many kinds of play. In play have a rule. By the rule game is played. I have interest in many kinds of play including football, cricket and running. In 2007 a sports programme was held in Jamda Block. In that programme I participated in two events and stood first in the running event. Then I was promoted to the District events where I also stood first in the 21 kilometres marathon and got a certificate and prize. The prizes were T-shirts, saree, glass and tiffin boxes. In our Mayurbhanj, 15 participants were selected, but play events only 3 selected. Two other participants were selected for the 14 kilometres marathon and stood first and second . Then afterwards on 20th December*

we were all admitted to the National events from Orissa State in Maharashtra but in Maharashtra I couldn't get a position. Also such two girls participated but did not end up in getting a position. From our Orissa team we participated in Kabadi, Koko, Dhanutir and marathon events. We had 4 girls in the junior girls Kabadi championship team. On 1st January 2008 we returned to our homes.

The Forms of Village Play

I will turn now to the level of intra-village children's play. Before discussing what their play represents for young Munda people's subjectivities, let us clarify what forms children's play takes. Typologies of play often reflect the three Greek classifications: *agon* (contests or competitions of players' skills); *alea* (games of luck/chance through dice, etc.); and *mimesis* (socio-dramatic play/make-believe dramas) (Spariosu, 1989; Frost, 2008). Caillois [Caillois, 1961 (English Translation) ; 2001 this version] added "ilinx" to this threefold. Ilinx refers to vertigo-inducing play which challenges our vestibular system's equilibroceptive and proprioceptive functions by disrupting normal subjective intentionality and selfhood. Swinging, spinning round and around, sliding, riding a moving platform, speeding, ascending to unusual heights all fall into this category. Caillois insists we may analyse any given social setting by interpreting the human expressions of any (or any combinations) of the above four forms of play [Caillois, 1961 (English Translation) ; 2001 version].

I found that the above four forms were indeed manifest in children's every-day play in Mayurbhanj and do reveal important aspects of their subjective, social and spatial experiences. However, I would like to add another hard-to-name play-type to this mix. *Ad hoc* "roaming around" (*ghurna/ghumna*), or "mucking around". It would include all of the enactments by young people when they are seemingly not doing much, moving with no fixed plan and opportunistically engaging with random minutiae of their spatial and social contexts apparently meaninglessly: picking up stones and throwing them away; following a line of ants as it climbs up a log; curiously watching a social exchange and giggling about it with a friend; gossipping while sitting under a tree; tinkering with things/pulling things apart and putting them back together; building and destroying a sand cave or structure; clambering over the rocky outcrops at the base of surrounding hills and idly exploring crevices and other rocky features; becoming distracted while bathing at the pond, to watch or create water ripples or splash and tease a fellow bather, etc. All these *ad hoc* enactments of play feed into the "ensemble of modes of perception, affect, thought and desire that animate acting subjects". The rural village provides a stimulating sensory and social environment for this (and other sorts of) play and many of my young informants told me they prefer living in the village than in town because they can move around freely to play with their friends.

The Relationship between Munda Child Subjectivity and Play

Considering the relationship between Munda children's subjectivities and peer play, I will approach the topic from two directions. First, how does their context shape their play and subjectivity? Second, how do peer players shape their social and spatial contexts?

Addressing the first question, context shaping peer play and subjectivity, it is worth comparing universal characterizations of the links between play and subjectivity and specific links between Munda peer play and child subjectivity. In terms of subjective experience, Sutton Smith (Sutton Smith, 1982) argues that all human play emanates from antecedent exchanges between neo-nates and primary adult nurturers that involve a back and forth between subjective experience and inter-subjective interactions. These take the following forms: *exchange routines* (i.e., mother responds comically to a sound made by baby, baby repeats the sound, mother comically responds and so on); *central person routines* (i.e., mother manipulates the situation or baby to provide increasing excitement such as in tickling or peek-a-boo games); *unison games* (i.e., mother and baby dance along or rock/sway together in unison or concert); *contest routines* (i.e., mother escapes as baby twists her nose, etc.), (Sutton Smith, 1982). These primordial routines lay the foundations of self and other related and stimulate subjective experience and expression. When children are old enough to begin playing with peers, their play performances are transformed versions of these early play-antecedent routines with each other, all of which modulate arousal to a climax and denouement(Sutton Smith, 1982). These peer performances strengthen subjective awareness and inter-corporeal social awareness at the wider level of age mate peers, just as they did between neonate and nurturer. In Mayurbhanj, carers and babies routinely enact various forms of play-antecedent exchanges from their earliest days[5] and such exchanges continue until the child is old enough to begin participating in village peer play with age-mates (at about four-five years old). The exchanges establish the peer subjective and inter-subjective identifications in ways that are deeply related to the sensory and imagined spatial and social landscape of the village.

Another universalizing proposition about play (or games in particular here) suggests that there is a universal template of game-purpose that incorporates one or several of the following challenges: "the chase"; "the race"; "the hunt"; "the harassment"; "the attack"; "the capture"; "the rescue"; and "the seduction". The game-purpose invokes subjective responses in players of both uncertainty and modulated arousal/fun/excitement (Sutton Smith, 1972). All of the games I played and observed in Mayurbhanj incorporated one or several of these challenges and invoke the above-mentioned responses. Kabadi for example involves chase, harassment, attack and capture. *Bahu chor* (bride kidnap) involves chase, attack/capture, rescue and harassment.

All the above abstract elements of play interactions occur in concrete spatial and social settings and the sensory-motor loops and imagined constructions of those settings shape the experience as the following anecdotes illustrate. We can now move from the universal to explore how peer play in Mayurbhanj invokes a distinctive performance and subjective experience that is both shaped by and shapes context.

It is a hot spring day and in a grove of tamarind trees a dozen men and boys sit upon a huge, granite grave-stone[6] in their Ho village. A few of them start a game of *pacheesh* using tamarind seeds as their dice. The game board was carved into the flat Ho grave-stone about half a century ago and still draws players for regular games today. The players are surrounded by young and old onlookers but a group of young boys breaks away to play their own more active game. Determining which player will be the first chaser, they start their own version of chasing. In this local version, players leap from one grave-stone to the next without touching the ground in between while being chased by the chaser. If a player slips to the ground, or gets tagged by the chaser, he becomes the next chaser and everyone flees from him while leaping from grave to grave. In the graveyard, situated in the centre of the village, the two adjacent games were underway: *pacheesh* players sitting quietly on a huge grave casting their tamarind seed dice, chasey players leaping wildly, yelling and screaming from grave to grave. In both cases, players were in tactual contact with graves of their ancestors, whose spirits they maintain regular contact with and who remain part of give and take of every-day life in the village is now unseen but in imagined ways. The experience of these socially interactive games can't be isolated from the context within which they are played. Players share a rhythmic coordination in their actions as the meanings of the game and the context intermingle. It is dusk in winter and a group of boys between the ages of ten and thirteen are playing a hockey variant they call *chakri* in a post-harvest rice field. Darkness thickens and it is harder to see the puck they've fashioned out of an old rubber *chapal* (thong). They head home in a group, each carrying the hockey sticks they've cut and carved for themselves. Two aspects of context interact with the subjectivities of these players. First, among them is a common understanding that it is risky to roam around in the dark alone, because of the presence of mischievous spirits who become active at night. Second, the players share a common sense about making their own toys and play props. The crafts of making whatever is needed for each game are taken-for-granted part of their play. Their self-made objects of play include carved cricket bats and hockey sticks, cloth or plastic bag balls, catapults, bow and arrows, rustic dice, game boards drawn directly on the soil, clay dolls, figurines and miniature pots, plates, cars and so on, to name just a few items. Sometimes one person becomes well known for their particular skill in making one or another item and they are recruited when a game needs that item. Other times there is a "good-enough" approach amongst all players. The manufacture of their own play props represent both the ways young people's peer play is both shaped by the context and shapes it. Their nonchalant readiness to craft their own play props is undoubtedly shaped by living in an environment in which many elements of daily life are locally produced, from food to local mud-brick and country roof tile houses, to tools made by the ironsmith, etc. Yet what children make and play with is shifting with each generation. Only one generation ago, cricket was never played in rural villages, according to many adult informants and now it is highly popular. In the past children would make their own "*kopra* balls" out of string and old cloth, today they make them out of discarded plastic bags. Tinkering now-a-days often involves pulling apart various electronic items and steadily the mobile phone is becoming an enticing object of digital entertainment and play. The kinaesthetic sensory-motor experiences of crafting simultaneously shape their own subjectivities and their identifications with and identities within local space. As young people make their play props they also shape the context, for the props are part of the technologies of life in the village.

In a secluded location under a large spreading shade tree, away from adult eyes, a group of girls enact a make believe drama on the theme of a marriage. They interweave references to their make-believe food items that will be served with dramatic narratives and conflicts, drawing on a combination of their own vivid imaginations and a mish-mash repertoire of transformed themes remembered from incidents in daily social life in their own families and village; village theatre performances, including tribal social issue themes; Chau dance-drama performances; and Bollywood films. Their hilarious and tragic story covers inter-gender relationships, social ostracism, threats, risks and love as they make sense of their own peer circumstances. Eruptions of creativity within their performances emerge from children set in their social, cultural and historical circumstances and comment upon and reformulate their own dilemmas. In these seemingly banal ways, young people at play begin to reflect on their subjectivities as narratives. Young people's subjective narratives effect subtle shifts in the social architecture of the village, just as their play sites become permanently shaped by their memory of their enactments.

It is also in the *ghumna*, "roaming around" play that children are being shaped by their context. Through *ghumna*, young people 'own' their spatiality and survey its intricate details. As I wandered with groups of children, they pointed out things that were invisible to my eyes, from edible items to pick and eat on the spot, to sacred symbols by the edge of the path, to elephant or other animal tracks. They also used their time to have frivolous, flippant or in depth heart to heart conversations with each other, debriefing each other about their problems. On one walk with two teenage girls who were friends and neighbours of each other, they spent the entire walk discussing how to deal with the situation of a drunken father of one of them causing the mother to run away back to her parents house, leaving this girl to have too much extra housework just at the time she should be preparing for an examination.

Peer Play and Transformations

Thus far we have considered ways that the universal elements of play are shaped by the particulars of the Odishan Munda social, environmental and cultural context and how these shape the universals of child subjectivity in contextually specific ways. We have also touched on some of the ways that Munda children in turn shape their context through their play. Certain sites within the village get memorialised because of children's play, the village road is happily associated with the cacophony of *kabadi* and cricket, certain large shade trees are associated with girls' dolls play, others are recognized as good for tree climbing games.

There are other intangible ways that peer play and the subjective experiences of it transform the social context. School-going children interact with their peers to make sense of the diverse experiences, expectations and trajectories that confront them *via* a common peer social cognition. They have to deal with the continuities and discontinuities between bodies of knowledge presented in school text books *versus* those encountered through engagement with field, forest and local community. In common they also deal with the circumstantial pressures that diverge in some respects from the experiences of their parents. Consequently their play itself changes its own shape and form, for children's peer play is a mode of interacting with context and experimenting with transformations. In Sutton Smith's words, it is "adaptive potential" (Sutton Smith, 1997) responding to "what is" and asking "what if?".

School contexts transform peer play by encouraging age-grade and gender segregated play, by prohibiting some of the games children play in the villages and promoting internationally popular gender specific competitive sports (prioritizing male-dominated sports such as football and cricket), by establishing temporal rhythms that constrain when students may play and by reinforcing peer play groups of school-going *versus* non-school-going children –for each group has daily work rhythms that determine which time they may play. Schooling also transforms play because the narratives and conversations that accompany students' peer play are inflected with shared understandings that come through participation in school, including shared understanding about the problems that students confront in relation to poor delivery of curriculum, coupled with high expectations that students will dedicate intensive hours of their day to school related tasks and to the common understanding of students who are still participants in agro-forestry occupations and negotiate multiple responsibilities.

Conclusion

In conclusion, amidst rapid transformation in tribal areas, such as in Mayurbhanj, Odisha, peer play provides an important venue for Munda school-aged peers to make sense of their subjective experiences as they are shaped by their village and school social and environmental contexts. It also provides a mode through which they develop peer understanding about their circumstances and enact performances that engage with, comment on and subtly shift social, cultural, technological and environmental contexts.

NOTES

1. The spirits include: village tutelary spirits worshipped by the village priest on behalf of all villagers (including the five pan-Santal national *bonga* recognised in all Santal villages and the spirit of the original founder of the village worshipped in a sacred site opposite the current chief's home); sub-clan spirits; household spirits; ancestor spirits; tutelary spirits of Santal '*ojhas*' (shamans); *Jom Sim* spirits; village boundary spirits (*siima bonga*); spirits beyond the village who live in mounds, hillocks, ditches, roadways, etc. (*bahire bonga*); water spirits living in ponds, rivers, streams, etc. (*rongo ruji, baghut bonga*); outsiders spirits (*deku bonga*) refers to all of the deities and divinities worshipped by people who are not adherents of *Sarna*, i.e., Jesus, *Krna, Kali*, etc., tramp/stray mischievous spirits which have to be scared away through magic or exorcisms (*bhuts, rakshas, ekagudia* etc.) Troisi, J. (1978). *Tribal Religion: Religious Beliefs and Practices among the Santals*. New Delhi: Manohar Publications.
2. Child names changed in this article in accordance with my research ethics protocol.
3. All names have been changed in keeping with my university research ethics protocol.
4. At dawn some of them would have duties to perform before going to school.
5. Elsewhere I have described some such exchanges carried out during infant massage routines Bowen, Z. 2012. *Children and Play in Mayurbhanj, Odisha*. PhD, The Australian National University.
6. In this particular graveyard there is a spectacularly large flat stone which was hauled from the mountains by all the men from twelve surrounding villages using human power alone, without machinery. The size of the stone correlates with the respect being offered to the ancestor whose grave it marks. When hauling the stones, they are placed on tree trunks, which are rolled.

REFERENCES

Bateson, G. 1972. *Steps to an Ecology of Mind*. New York: Ballantine Books.

Berlyne, D.E. 1960. *Conflict, Arousal and Curiosity*. New Yok: McGraw-Hill Book Company.

Bowen, Z. 2012. *Children and Play in Mayurbhanj, Odisha*. PhD, The Australian National University.

Caillois, R. Barash, Meyer 1961. (English Translation 2001 this version). *Man, Play and Games*. USA, The Free Press of Glencoe Inc, Reprinted by Simon and Schuster Inc.

Carrin, M. 2012. "Two Peripheries: Teh Billavas of Karnataka and the Santals of Orissa," *In:* M. Carrin and L. Guzy (eds.), *Voices from the Periphery: Subalternity and Empowerment in India*. New Delhi: Routledge.

Eisen, G. 1988. *Children and Play in the Holocaust: Games among the Shadows*. Amherst: The University of Massachusetts Press.

Factor, J. 1988. *Captain Cook Chased a Chook : Chldren's Folklore in Australia*. Victoria, Australia: Penguin Book Australia Ltd.

Frost, J., Sue Wortham and Stuart Reifel. 2008. *Play and Child Development*. Upper Saddle River, New Jersey, Columbus, Ohio: Pearson Merrill Prentice Hall.

Geertz, C. 1973. *The Interpretation of Cultures: Selected Essays.*

Groos, K. 1901. *The Play of Man.* New York: Appleton.

Hansda, G. 2008. *Personal communication.*

Hardman, C. 1973. "Can There Be an Anthropology of Children?" *Journal of the Anthropological Society of Oxford,* IV(2): 85-99.

Hembrom, T. 1996. *The Santals: Anthropological-Theological Reflections on Santali and Biblical Creation Traditions.* Calcutta: Punthi Pustak.

James, A. 2007. "Giving Voice to Children's Voices: Practices and Problems, Pitfalls and Potentials", *American Anthropologist,* 109 (2): 261-272.

James, A., C. Jenks and A. Prout. 1998. *Theorizing Childhood.* Cambridge, UK: Polity Press in association with Blackwell Publishers Ltd.

James, A. and A. Prout. 1990. *Constructing and Reconstructing Childhood: New Directions in the Sociological Study of Childhood.* Hampshire, UK: Falmer Press.

Kennedy, D. 2002. "The Child in Post Modern Subjectivity", *Educational Theory,* 52(2).

Lancy, D. 1996. *Playing on the Mother Ground: Cultural Routines for Children's Development.* New York: Guildford Press, Guildford Publications Inc.

Morrow, V. 2004. "Children's Social Capital: Implications for Health and Well-being", *Health Education* 104 (4): 211-225.

Nieuwenhuys, O. 1994. *Children's Lifeworlds: Gender, Welfare and Labour in the Developing World.* London: Routledge.

Ortner, S. 2005. "Subjectivity and Cultural Critique", *Anthropological Theory,* 5(1): 31-52.

Piaget, J. 1951. *Play, Dreams and Imitation in Childhood.* Melbourne: London/ Toronto: William Heinemann Ltd. in association with the New Education Fellowship.

Pradhan, B. 2011. "Panchayati Raj and Tribal Development in Orissa: An Overview," *International Journal of Current Research,* 3 (November 11): 252-258.

Pramanik, R. 2007. "Overburdened School-going Children: Reflections from a Small City in India", *In:* D. Behera (ed.), *Childhoods in South Asia.* New Delhi: Longman.

Spariosu, M. 1989. *Dionysus Reborn: Play and the Aesthetic Dimension in Modern and Scientific Discourse.* Ithaca, NY: Cornell University Press.

Sutton Smith, B. 1972. *The Folkgames of Children.* Austin and London: University of Texas Press for the American Folklore Society.

Sutton Smith, B. 1982. "Performance Theory of Peer Relations", *In:* K. Borman (ed.), *The Social Life of Children in a Changing Society.* New Jersey: Lawrence Erlbaum Associates Inc.

Sutton Smith, B. 1997. *The Ambiguity of Play.* Harvard: Harvard University Press.

Troisi, J. 1978. *Tribal Religion: Religious Beliefs and Practices among the Santals.* New Delhi: Manohar Publications.

Turner, V. 1982. *From Ritual to Theatre: The Human Seriousness of Play.*

Vygotsky, L. 1966. (first published 1933). "Play and its role in the Mental Development of the Child", *Voprosy Psikhologii,* 6.

TEN

PLAY, NARRATIVES AND GENDER: Understanding Children's Folklore in Context

S. SIMON JOHN

Introduction

The study of folklore in context is important in understanding the functioning of traditional societies. The term "folklore" was first coined by a British antiquarian William J. Thoms in the year 1846 to replace the phrases such as popular antiquities, the lore of the people, the manners, customs, observances, superstitions, ballads, proverbs, etc., of the olden times and it was widely accepted by the scholarly community. The term "folklore" consists of two words, "folk" and "lore", the former is a sociological category and the latter is a cultural category. Dundes (1965: 2) asserts that the term "folk" can refer to any group of people who share at least one common factor. It does not matter what the linking factor is. It could be a common occupation, language, or religion, but what is important is that a group has some traditions that it calls its own. Don Ben Amos (1971) defined folklore as artistic communication of small groups. George H. Schoemaker (1990) classified folklore into verbal folklore and non-verbal folklore. Richard M. Dorson (1972) classified folklore into four categories—oral narratives, performing folk arts, customs and practices, and material culture. Thus the study of folklore includes myths, epics, legends, riddles, narratives, proverbs, lullabies, lamentations, tongue twisters, anecdotes, songs, jokes, life cycle ceremonies, plays, pastimes, rituals, customs, practices, dance, music, theatre, fairs, festivals, material culture, etc., that are orally or aurally transmitted from generation to generation. These standard classifications of folklore are not purely independent but interrelated in nature, particularly in the Indian context. For instance, myths are performed through performing folk arts and also enacted in rituals; songs are associated with traditional occupation; music is associated with dance; and material objects are associated with rituals and performances; while songs and narratives are associated with games. Similarly the classification of "genre" is also a complex one. For instance, a *therukoothu* performance in the northern region of Tamil Nadu which is popularly known as a "folk theatre" form is culturally considered as a "ritual" by the people and *devarattam* which is popularly known as a "dance" form is actually termed as *vilayatu* (play) by the ethnic group. However, these classifications and understanding of genres help to identify and differentiate the various forms of expressive traditions.

Some of the important characteristics of folklore include among others, the element of traditionality; vernacular, oral or aural transmission, and not in written form; contextual; absence of individual authorship; based on a community or region; and having the element of versions and variations. Bascom (1954) argues that folklore can serve four primary functions in a culture. One, it lets people escape from repressions imposed upon them by society. Second, it validates culture, justifying its rituals and institutions to those who perform and observe them. Third, it is a pedagogic device which reinforces morals and values and builds wit. Fourth, it is a means of applying social pressure and exercising social control. These primary functions of folklore can also be seen in children's folklore, particularly the first one and the third one.

Children's folklore is one of the important areas of folklore studies. Children are the fundamental unit of every society and universal symbol of future potentiality as well as the carrier of the heritage of the past. Kerenyi and Jung (1969) stated that the child reflects the infancy of the world and the beginning of life, and the child represents innocence, purity, wonder, receptivity, freshness, non-calculation, absence of narrow ambition and purpose. Understanding of children's world by an adult is always a mystery because the adult always tries to understand the child through the eyes of adulthood. In the beginning of life, children fully depend on adults in order to fulfil their needs, and the adults reciprocate this need by looking after them through various child rearing methods guided by a society's norms. It is important to note how children express their needs and the way adults understand it. The needs and habits of children are constantly changing according to their age and sex. There will be no progress in the process of socialization if a child is unable to change his or her habits according to the expectations of the particular society. Whatever the child learns from the peer group or social group are the reflection of the "culture" of the particular society, in a way, the habits becomes their culture. In this manner, folklore serves as an important medium in the process of socialization.

Children's Folklore: Meaning and Definition

In the West, children's folklore is an important subject matter and number of studies has been done on children's folklore particularly on the cognitive science. Jean Piaget (1951, 1965, 1969, and 1973) carried out an extensive research on children's play activities in order to understand the cognition of the child. Sutton Smith (1979, 1981, 1986, and 1995) has studied children's play activities in order to understand the cognitive and social development of children. Alan Dundes have used psychoanalytic theory to interpret children's folklore text. Similarly, in the early 1970s, the students of folklore and linguistics in the University of Texas used children's abilities to replicate jokes, riddles, and other minor genres of everyday folklore as measures of the cognitive and linguistic development of children under the supervision of Richard Bauman. However, study children's folklore is the most neglected area in India. There are a number of "collection" of children's tales, games and songs in vernacular languages, however, a proper analytical research on children's folklore is lacking in the Indian context.

This chapter is an outcome of my larger research on "Children's Folklore: Functions and Socialization" which was carried out among the children belonging to Pallar—an indigenous agricultural community domiciled in Thuiruvenkatanathapuram village in southern Tamil Nadu. The empirical data was collected through fieldwork among children through observation, participant observation, and interview method.

It makes sense to differentiate between "folklore for children" and "children's folklore". From the communicative point of view, "folklore for children" serves the hierarchical and unidirectional inter-relationship of adult and child. This is used by the adults to sooth a child, to activate a child, for dictatic purposes, for fun and amusement through which the communication between adult and child takes place. For instance, lullabies, story telling and rituals performed by adults to children are basically unidirectional in nature. The important function of "folklore for children" is to bring the cultural nuances within the reach of the child and to make him or her familiarize with culture. Folkloric text provides for the child the most elementary model of the world. Through this the adult leads the child into the surrounding animated world and into the society of adults, among whom the child is accorded a place.

On the other hand, defining children's folklore is always a challenging task because it is dynamic, varies from place to place, time to time, age to age and gender to gender. For children, folklore is primarily an amazing and exciting activity which lets them express their play, narration, singing, dancing, joking, etc. Osorina (1986) defines children's folklore as the sum of various forms of activities of a children's group that have a tendency to repeat themselves from generation to generation of children and that are intimately linked to the age and sex related peculiarities of psychological development and to the nature of socialization of children within the limits of a particular culture. Sierra (1995) described children's folklore are those that are passed from child to child, generation to generation, and informally by oral communication. They come in variety of forms and types. Children's folklore is fundamentally co-operative, such as dramatic and singing games and hand-clapping games. For practical purpose, I understood children's folklore as a set of activities or body of knowledge which is orally transmitted from generation to generation and repeatedly performed by the children belonging to a particular region or culture, primarily for their own pleasure and entertainment. It consists of verbal and non-verbal plays, games, pastimes, stories, rhymes, jokes, riddles, etc.

The adult terminologies like game, play, pastime, leisure and recreation are very difficult to apply among children. During my fieldwork, whenever I asked "what are you doing"? to the children during their leisure time, they replied, "*naan vilaiyaditu iruken*" meaning, "I am playing". For children, every leisure activity is a "play"—it can be performed alone or in a group; it can be cooperative or competitive, and it can be verbal or non-verbal. Telling a story, or listening to one, singing a song, dancing, swimming, drawing or scratching on the walls, joking, running here and there, climbing a tree, riding a wheel, whistling a whistle are all "play" for them.

Fieldwork among Children

It is worth mentioning here about my own fieldwork experiences among Pallar children of southern Tamil Nadu. Doing fieldwork among children was always a challenging task because children performed their folklore with their peer group primarily for their own pleasure, entertainment and happiness. They were least bothered about "research" and the "researcher", and the purpose and importance of "research" cannot be explained to them. The methodological ideas of "contact", "lead", "questionnaire" and "interview" have very little or no role at all when doing fieldwork among them. Generally, they neither play in front of adults and outsiders nor allow adults to take part in their play. They stop playing and disappear the moment they see adults in their play context. For children, "play" is most important and dearest to their heart. At times they mock and make fun out of the researcher too! It took me several weeks to get familiarized with the children of the said village, and for them to accept me.

On the first day of fieldwork, when I approached a child and asked her name, she called out to her parents and informed that one *poochandi* has come! *Poochandi* is a character in stories referring to the person who kidnaps children; and so parents usually used to threaten children that if they do anything wrong, *poochandi* will come and take them! After this incident I decided not to interact with any children for some time and I started taking photographs of the village surroundings everyday. When children saw me taking walking around with the camera and clicking pictures everyday, they started approaching me since their curiosity was piqued. Slowly they came near and started asking me to take their pictures, and requested me to show the pictures to them. When I listened to their excited talks, took their pictures, showed their images to them, they would happily smile, laugh, and run away! Once their curiosity was aroused, and they found a willing participant in their demands of picture-clicking, I was no longer a stranger. Thereafter, I started carrying chocolates, and whenever they approached me I gave them the chocolates, conversed with them briefly keeping my "research" for another day, and slowly I became their "big" friend. They started sitting around me, some even climbing on my shoulders, riding my motorcycle with me, telling me all their stories, until finally, they refused to let me go home in the evening ! Everything became easy when I became their friend—they played, danced, told stories, joked among themselves, and even with me. In fact I became a child, a part of their peer group in all their play activities.

Classifications of Children's Folklore

Classification of children's folklore is an important tool to understand the various genres and its functions in the world of children. Children's folklore may be primarily classified as follows:

Early, Middle, and Later Stage

It was observed during the fieldwork that there are specific play activities for each age group and, therefore, children's folklore may be classified on the basis of different age groups. Generally children during the early stage, i.e., below four or five years of age normally play alone with a lot of material objects like wheels, toys, stones, sand, shells, leafs, etc. Even if they play together with other children, there will not be any co-operation among them and everyone plays their own game according to their ability and imagination level. During the middle stage i.e. between ages five and nine, children perform their play activities with their peer group. During this stage the play activities are performed in a semi-organized manner. Imitation, cooperation and competition can be found during their play activities in this stage. Children in the later stage i.e., between nine and fifteen years perform their play activities in a very organized way. In this stage, gender plays a significant role in their play. Till the middle stage, both boys and girls play some games together but in the later stage they play games which are specific for their gender.

Verbal, Non-verbal and Both

Children's folklore can also be classified on the basis of the content and nature of play activities. Verbal play consists of storytelling, riddling sessions, joking, singing songs and rhymes. Non-verbal play consists of physical activities and material objects, for instance plays like *kannam poochi* (hide and seek), *pamparam* (top), *Koli* (marbles), *kalaichi kal, thayam* (board games), etc. There are many play activities which consists of both verbal and non-verbal, for instance imitative or dramatic plays like *amma appa* (mummy daddy), *petty kadai* (petty shop) and many girl's plays consists of rhymes along with physical game.

Gender

As mentioned earlier, gender plays a significant role in children's folklore. In every culture there are specific play activities for boys and girls and, therefore, children's folklore can be classified on the basis of gender, i.e., boy's games, girl's games and both together. For instance most of the board games and rhymic games are performed by girls and games like *pamparam*, *koli*, *kallan police* (police and thief), *maram eari kurungu* (monkey climbing tree) are played by boys. Both boys and girls play together in imitative games like *amma appa*, *petty kadai* and also plays like like *kannam poochi*.

Competitive and Cooperative

Children's folklore can be classified on the basis of the nature of the play activity. Certain play activities are competitive in nature and at the end of the play there will be a winner/runner and punishment, for instance marble and top game; and certain play activities are purely cooperative in nature, there will not be any winner and punishment, for instance *samaiyal vilayattu* (kitchen game), *petty kdai* and *amma appa vilayattu*.

Rules

Children's folklore may be classified on the basis of method of playing, i.e., 'rules'. Certain play activities have a traditional mode of play which should not be violated by the players and certain play activities are without any prescribed rules. For instance board games, *pamparam, koli* are having prescribed rules and the rhymic and imitative plays games falls under the play without prescribed rules.

Children's folklore can also be classified into imitative and non-imitative plays. The nature of children's folklore is purely contextual in nature and varies from culture to culture and time to time. These classifications are just to understand the nature of children's folklore and should not be considered as a standardized and watertight compartment.

Characteristics of Children's Play

The understanding of children's world is a difficult task for adults since they try to understand children through the eyes of adults and not through the eyes of children. Since children's folklore is a unique segment of folklore studies, it is pertinent to explore its characteristics. Apart from the general characteristics of folklore mentioned earlier, the following are some of the unique characteristics of children's folklore observed during the fieldwork among children.

Children's folklore is primarily performed by children for their own pleasure and entertainment. They are experts in their play activities and they decide how, when, where and what to play. For instance while playing "petty shop" game, the required space, materials and its symbolic meaning, time duration of the play are all decided by children spontaneously during their play.

There are unwritten rules for certain children play activities which are orally transmitted from generation to generation. These unwritten rules are simple in nature and easy to remember. For instance, there are different kinds of play in the "game of marbles" and each kind of play is having certain prescribed rules like how many marbles should be used, the shape, size and distance of the space, and method of playing marbles. These rules should be followed by the players.

The rules of children's folklore differ from place to place. Additionally, according to their wish the rules are modified by the children while playing. This repetition and alteration of rules are one of the important characters of children's folklore. For instance, children formulate the rules before they start the play of "hide and seek". The numbers to be counted by the children who close his or her eyes, how to close the eyes—by hands or by cloth, in which position and where should he or she should close eyes, etc., are all determined by children before start their play and every time they may alter the rules too.

Another important character of children's folklore is that there is no formal classes to learn these play activities. Children learn their play activities through observation and participation. Sometimes, those children who are not familiar with certain games are not included in the game played by older children. For instance when seniors play *kabaddi* or board games, they do not allow children to take part. In this situation, the juniors observe the seniors play and then they play along with their peer group.

There is no need for expertise to perform children's folklore. All interested children can perform children's play. However, certain qualities or skills are required to excel in their play. For instance, children require memory and narration skill for storytelling and rhymic play, observation skill is required to play imitation play like *petty kadai* and *amma appa* game, concentration is required to play *pamparam, koli* and board games, physical strength is required for *maram eari kuranku*, *thotu piduchi* (running race), etc.

Some of the children's plays are competitive in nature and some are cooperative in nature. For instance, *koli, pamparam*, board games, *maram eari kuranku, pillaiyar panthu,* etc., are competitive in nature and games like *petty kadai*, *samaiyal*, *amma appa* are cooperative in nature.

Most of the children's traditional play does not require any items produced in factory. They play their games with available materials in their place. Stones, sand, a stick, papers, leafs, empty boxes, bricks, shells, etc., are all play materials for children. *Kichu kichu thambulam* is a game played by two children. Here, a heap of sand is adjusted to the size of one foot long and few centimetres high. Then one player takes a small object like a seed or coin or stone in his hand and moves his hand from the starting point of the sand heap to the end within the sand. While moving, somewhere he leaves the object inside the sand and keeps moving his empty hand further. The other child does not know where the object was kept. After this act the child has to guess and select a palm sized space in the sand heap to find out the object. The child is considered a winner, if he or she finds the object in the selected space and the winner starts the game again.

For children, play is always voluntary in nature and primarily for their own pleasure and entertainment. They do not have any particular time and space for their game. Most children's play begins spontaneously and ends when they feel that is enough for the day or stopped by adults.

Children know that their play is for their entertainment and is, therefore, not "true". For instance, those who are playing *petty kadai* game or *amma appa* game or *kallan police* game know that their role is only an imagination.

Gender Construction through Children's Folklore

The specific roles for men and women is orally transmitted from generation to generation and practiced traditionally in every culture. The social construction of gender begins as soon as a child is born. Specific rituals, names, dress codes, ornaments, play activities for boys and girls all serve as a medium of constructing gender. These gender traits are reflected in the early stage of children's folklore in the form of imitative play. The following illustrations clearly show how gender is constructed through play.

Amma appa vilaiyattu (mummy daddy play) is played by a group of children—two boys and two girls—between age four and seven. The older boy plays the role of the father and the older girl plays the role of the mother, while the other children play the role of the daughter and son. The space of the game is usually in a little narrow area in the portico. The game commences with the collection of sand from nearby areas, and the building of a four-walled sand house without roof. Thereafter, all the children act as if they woke up from their sleep in the early morning. The "mother" starts drawing the traditional *kolam* (traditional line drawings) in front of the house with the help of sand and her "daughter" helps her. Meanwhile the "father" gets ready to go to the "paddy field" and the "son" gets ready to go to school. Soon after the drawing of *kolam*, the girl who is acting as mother starts "preparing coffee" and the girl who is acting as daughter serves it to her "father" and "brother".

After having coffee, the "father" and "son" go out for their respective jobs to carry out their duty. The "mother" and "daughter" get busy in "cooking". They collect materials like stones, leaves, paper, shells, etc. and act as if they are cooking. An oven is made of three stones and dry coconut shell is used as utensils. They symbolically make fire and start cooking. The sand symbolizes rice, the stones symbolize the oven, the coconut shells symbolize utensils and the leaves symbolize vegetables. When cooking is in progress, the children who are enacting the role of father and son return home, they wash their hands and face, and ask loudly, "Is meal ready"? The "mother" replies that it will be ready in a few minutes and thereafter the "daughter" starts "serving" food to her "father" and "brother". Soon after the meals the "father" again goes back to the fields and the "son" to school. The "daughter" cleans the place and takes away the plates and the "mother" washes the utensils. Finally, the "daughter" sweeps the floor. This game goes on and continues till an adult interrupts and tells them to go home.

The above is an imitative play performed by children which reflects the children's family—what they have seen in their homes and in their neighbourhoods. Specific roles for men and women are traditionally prescribed in every culture. The studied region is patriarchal in nature, and men are seen to be domineering and are engaged in works outside the home like purchasing, maintaining the agricultural fields, community service, etc., while women are mainly confined to their homes—doing household jobs like cooking, cleaning, washing clothes and utensils, etc., in addition to their works in agricultural fields during day time. Also, the male children are given preference in the society in terms of education, property, etc. These cultural traits are reflected in the everyday life and thus children belonging to this society observe these practices associated with their gender prescribed by the society. These observations are reflected in their imitative plays which reinforces their role in the given society. There are many other plays played by girls and boys which clearly reflect the role of gender in children's folklore. The plays performed by girls are soft and cooperative in nature with less physical activities. The space for their play is mostly near their houses, particularly for the girls belonging to the age group of above eight years. Moreover children belonging to this age group are not allowed to play boys' games and to play along with boys. They are expected to play only the games prescribed to girls and with girls.

Boys enjoy more freedom when they grow older. Their plays are more competitive in nature with more physical activity, stringent rules and the space for their play is always away from home and they have more liberty to play what they want. For instance, *pillaiyar panthu* is a game normally played by boys. *Pillaiyar* in Tamil refers the Hindu god Ganesha and *Panthu* refers to a ball. A group of children, generally boys, play this game. The players are divided into two and they keep a brick in the ground which is known as *pillaiyar.* Team *A* will throw a ball from a certain distance to hit the *pillaiyar*. Each player gets three chances to hit. If a player hits the *pillaiyar* and knocks it down, then the players belonging to team *A* will safeguard the *pillaiyar* from team *B*. The objective of team *B* is to touch the *pillaiyar*, without being hit by the ball by Team *A*, and the objective of team *A* is to hit the players belonging to team *B* before they touch the *pillaiyar*.

Team *A* hides the ball so that team *B* does not know who holds the ball. Everyone in team *A* pretends as if they are having the ball and waits for a suitable time to hit the team *B* players. Team *B* is considered a winner, if they can touch the *pillaiyar*, and team *A* will be considered winner, if they hit the players of team *B*. The winning team will get the opportunity to knock down the *pillaiyar*.

This play explains the nature of boys' games. However, they will be mocked by others if they play girls' games. These examples clearly reflect the social construction of gender and how folklore serves as a medium for socialization.

Cognitive Development through Children's Folklore

Researches clearly prove that children's folklore plays a vital role in the cognitive development of child. Bettelheim (1976) explains why children are attracted to tales. For the child it is not an amusement. Significantly, it is the need to understand itself in this complex world, with which it must come to grips. The child needs ideas as how to bring its inner house into order. It needs a moral education which subtly and by implication only, conveys to it the advantages of moral behaviour, not through obstruct ethical concepts, but through that which seems tangibly right and, therefore, meaningful. The psychoanalysis confirms the great influence of folk tales upon the mental like of children. One reason for this great influence is that the tale offers fantasy materials which suggests to the child in symbolic form what the battle to achieve self-realization is about and it guarantees a "happy ending".

The following *kosuvanar kathati* (mosquito tale) which is collected in the field will explain the unique character of children's narratives.

> *Once there was a mosquito in a village. One day it wore its best silk sari and went out in search of bridegroom. It came across a spade and asked, "O Spade! Would you like to marry me"? The spade replied, "I will do all sorts of works for you. I will cut the plantain trees, I will cut the grass, and even I will cut you into pieces". Hearing this, the mosquito replied, "I don't like you".*
>
> *After some time the mosquito found a donkey and asked, "O Donkey! Will you marry me"? The donkey replied, "I will do any work for you, I will wash your clothes. I will bundle your clothes and carry. When I see the ash I will roll on it. Even I will trample you". By hearing this, mosquito went away saying, "I don't like you".*
>
> *After some time the mosquito met a rat and asked, "O Rat! Will you marry me"? The rat replied, "I will bring grocery, whatever you don't have, I will steal and bring". Hearing this, the mosquito felt happy and married the rat.*
>
> *One day when the rat was brushing his teeth, the mosquito went into its nostrils and died. The rat sneezed, made paste of the mosquito, put it on a plate and left it upon the sea and immediately after that the sea water turned dirty.*
>
> *At that time a wild elephant came to the sea to drink water and saw the dirty sea. It asked, "O Ocean! You used to be clean*

always. But why are you so dirty today"? The sea replied, "The rat has made a paste of his wife mosquito and left it on me and that's why I have become dirty". By hearing that, the tusk of the elephant got broken. Following that, all the leaves of the banyan tree withered.

At that time a domestic elephant came to the banyan tree and asked, "O Banyan tree! You look green always. What happens to you now?" The banyan tree replied, "The rat has made a paste of his wife mosquito and left upon the sea and it became dirty and by hearing that, the tusk of the tusker got broken and I withered all my leaves".

On hearing this, eyes of the domestic elephant became blind and it walked slowly and stood upon the ridge of a field. The ridge saw the elephant and asked, "O Elephant! What happened to you? How did your eyes become blind"? The elephant replied, "The rat made his wife mosquito into a paste, laid it on a plate and left upon the sea, the water of the sea became dirty, the tusk of the tusker broke, the leaves of the banyan tree got withered and my eyes became blind".

On hearing this, the ridge became crooked. A farmer came there and asked the ridge, "O Ridge! You always used to be straight. How did you become crooked now"? The ridge replied, "Listen to the story, 'the rat made his wife mosquito into a paste, laid it upon a plate and left in the sea. The water of the sea became dirty, the tusk of the tusker got broken, the leaves of the banyan got withered, the eyes of the elephant turned blind and I became crooked' ".

On hearing this farmer dropped his plough and broke it. The farmer's wife came there and saw the broken plough. She asked, "What happened? How was the plough broken"? The farmer replied, "Listen to the story, 'the rat made his wife mosquito into a paste, laid it upon a plate and left in the sea. The water of the sea became dirty, the tusk of the tusker got broken, the leaves of the banyan got withered, the eyes of the elephant turned blind, the ridge became crooked and I broke my plough' ".

On hearing this woman dropped the pot and came back to her home. There her parents asked, "What happened to you? Why did you break the pot"? The woman replied, "Listen to the story, 'the rat made his wife mosquito into a paste, laid it upon a plate and left in the sea. The water of the sea became dirty, the tusk of the tusker got broken, the leaves of the banyan got withered, the eyes of the elephant turned blind, the ridge became crooked, my husband broke his plough and I broke the pot'."

On hearing this, the son tore all the books. When he went to school, his teacher asked him, "Where are the books"? The boy replied, "Sir, listen to the story, the rat made his wife mosquito into paste and left in the sea, the water of the sea became dirty, the tusk of the tusker got broken, the leaves of the banyan got withered, the eyes of the elephant turned blind, the ridge became crooked, my father broke his plough and my mother broke her pot and I tore all the books'."

On hearing this teacher demolished the school!

The above stated children's narrative clearly reflects that the children have the creative ability to narrate a tale out of anything and everything and learn the formula and skills of narration through tales. Telling and listening to tales helps children to develop their cognitive skills and through their imagination they brought the surrounding world within their reach. The significant "formula" of this tale is "repeating" the events again and again in order to lengthen the narration. According to the imaginary skills children add several additions to this tale and, therefore, there are several versions available of this tale. But the tale always ended up with torn books and demolition of schools, which is the happy ending for children. This tale clearly reflects one of the primary functions of folklore—folklore lets people escape from repressions imposed upon them by society. Normally children in the studied region are not interested in going to schools and reading books and they are forced by the adults to go to school. This suppressed emotion of children which is imposed by adults upon them is expressed through the form of children's narrative and they tore their books and destroyed the schools in their tale, as a happy ending.

Conclusion

Children's folklore is the basic subject matter to understand the various aspects in the process of human life. The social construction of body, gender, cognition, skills, attitude, personality development, language learning, assimilation, adaptation and the impact of globalization can be studied through children's folklore. This chapter tried to understand the possible classifications, characteristics and functions of children's folklore of a particular time of given society. However, generalizing children's folklore will lead to misunderstanding the world of children belonging to different cultures. As Peter Clauss (1986) mentions, children's folklore should be studied along with particular socio-cultural context and not just only the text. Children's folklore is always dynamic in nature and differs from place to place, culture to culture, gender to gender, age to age and time to time. Children's folklore helps children to learn and express the socio-cultural-psychological-topological elements to which the child belongs. In short, children's folklore serves as a medium of socialization or enculturation. The "experience of childhood" is very close and dear to every adult and it becomes nostalgia when one crosses our childhood. In fact, one of the important methodologies of collecting children's folklore is from the memories of every adult.

REFERENCES

Bascom, W. 1954. "Four Functions of Folklore", *The Journal of American Folklore*, 67 (266): 333-349.

Beettlheim, B. 1976. *The Uses of Enactment: The Meaning and Importance of Fairy Tales*. New York: Vintage Books.

Ben Amos, D.1971. "Towards Definition of Folklore", *Journal of American Folklore*, 84: 3-15.

Clauss, P.J. 1986. "Playing Cenne: The Meaning of Folk Game", (pp. 265-293) *In*: S. H. Blackburn and A. K. Ramanujan (eds.), *Another Harmony: New Essays on the Folklore of India*. Oxford: Oxford University Press.

Dorson, R.M. 1972. *Folklore and Folklife: An Introduction*. London: The University of Chicago Press.

Dundes, A. 1965. *The Study of Folklore*. Engelwood Cliffs, N.J.: Prentice-Hall.

Kerenyi, C and C. Jung. 1969. *Essays on a Science of Mythology*. NJ: Princeton University Press.

Osorina, M.V. 1986. "Modern Children's Lore as an Object of Interdisciplinary Study", *Soviet Anthropology and Archaeology*, XXV (1): 27-48.

Piaget, J. 1969. *The Psychology of the Child*. New York: Basic Books.

____. 1951. *Play, Dreams and Imitation in Childhood.* New York: W.W. Norton.

____. 1965. *The Child's Conception of the World.* Totowa: Little Field Adams.

____. 1973. *The Child and Reality: Problems of Genetic Psychology.* New York: Grassman.

Schoemaker, G. H. 1990. *The Emergence of Folklore in Everyday Life: A Field Guide and Source Book.* Bloomington: Trickster Press.

Smith, S. 1995. *Children's Folklore*, London: Garland Publishing.

____. 1979. *Play and Learning.* New York: Gardner.

____. 1986. *Toys as Culture.* New York: Gardner.

Sierra, J. and R. Kaminski. 1995. *Children's Traditional Games.* Arizona: Oryx Press.

ELEVEN

'KEEPING HOUSE' AND 'HERDING COWS': Games Played by Garo Children

QUINBALA MARAK

Recreational activities have been classic ethnographic concerns, and questions about the distributions of games were asked early in the history of anthropology (Tylor, 1879; Hodge, 1890; Dorsey, 1891; Daniel, 1892; Stevenson, 1903). A wide range of recreational activities are termed games and they are variously defined. A game is a recreational activity, after Roberts *et al.* (1959: 597), characterized by organized play, competition, two or more sides, criteria for determining the winner, and agreeing upon rules. The games played may be classified in terms of distinctive patterns of play. The outcomes are determined primarily by the physical abilities of the players, some by a series of moves, each of which represents a player's choice among alternatives, and others either by non-rational guesses or by reliance on the operation of some chance device such as a die; and some are determined by combinations of these patterns. All these ways of determining outcomes are widely distributed among the societies of the world, and can be classified into those of physical skill, strategy, and chance.

Despite the interests in games (of adults), children's games were not systematically studied as a part of child socialization until much later. Children's plays were not always seen to contribute significantly to this socialization process and so it was seldom investigated (Schwartzman, 1976, 290). Some ethnographers, however, started to look at children's games as an important part of growing up years, and started to view play as imitation and preparation of adult life (Mead, 1934; Malinowski, 1960; Turnbull, 1961; Loizos, 1969). Loizos (1969: 236) for instance, tended to view it as practice for adult activity. Children's role play has been interpreted from this perspective and in this way the seemingly non-purposeful actions of play are transformed into activities functional for the continuation of the social order. Thus, "ordinary" play allowed the child to imagine himself or herself in various social roles and by so doing to "build up" his or her own character (Mead, 1934: 151-159).

This chapter discusses the games played by children belonging to the Garo tribe. The games mentioned here are not all of physical skill, strategy or chance (after Roberts *et al.*, 1959), but also games played by children that cannot be categorized into any of the above. These are essentially children's games, where adults at times play along. Interestingly, the study of children's games among Garos reveals much more than mere recreational activity. It tells not only about the matrilineal societal set-up of the Garos, but also how Garo children are socialized into adult roles. Thus here we try to look at two aspects: (1) How games act as a socializing agent among Garos; and (2) How much of a society is revealed through these games. It is understood that all games cannot be elaborately discussed, and, therefore, here we try to look at two of the most popular games played by children in all Garo societies as part of their growing up years.

The Matrilineal Garos

Garos are a tribal group living in the Garo Hills region of Meghalaya, and in other neighbouring States such as Assam, Nagaland and Tripura (India), and across the political divide in the northern parts of Bangladesh. They call themselves *Mande* or *Achik Mande* which means "man", and are referred to by others as Garos. Linguistically, they belong to the Tibeto-Burman group, and their lores talk about different waves of migration in the prehistoric past from a place called Torua in Tibet. They are divided into nine sub-tribes (after Majumdar 1980: 19), such as the Awe, Chisak, Matchi-Dual, Matabeng, Ambeng, Ruga-Chibok, Gara-Ganching, Atong and Megam. These sub-tribes speak different dialects of the Garo or Achikku language. Originally, there were two clans – the Sangma and Marak, but at present three clans such as the Momin, Areng and Shira are found which are said to be splinter groups of the former two (Sangma,

1981). Each of these clans has a number of sub-clans which are exogamous in nature and are by themselves many times taken to be clans.

The Garos are not only a community in the threshold of culture change due to factors of modernization and urbanization, but an exemplary one due to their attempts of clinging on to the traditional cultural patterns and values, which is strongly based on matrilineal kin ties. In a Garo society, the lineage, inheritance, succession, and residence is from mother to daughter. For instance, a child takes the mother's clan (or lineage) name. Thus, when a child is born, he or she becomes a member of the mother's clan. A daughter inherits the parental home and landed property, as well as the responsibility towards elderly relatives, relatives in need and unmarried younger siblings. Usually, the eldest daughter is the inheritress known as *nokna dongipa mechik* (daughter for the house), but failing which any of the daughters can be made the inheritress. The bulk of the property thus goes to the *nokna* but according to affordability, the other daughters too receive small plots of land for setting up independent houses after marriage. Post-marital residence is matrilocal, with the groom moving into the bride's mother's house. If he marries the *nokna* he continues to reside there making it his permanent home, but if he marries a non-inheritress daughter then within two or three years he moves out and sets up an independent house in a plot gifted by his wife's family. Succession to the post of chieftain or *nokma* whose office is still seen in Garo Hills is matrilineal, i.e. it passes from a father to the son-in-law through the daughter. Thus, it remains in the same matrilineal family and clan. In such cases the groom for the inheritress daughter of the *nokma* preferably has to be the father's real or classificatory nephew. In the Garo matrilineal system, women are the owners of property and the ones whose lineage passes along. However, the position of men and boys is not neglected. On the contrary, as the father and maternal uncle, he wields power over his family and his sister's family. In the matters of his matri-clan, he occupies the most powerful position. A Garo woman thus appears to be a mere custodian, while all decisions are taken by men.

The Garos are traditionally shifting cultivators, cultivating a plot of land on rotation basis and moving along with the plot. But for centuries now, they are more or less settled in certain pockets towards the hilly areas. In Garo Hills, land is owned not only by the village but by matrilineal clans through the office of the *nokma*. In such a scenario, how much of land (for shifting cultivation) is to be given to an individual will depend on the *nokma* and the family's ability to cultivate.

Traditionally, they were animists following what is now known as the *songsarek* religion, with a belief in numerous spirits, some benevolent others malevolent, and to appease whom a number of rituals were conducted. However, with the coming of Christianity much has changed in the religious sphere and today only a few Garos practicing the traditional faith can be seen.

In Assam, Garos live in a number of districts such as Kamrup, Goalpara, Karbi Anglong and Sonitpur. This chapter is based on the Garos of Gohalkona a village in Kamrup district, Assam. This village is uniquely situated between the predominantly caste populated areas of Assam and the Khasi Hills of Meghalaya. It falls within Boko Police Station, Kamrup District, though it is only a few kilometres away from Nongstoin, West Khasi Hills (Meghalaya). Gohalkona has 258 Garo households, with a total population of 1367, males numbering 632 and females 735. The Garos of the village are all Christians, majority of whom are American Baptists. The mainstay of the Garos is agriculture, and every household does some form of cultivation or the other. There are only 29 individuals engaged in some kind of service/jobs ranging from school teachers to peons, drivers and security guards. Besides agriculture, a few engage in sericulture, carpentry, weaving and basketry as well. The main source of water is private wells. The Public Works Department (PWD), Assam had set up points for public water supply twenty years back, however, till date these points have not yielded any water. The village boasts of a Garo medium lower primary, middle and a high school, run on government aids, but with non-Garo teachers who are regularly absent. The village has no Public Health Centre (PHC), and thus for common ailments such as cough and cold, traditional methods of treatment are used. For sicknesses that cannot be cured through traditional means, the sick are transported with great difficulty to the Boko government hospital at a distance of 7 kilometres. The village has not been electrified, the roads have not been pitched and, therefore, during monsoon the village is marooned. The data is collected first hand through observation and interview.

Bringing Up a Garo Child

As far as the upbringing of a child is concerned, it is seen that not only the immediate family such as parents and siblings play a role but also uncles, aunts, cousins who might not be related through blood but who belong to the same clan. Children are looked upon as God's gift, and children of either gender are welcomed (Marak, 2012). When a girl is born, there is much celebration for she is looked upon as one who will bring numerical strength to the clan, but also will carry forth the family (and clan) name. When a boy is born, he too is welcomed with great funfare for he is looked upon as the one who will be the backbone of the sister, and niece. The boy, as the maternal uncle, plays the most important role in a child's life, and occupies a very important position, at par with the position of the parents, if not more.

When a baby is born, it is usually the mother, the grandmother and other female members of the family who look after it. At times, a young girl called *bisa rodilgipa* is hired to look after the baby and child. Notwithstanding the parental instincts the underlying feeling is that just as a baby is looked after now, it will one day do likewise to the aged parents and grandparents. Like many societies, among the Garos too, a number of beliefs and practices exist regarding conception, pregnancy, child birth and eventual upbringing of a child (Medhi and Marak, 2001). Diet control comes into the picture after confirmation of pregnancy. Interestingly, it is believed that an expectant mother should not take food too rich in protein and carbohydrate, otherwise the baby would be obese (*biltomtom dake milgen*). The pregnant woman is not given cold food, and allowed to eat whatever she craves for, such as bits of clay utensils or mud plaster, else it is believed the baby will have overflowing saliva (*kuchi onggen*).

Child birth is usually taken care of by the midwife (*kamal*), who also gives the first bath to the baby. Delivery for Garo women is said to be fairly easy, and there are no known cases of women having died of child birth in the village unless it led to other complications. The room where the pregnant woman sleeps doubles up as the delivery room. As soon as the baby is born the umbilical cord is cut off with a clean blade about three inches from the child's navel. The displaced placenta is then gently buried in the garden. If thrown across a river, it is believed that the woman will never conceive again. The still attached placenta (*gandil*), when it shrivels and falls off, is washed, dried and kept preserved in a bottle. This is used for medicinal purposes later for child ailments. Breast feeding takes place almost immediately, and continues till about two and half years when weaning starts slowly, which, however, may be advanced if another child is expected. If there is lactation before birth, it is believed that the child will not live long.

Until the mother sufficiently recovers, the baby is attended to by the grandmother and the mother's sisters. The baby is placed in a warm, dry wrapping and kept in a safe place after the *kamal*'s bath. However, as the mother regains her strength, she starts looking after the baby and carries the baby on her back as she goes about her daily duties. For the first few months, the baby defecates and wets his/her bed regularly. By the eighth and ninth month the child is regularly taken out to the backyard for defecation and given toilet training. By this time exercise and play become a daily routine. The grandmother regularly massages the baby with mustard oil, and while massaging some amount of play is also engaged in such as tickling, and moving the arms and legs.

When a baby starts to toddle, it is no longer considered a baby, but a child (*bisa*) in Garo nomenclature. He/she continues to be given attention by parents and grandparents and never left alone till they turn four or five years. By this time, in village Gohalkona, children are sent to pre-schools to keep them busy, and so that they might learn a few things before starting school. When an infant becomes a *bisa,* the socialization process starts through imitation and discipline. The young girl-child starts playing setting-up-house with friends, where she imitates processes of food collection and cooking as well as serving it to friends. Friends taking part in such an imagined eating process make appropriate verbal responses like "*to•aha*" (tasty), "*saataikubo*" (serve me more), and "*kari nangja*" (less salt). On the other hand, young boys make their own play-groups, and it is usually boisterous activities like *matchu-saria* (cow-herding) and *sikarna* (hunting). Imposition of mild discipline and task assignments go a long way in the whole socialization process (Marak, 2006; Marak, 2010).

Games Played by Garo Children

Much of the recreational activities of Garo children are referred to as *kala* (games). Children's games as opposed to adult games are referred to as *bisani kala* even though games such as football are played by adult men. However, not all recreational activity can be termed games, even though a large amount of time is spent on them. For instance, a whole range of recreational activity in which children engage in are listening to stories, and singing songs. On the basis of what children play during different age groups the following classification can be made.

Table 11.1: Types of Games played by Garo Children.

Age Groups	*Games played by girls*	*Games played by boys*
1-5 yrs	Playing with dolls, keeping house, play-acting, racing, skipping, hide and seek, blind man's buff	Racing, hide and seek, herding cows, blind man's buff, football
6-10 yrs	Chasing each other, blind man's buff, *haodudu, gut-gut,* keeping house	Playing with marbles, chasing each other, blind man's buff, *haodudu,* football
11-15 yrs	*Sue ginda*, tug of war, *haodudu, gut-gut, umphi kala meakol*	*Wapong sala, wapong sika, sue ginda, dang guti,* tug of war, *haodudu, meakol,* football
16+ yrs	*Daria banda,* tug of war, *haodudu, gut-gut, matcha kala, meakol*	*Wapong sala, wapong sika, dang guti, daria banda,* tug of war *haodudu, matcha kala, meakol,* football

The above listed games are all outdoor games. Even playing with dolls take place outdoors and not within the confines of the house. Garo children are never seen spending the day indoors, unless they are indisposed. They play outside the whole day or help elders in their daily activities. In fact, it is believed that a child who stays indoors is a lazy one, and laziness is a characteristic Garos abhorrence. Except infants, children of all age groups are assigned certain tasks around the house which could include sweeping the house and courtyard, fetching water, fetching stools and chairs for guests, cutting vegetables, laying the plates, washing utensils, feeding and washing the pets, help in carrying the field produce and other such tasks (Marak, 2010). But once the tasks are complete, or even in between the tasks, they do find time to play games. A few children with younger siblings are seen babysitting them or looking after them fulltime. Many carry their younger siblings along as they play with friends. Thus it is not an uncommon sight to see a boy or a girl of 5-10 years carrying a sibling of 1-2 years on their back and playing hide and seek with friends. Due to the number of tasks they have to complete, older children usually get time to play in the late afternoons, early evenings or during holiday seasons (for students), and lean seasons during the agricultural cycle.

Some of the traditional games played by children include *wapong sala, wapong sika, sue ginda, dang guti, meakol, matcha kala* and others. *wapong sala* and *wapong sika* are played by boys to test their strength. A piece of *wapong* (bamboo) is procured and this is caught by the two boys at the ends, and at the word "go" they start pushing or pulling each other. The one who can over-push or over-pull is the winner. This is played publicly during festive occasions. *Wapong sala* refers to pulling the bamboo, and *wapong sika* refers to pushing it. *Sue ginda* and *dang guti* are games that require skill, the former played with the help of *sue* (beans), and the latter with a stick and ball. Another game requiring skill is *umphi kala*, which is played by girls with a set of five stones; and *gut-gut* requiring the strength and skill to stand on one foot. *Matcha kala* resembles chess to some extent and is played by both boys and girls with certain markings on the ground. This is a mental game where one player plays with *matcha* (tigers) and another with *matchu* (cows), the aim being to eat up all the cows, or to strategically block the tigers' way. Another similar game is *meakol*, the intention behind being to acquire as many stones as possible. The game of *haodudu* is similar to the Indian game of kabaddi. However, the most popular game played by teenagers is *daria banda*, played by two parties in a pre-drawn court, the intention behind being to block the movement of the opposing team.

On the basis of the kind of games played whether of skill, strategy or chance, the following classification can be made which is shown in Table 11.2.

An overview of the games reveals the following: (1) Strategic games appear only after 6 years or so. This could be so since the children are not yet mature enough to understand strategy etc.; (2) As children become older, boys tend to play games more of physical strength and skill, while girls play games which need skill together with strategy and chance. This is echoed in their social behaviour too, as boys become more and more outgoing and begin to lay stress on physical strength, while girls become shy and prefer not to play games of strength.

Some popular games which cannot be clubbed into any of the above three are "playing with dolls", "keeping house" and "herding cows". Keeping house (*nok kala*) is a game played by a young girl alone with imaginary friends who help her cook, and keep house or drop in for tea, lunch and dinner; or with other young girls who may be sisters, cousins

Table 11.2: Classifying Garo Games.

Age Group	*Games played by girls*					*Games played by boys*		
	Physical skill	Strategy	Chance	Others	Physical skill	Strategy	Chance	Others
1-5 yrs	Racing Skipping		Hide & Seek, Blind Man's Buff	Playing with dolls, keeping house, play-acting	Racing Football		Hide & Seek, Blind Man's Buff	Herding Cows
6-10 yrs	Chasing each other		Hide & Seek, Blind		Chasing each other	Marbles		
	Haodudu, Gut-Gut		Buff		Haodudu, Football			
11-15 yrs	Tug of war *Gut-gut,*	*Umphi kala*	*Meakol*		*Dang guti* Tug of war, *Wapong sika, Wapong sala,* Football,		*Meakol*	
	Sue ginda Haodudu				*Sue ginda Haodudu*			
16 + yrs	*Daria Haodudu*	banda, Gut-gut			*Dang guti* Tug of war, *Wapong sika, Wapong sala*			
	Tug of war	*Matcha kala*	*Meakol*		Football,	*Haodudu*	*Meakol*	

or neighbours. In this game, young girls usually imitate their mothers and "make" tea, lunch and dinner. Each girl would have her own demarcated area as her "house" and would visit each other and offer "food". Boys are usually not a part of this game. If one is, then he would be only a guest and hence offered food and drinks. He could also be sent off to the "markets" to buy food or to the "shifting fields" to collect firewood or rice, etc.

On the other hand, herding cows (*matchu saria*) is a game played by young boys in which they take turns to act as cowherd while all the other boys act as cows that are taken out to graze. Some use strings to tether the "cows" to trees, or use a stick to move the "cows" along to the grazing fields. At times there could be a "tiger" lying in wait to pounce on the "cows", and this would be followed by frenzied running and jumping either to "kill" the "cows" or the "tiger".

As children grow older physical skill and strategy become more important. When younger they played chance games and others which by anthropological definition do not fall under the category of "games". Secondly, a clear cut gendered distinction can be seen not only in the types of games played, but also in the segregated manner of playing the games. For instance, girls will play racing among themselves, and boys among themselves. Thus, physical contact between the two becomes less and less as they grow older.

Games and Societal Behaviour

Children learn games through imitation. They usually imitate older siblings, and very rarely are they taught the rules of the game. It is merely by imitation and experience alone that they learn different games, both traditional and otherwise, which they play. Many children, interestingly, are seen to add some new dimension of their own through imitation. Three decades ago, in a game involving "keeping house", the utensils used were coconut shells, leaves, discarded covers of bottles and tins. A decade back, young girls were playing with the same items in addition to plastic utensils sold in the markets.

Geronima[1] said, "My eldest daughter Geroni saw colourful plastic utensils in the neighbour's house. She demanded that we buy her the same. Her father had to go to the Boko market 7 kms away only to buy the set for 30 rupees". Geronima had two more children since, and the third child is named Zida, aged 4 years. "Zida", she continued, "plays 'keeping house' the whole day. We watch her and we laugh at what she says"! An observation of Zida's play with her friend Doris was rather revealing.

> *Doris: Is anyone home?*
> *Zida: Aiao! You have come! Please come in! I was just talking*

about you to my husband yesterday!
Doris: What are you cooking?

Zida: There is nothing in the house today! I have sent my husband to buy pork from the market. Please eat and go. Let me make some tea for you, with tabulchu (tapioca) which I dug out yesterday. Oh, you should have seen the tabulchu this year! It's so bad! I was thinking of selling it in the market but now what shall I wear for Christmas?

This conversation continued with frenzied talking and "cooking" for her friend. In the afternoon Geronima's youngest aunt paid a visit bringing along her youngest son of the same age as Zida. By relation the young boy was Zida's uncle (*mama*). This young boy was asked by the elders to go see what Zida was doing behind the granary. When Zida saw him, she again had a very interesting play-acting [As soon as she saw him she ran to meet her grandmother and ate the biscuits which was offered]. However, after the biscuits were consumed, she went back to her game of 'keeping house'.

Zida: Do come in, mama! How are you? I was just talking about you to my friend.
When her mama did not reply, she continued: There is nothing in the house today. Please sit. Sit. Let me make tea for you.
Then she started 'cooking' and as she was cooking she suddenly remembered something and called out to her friend Doris.
Zida to Doris: Let us slaughter a rooster (do'o bipa). *Go and find a big rooster! Let us slaughter a big rooster for mama!*

An observation of this game revealed how a young girl imitated not only the activities of the mother but also carried on a conversation on similar lines. A maternal uncle plays a very important role in a Garo society and, therefore, assumes the highest status in a family. Thus whenever a *mama* (maternal uncle) from a faraway place, visits, he is usually given the "best" available food thus showing respect. Usually the biggest rooster or the biggest pig is slaughtered and nearest kin members living in the village is invited to a feast. In the village of Gohalkona, besides paddy, many other vegetables and root crops are grown. *Tabulchu* (tapioca) is a popular root crop which is considered a traditional crop. Zida's mother, in the winter's just after harvest, sold tapioca, potatoes and yams in the weekly market (which sits on Thursdays) in order to buy Christmas clothes for her three daughters.

From the study of games it is seen that some are gendered. For instance, keeping house, playing with dolls, *gut-gut* and *umphi kala* are girls' games, while *wapong sika*, *wapong sala*, *dang guti*, and football are boys' games. In the recent past a few girls are also seen taking part in football and *dang guti*, but *wapong sika* and *wapong sala* are traditional games played by boys and men alone to test their strength. Girls do not allow boys to play keeping house with them, and if they do, the latter only act as guests who have dropped in, or are send on errands to the "shop" to buy "eatables". Boys too do not allow girls to play herding cows with them, and if some girls want to, then they are ridiculed and chased away.

Some games such as *daria banda* are, however, played together by both boys and girls. An observation of such a game showed that it was not free from social undercurrents. A young boy of 14 years was guarding his team's court so that none of the opposing party passes by, when a girl from the opposing team sailed through without any hindrance from the boy. His team mates ridiculed him calling him an "idiot", but nevertheless, laughed at the whole incident. On enquiry it was found that the boy and girl belonged to clans which were preferred in marriage and, therefore, this led to a peculiar situation. Garos strictly follow clan exogamy, with some categories being preferred. For instance, cross-cousin marriage is the social norm especially the MBD (mother's brother's daughter) type of marriage. In this occasion, the young boy belonged to the same clan as the girl's father, making this a case of classificatory MBD. This being the state of affairs, even the slightest physical contact was avoided by both the children since it could lead to further embarrassment and ridicule.

In terms of movement of children while playing games, it is seen to be much restricted for girls. They are to stay in or near the house. Upto 6 years or so, girls are made to stay within 100 metres of their homestead, while boys of that age freely move around to the neighbours' houses, etc. When a girl reaches her teens, she gets the liberty to play in the neighbourhood, culminating towards playing in the village field or near the school house when she is 16 years or more. On the other hand, when a boy is in his teens he is seen moving to different areas of the village, often visiting neighbouring villages for football tournaments when he reaches 16 years or more. Thus the radius of movement is much wider for boys than the girls.

When children are below 6 years, parents and older siblings usually keep an eye on them. When a boy is seen playing with girls he is usually rebuked, "Go and play with your friends", "What you are doing"?, "You are behaving like a girl"! At times they would discuss the child within ear shot and mention how he is "just like a girl". Similarly, girls wanting to play with boys are rebuked by saying how she is "just like a boy". Shaming a child is one of many ways in which Garos try to socialize a child in the "correct" behaviour (Marak, 2006). Thus being ridiculed constantly forces an aberrant child to start playing the "correct" girl games or boy games. Another orientation that takes place is how to behave correctly towards kin members who are friends. A boy or girl might have an aunt or uncle of the same age-group and thus be play mates. But if the aunt or uncle, in the excitement of the game is found to be treated "derogatively", the children are rebuked publicly, and at times physically punished.

Tobias, a 24 years old young man, narrated how he was thrashed by his father when he had tethered his maternal uncle Bijon (who was acting as a "cow") to a tree. When he did it the first time he was scolded and asked not to repeat, but when he was caught repeating, he was beaten with a stick. Tobias passes off the childhood incident as something shameful and says, "I did not know the importance of the *mama* (maternal uncle) then, for I was just a child. Now of course, I would never do that to *mama* Bijon, and if I even think of doing it *mama* Bijon will thrash me"!

Games which do not follow general rules but are rather created by the children themselves are also found plenty in the village. In fact, an important play engaged by young children is play-acting. These are imitations of adult behaviour, whether incorporated in keeping house, playing with dolls, or herding cows. One interesting play-acting I witnessed was when a young girl of 5 years placed all her dolls in a row along with her toddler brother. She took on the role of her kindergarten teacher, and was teaching them poems. Some non-traditional indoor games like ludo, snakes and ladders, carom, etc., are also played, however, the recent craze of computer games in cities is yet to reach the village under study.

Conclusion

In many communities we find that the child passes through a period of almost complete detachment from home, running around, playing about, and engaging in early activities with his playmates and contemporaries who become most important to them. In such activities it is seen that children learn how to behave too.

A study of games played by Garo children thus reveals interesting facets of Garo society. Garo children start off by playing games of physical skill, and later move to those of strategy, skill and chance. This seems to be in tune with their mental and physical development. It is also seen that the radius of movement for girls is restricted even while playing games. It widens to some extent when they grow older. On the other hand for boys right from their childhood the radius of movement is much wider often leading to outside the village.

Through these games the social behaviour of children is monitored by the elders indirectly, and by peer groups directly. For instance when girls play keeping house elders would encourage them playing along and saying "It's very tasty", "Wont you offer me tea"?, "Where is the meat"? etc. If a boy is seen playing with the girls he is subtly rebuked and told to play with his friends and not with the girls, thus guiding him into realising that it is not "correct" behaviour for a boy to keep house. Contrastingly, it was "correct" behaviour for a boy to graze cows.

The status given to matrilineal kin is upheld while playing games by children too. Thus when children of the same age group play together, they could be related not only as siblings or cousins but also as uncles and aunts. In such cases through repeated admonishments by elders, if required, the maternal uncle (and aunt) is not only not called by name but also not made fun of. Peer pressure also to a large extent regulates their sexual behaviour too.

Like children everywhere, Garo children love to imitate their adults. Thus, at an early age girls and boys are "keeping house" and "herding cows" [after Turnbull (1961: 129)] who studied Mbuti Pygmy children). And one day they find that the games they have been playing are not games any longer, but the real thing for they have become adults!!

NOTE

1. The Garos consider it improper to call married men and women by their name. As a result they are called by the name of their first child, with the suffix "*pa*" for father and "*ma*" for mother. If they have a grand-son, or a grand-daughter, then they are referred and addressed as so-and-so's grand-father or grand-mother. A couple having no surviving children will be called *memangpa* and *memangma*

(*memang* = ghost). In case of barrenness of a woman, the couple will be known and called as the uncle or aunt of so and so. In this and in several ways, they try to avoid calling them by their given names. It is only on rare occasions that they are addressed or referred to by names. It is always considered impolite to call elders by their names.

REFERENCES

Daniel, Z.T. 1892. "Kansu: A Sioux Game," *American Anthropologist*, 5: 215-16.

Dorsey, J.O. 1891. "Games of Teton Dakota Children", *American Anthropologist*, 4: 329-46.

Hodge, F.W. 1890. "A Zuni Footrace", *American Anthropologist*, 3: 227-31.

Loizos, C. 1969. "Play Behaviour in Higher Primates: A Review", (pp. 176-218) *In:* Morris, D. (ed.), *Primate Ethology*. Garden City, NY: Doubleday.

Majumdar, D.N. 1980. *A Study of Culture Change in Two Garo Villages of Meghalaya.* Guwahati: Gauhati University Press.

Malinowski, B. 1960. *A Scientific Study of Culture*. New York: Oxford Univ. Press.

Marak, Q. 2006. "Discipline in Child Rearing Process: A Case Study of the Garos of Assam", (pp. 295-304) *In:* A. K. Haldar and P.K. Bhowmick (eds.), *Societies and Culture in India, Vol. I*. Kolkata: RNB.

____. 2010. "Sex Typing of Children's Tasks: A Study among the Garos of Assam", *The Oriental Anthropologist*, 10 (2): 301-10.

____. 2012. "Are Daughters Preferred in a Matrilineal Society? A Case of the Garos of Assam", *The Anthropologist*, 14 (1): 49-56.

Mead, G.H. 1934. *Mind, Self, and Society: From the Viewpoint of a Social Behaviorist*. Chicago: University of Chicago Press.

Medhi, B.K. and Q. Marak. 2001. "Child Rearing Practices among the Plains Dwelling Garos of Goalpara District, Assam", *Man and Life*, 27 (3 & 4): 213-22.

Roberts, J.M., M.J. Arth and R.R. Bush. 1959. "Games in Culture," *American Anthropologist*, 61: 597-605.

Sangma, M.S. 1981. *History and Culture of the Garos*. New Delhi: Books Today.

Schwartzman, H.B. 1976. "The Anthropological Study of Children's Play", *Annual Review of Anthropology*, 5: 289-328.

Stevenson, M.C. 1903. "Zuni Games", *American Anthropologist*, 5: 468-97.

Turnbull, C. 1961. *The Forest People*. New York: Simon & Schuste.

Tylor, E.B. 1879. "On the Game of Patolii in Ancient Mexico and its Probable Asiatic Origin", *Journal of the Royal Anthropological Institute*, 8: 116-29.

TWELVE

LEISURE TIME ACTIVITIES OF TRIBAL CHILDREN IN A SLUM SETTING

NIBEDITA NATH

Introduction

Leisure refers to the time when one is absolutely free from routine, systematic, gainful and purposeful work "Leisure is the time during which somebody has no obligations or work responsibilities and, therefore, is free to engage in enjoyable activities" (Microsoft Encarta Reference Library, 2005). Leisure should be distinguished from free time. Free time includes leisure as well as other activities that take place outside the scope of gainful employment.

To social scientists, leisure is essentially "time spent not in paid work" (Kleemeier, 1961). Bogardus (1960) says that "The develop-ment of increased leisure time does not necessarily give people more time for social problems or social control. People everywhere seem to have a longing for freedom from the struggle for subsistence, for time, resources and opportunities to enjoy". The object of leisure was "the pursuit of excellence, unrelated to the necessity of earning one's living" (Bhattacharya, 2003: 70). Dressler and Willis (1969) rightly points out that "possession of leisure was and is a marker for the distinction in social class, separating the elite from the non-elite". Roberts (1970) writes that "the population, time and money create leisure interests on an unprecedented scale".

Bose (1957) in his study found that "urbanization urges people to take upon themselves the responsibility of providing entertainment, the chief form of leisure. This personalized leisure then is moulded according to personal preferences". On the other hand Roy Burman (1957) has pointed out that "leisure is always personal, both in industrial and pre-industrial societies, though it is society that makes available leisure to individuals or groups of individuals in significant forms".

Leisure and Childhood

Leisure and childhood are inseparable. Not recognized by law, but of paramount importance, is the child's right to a happy childhood. Childhood is the golden phase of life. It should pass amidst an environment of joy and happiness so that the child can prepare himself to face the upcoming adult life which is full of problems and complications. Leisure must be understood as children's own time and space when they can do what they want, in the way they want. This time should not be misappropriated by education or work. Leisure is a time for children for games and sports or artistic or literary activities that gives children pleasure and helps to come out of physical and mental pressure. Leisure is not only recuperative but also productive. For children, leisure activities are learning experiences, particularly those which are interactive and participative. Leisure and recreation play an important role in the well-being of the children.

In this materialistic world, the parents are becoming quite ambitious. They have high expectations from the parents in terms of educational achievement and co-curricular activities. They hardly give importance to play and recreation of the children. Therefore, the children have become hard pressed and they hardly find sufficient leisure time. As they grow up their leisure time decreases. Leisure time activities are replaced by academic activities and curricular activities. Further due to modernisation and globalisation the forms and places of spending leisure time have changed.

The general conception of childhood as a period free from responsibility, conflict and full of fluttery, play, leisure and opportunity is quite unrealistic in the context of slum children. It is because they are the children who live amid economic stringency, social insecurity, psychological stresses and tensions, environmental pollutions and cultural fission. Childhood in slum is characterized by hard work, absence of leisure and lack of any opportunity. Countless children in slum settings advance almost directly from infancy into adulthood, and if they ever experience childhood, it is only a fleeting stage (Behera and Trawick,

2005: 5). Delimitation of childhood has occurred due to several reasons. The hard realities of worst kind of life are experienced by the slum children at a very early age during childhood. The childhood of slum children can be referred to as 'ruined childhood' and the worst ages of their life in contrast to the common designation of childhood as best phase of man's life filled with play, leisure and recreation. Against this background here we make an attempt to take a stock of the leisure time activities of the tribal children in a slum setting.

Objectives of the Study

The objectives of the present study are:

1. To find out the leisure time activities of the migrated tribal children in a slum setting.
2. To explore the gender differences in the leisure time activities of boys and girls.
3. To analyse the impact of poverty on the choice of play and leisure time activities of children in a slum setting.

Significance of the Study

In a typical anthropological mind-set "tribal" refers to the people who live in remote areas. However, in recent times tribal population in cities is increasing gradually due to large scale immigration in search of livelihood in the cities. So far there have been very few systematic and holistic attempts to study the tribal in the urban setting. Thus, the study is significant from the anthropological point of view as it deals with tribal in urban setting.

Methodology

The study was conducted in a slum Dhuturapara of Sambalpur city in western Orissa. Initially census survey was done covering all the households of the sample slum Dhuturapara. All the migrated tribal households (Munda[1], Kondh[2], Gond[3], and Oram[4]) were selected as sample households. Children in the age group of 2-18 were selected as samples for the study. Data were collected through observation, interview, free listing and group discussion methods. The sample slum Dhuturapara coming under Ward No. 7 is the largest and oldest slum in the city. It is located close to the National Highway No. 42. Some of the basic features of our sample slum are presented below:

- Over congestion leading to lack of proper ventilation.
- Chronic poverty.
- Malnutrition and high rate of morbidity.
- Low level of education of the children and their parents.
- Insanitary and unsatisfactory living conditions.
- Lack of basic civil amenities such as inadequate and unprotected water supply, absence of underground sewage, drainage, electricity, concrete lanes and public toilets.
- Engagement of the people in the lowly-paid jobs in the informal sector.
- Increasing intensity of drug addiction, child labour, indebtedness, juvenile delinquency, unemployment, social tensions, social disturbances, etc.

Results

Play Activities (Games and Sports) of the Sample Children

Due to resource constraint, the sample children are deprived of modern means of leisure and recreation. However, they have their own ways and means for merry-making and rejoicing. Play is a part of life and a pastime of certain age group and specific categories of the sample children.

Manhas *et al.* (2003: 393) write that "play is the royal road to childhood and is an integral part of the children's lives. It is the natural unfolding of the germinal leaves of childhood. It is a self-chosen activity that is undertaken for its own sake without external force or compulsion". Play is helpful in the overall development of the children and facilitates their cognitive development (Piaget, 1962). "Children have a natural tendency to play. Irrespective of whether children have space, material and other children to play with, play is a part of their daily life. They convert almost anything into a play material or play activity. Under all circumstances, children create play spaces those are safe, inexpensive and yet with scope for innovation and fun, fostering the spirit of playfulness during childhood" (Oke *et al.,* 1999).

Generally, the pre-school children and children of the lower and upper primary school-going age of both the sexes spend most of their leisure time by playing different types of game. Besides the different kinds of game and sports that have a specific nomenclature, children are observed to engage in a variety of other activities, which do not possess any recognition or designation. These include mud play, water play, play with garbage, etc., of the pre-school children. There is insufficient space for children to play in a slum setting.

A large variety of games and sports are popular among Munda boys and girls. Roy (1968: 272-273) has roughly divided all games[5] played by the Munda into three classes, namely (i) Athletic sports; (ii) Popular juvenile pastimes; and (iii) Dramatic games. The indigenous athletic games include *phodi* and *khati* and the sports include *gobar-hot-ko-khel*, *hengahal*, and the *hardang*. Juvenile games include the popular pastimes of the Munda cowherds and other lads, viz., *chhur*, *til-guti*, *kouri-inu*, *dundu-khel*, *bhoura-inu*, *uku-inu*, *hunt the slipp*er and *marbles knuckle-bones*. Dramatic games include the most interesting class of *Mundari* games. They are meant to combine amusement with instruction, and are generally played in the evening. *Kantara-kantara* is a typical of this category of game (*ibid.*). The other dramatic games are *didi-inu* and *tuyu oro sim inu*.

Majority of the games mentioned above are not played by the sample Munda children in the slum setting. Some of the sports and games cited above have totally disappeared. The reasons behind this are change in habitation, culture, economy, lack of large open space and switching over to other non-traditional games under the influence of neighbouring culture. Though there has been a change in types of game and sports, the inclination of the Munda children for games and sports has remained unchanged. Roy (1968: 271) rightly states that "conversion to Christianity does not impair the Munda's love of sports. Under the excellent guidance of European Missionaries, converted Munda boys have formed excellent hockey teams and further developing their other national games and sports". Some sample boys and girls have joined some sport club and a few of them have represented the State and own prizes in athletic, kabadi, football, etc.

An attempt is made to provide an account of the nature and type of play, the sample children are engaged in. Some of the common games normally played by the sample children are: *puchi*, *bichhu*, *kit kit*, *gengti*, *kachi-kudi*, *daudan*, *sabundes*, *ball khel*, *bati khel*, *gilli-danda*, *restif*, *nadi ki pahad*, *kabadi*, *bis amrut*, *rang rang kiska rang*, *current pass*, *tala chabi*, *cup plate*, *chhada chain*, *patar patar kiska patar*, *bagh chhel*, skipping, chess, ludo, carom, football, cricket, card, etc. Besides all the above games, a traditional game restiff, known as *uku-inu*, in earlier times, is played even today by the Munda children.

Some games like *kit kit*, *bis amrut*, skipping, marble, football, cricket, etc. are also played by the school-going children either in recess or in game period. The pre-school children and children of LP and UP school age usually play different types of game in the streets and open spaces within or close to the slums. Games like chess, ludo, carom, football, cricket, etc. are mostly played by the adolescent boys. Outdoor games, like football and cricket are played beyond school hours in nearby college ground, police ground, or open space close to the slums. Indoor games such as chess, carom, card, ludo, etc. are played in clubs, verandahs, open spaces, or even on ground near betel shops within the slums and others are played in streets or small open spaces within the slums.

Decision regarding playing a particular game is made according to the number of children available to play, particular time of day and the number of hours in their hand to play. Sometimes call from the parents or the requirement to perform a particular household job at a specific time forces a child to leave the game half way through. Hence, sometimes a game ends without any result.

Table 12.1: Gender-specific Play Activities of Slum Children.

Sl. No.	*Games of Players*		
	Games played only by girls	*Games played only by boys*	*Games played only by boys and girls*
1.	Puchi	Daudan	Restiff
2.	Gengti	Sabun-des	Nadi ki pahad
3.	Bichhu	Ball khel	Kabaddi
4.	Kachi-kudi	Bati khel	Bis amrut
5.	Kit kit	Gilli-danda	Rang rang kiska rang

Games and Sporting Activities of the Munda Christian Children during Festive Occasions

The Munda Christians of Dhuturapara conduct sports meet and organize various sports and games for children and adults in auspicious occasions like Christmas, New Year, etc. These sports meet plays an important role in spreading the fragrance of joy and happiness particularly among sample children of Christian background. Games like running race, potato spoon, thread and needle, *puchi*, chocolate eating, musical chair, bucket-ball, pot breaking, fancy dress, *gadu paen* (balancing pottery filled with water), skipping, lighting candles, etc., are organized by the community for different age and sex groups.

The boys take part in chocolate race, running, bucket-ball and lightening the candle, etc. whereas the girls take part in varieties of games such as pot breaking, thread and needle, musical chair, skipping, *gadu paen*, *puchi*, etc. All the children are divided into three groups on the basis of their age. The first group consists of children up to the age of eight, the second group is formed by children between nine and fifteen years of age and the third group consists of those who are above fifteen years of age.

Chocolate eating is organized for children below nine years old. Running race is done separately for different age groups. Both the boys and girls up to eight/nine years of age jointly participate in running and chocolate race. Running race, potato race, thread and needle, skipping and fancy dress competition are organized for the sample girls up to fifteen years of age. Girls above fifteen years of age participate in lighting candle, *gadu paen*, pot breaking and musical chair. Bucket-ball and lighting candle competition is organized for boys above fifteen years of age.

The sample children are not economically sound and, therefore, do not possess any formal/commercial play materials. When children of the affluent class in the city play with sophisticated toys; slum children manage with empty bottles and scraps of paper, etc. These children move out of home, spend time on the street with sands, scraps, marbles, etc. In spite of harsh economic conditions and lack of sophisticated play materials, the slum children exhibit remarkable ability to make

Table 12.2: Play Activity of Children of Different Age Group.

Sl. No.	*Sports*	*Boys*	*Girls*	*Age Group*		
				Up to 8/9 years	*9/10 years to 15 years*	*Above 15 years*
1.	Chocolate Race	□	□	□		
2.	Running	□	□	□	□	
3.	Puchi		□	□		

(*Contd.*)

Table 12.2: (*Contd.*)

Sl. No.	*Sports*	*Boys*	*Girls*	*Age Group*		
				Up to 8/9 years	*9/10 years to 15 years*	*Above 15 years*
4.	Potato race		□		□	
5.	Thread Needle		□		□	
6.	Skipping		□		□	
7.	Fancy Dress		□		□	
8.	Pot Breaking		□			□
9.	*Gadu Paen*		□			□
10.	Musical Chair		□			□
11.	Lightening Candle	□	□			□
12.	Bucket and Ball	□				

improvisation of whatever little is available in their environment. The environment and surrounding plays a vital role in the play activities of the sample children. They use the pebbles, marbles, broken earthen pot, long stick, small piece of wood, mud, water, bottles, bottle caps, plastic spoons, syringes, polythene bags, wrappers, cartons, pieces of bricks, stones, as play materials and make their own rules to start up a game. In some cases children make use of natural objects in their original form itself. While in other cases, the children are found modifying the natural properties or objects to use them as play materials, viz., children make utensils out of mud. Sometimes they play certain games which involve no play material. Despite limited space and play materials, play is part and parcel of sample children's daily life. It is so indispensable part of their lives that they try to convert any activity into play activity and any material into play material.

Play with certain nasty things causes some diseases among the pre-school children. Certain types of game invented in modern days that are

Table 12.3: Taxonomy of Play Materials Used by Children.

Sl. No.	*Play/Games/Sports*	*Materials Used*
1.	Puchi	Nothing
2.	Gengti	Small stones/pebbles
3.	Bichhu	Chalk/charcoal and broken clay tile and earthen pot
4.	Kachi-kudi	Mud, water, plastic spoon, bottle and caps
5.	Kit kit	Chalk/charcoal and broken clay tile
6.	Daudan	Nothing
7.	Sabun-des	Plastic ball, broken clay tiles and earthen pot
8.	Ball khel	Ball
9.	Bati khel	Marbles
10.	Gilli-danda	Small piece of wood and long stick
11.	Restiff	Nothing
12.	Nadi ki pahad	Nothing
13.	Kabaddi	Nothing
14.	Bis amrut	Nothing
15.	Rang Rang kiska rang	Nothing

available in markets entertain children and at the same time enhances brain development. But the poor sample children have no knowledge or access to such games due to cost factor.

Discussion

The small children below eight years of age get more leisure than the grown-up children. Children up to the age of five/six have nothing to do, but have a good time all day long. They are free to play (Mead, 1928: 121). Prior to that the child is closely confined and after age seven, the child becomes an integral part member of the family working unit (Lancy, 1996: 110). The small children get more leisure than older children. Most of the time, the older children remain busy in some work or the other either inside or outside the house. Thus the older children in slums get relatively less leisure time compared to the children of well off urbanites. Unlike the leisured[6] children of the affluent societies, the children in slum have to work for a living.

For the pre-school children, most of the time in a day is leisure time. The sample school-going children get leisure only during some scheduled time like recess and game periods in school and a few hours after returning from school. However, during holidays they get some extra time for leisure and recreation. Unlike the non-school-going or dropout children, evening is no time of relaxation for the school-going children. Many of them symbolically sit for reading during evening hours without taking their study seriously. For the non-school-going children between nine and eighteen years of age, the left out time beyond the working hours is the leisure time. Wage earning children get enough leisure time during the off season, when they do not get enough scope for earning wage.

No doubt the school-going children get some time to play in the school during the recess and game period. But they do not get away from the work which they are expected to do back at home. School-going children, particularly girls, perform their part of work in house before going to school and again after returning from school. So after completing the work, they neither have the stamina nor time to play. They rather prefer to gossip, sleep, and watch TV during the little leisure time they get. While narrating her everyday experience, a girl reading in class 6th told:

> "*In holidays I usually get time to play. The day I go to school, morning time is spent for attending household work and study. Returning from the school, I do the routine work, viz., bringing water, washing utensils and the like. Though I get a little left out time in the evening for playing, yet I prefer to sleep, gossip or watch TV as I feel tired after completing the household work*".

Play is essential for all children, be it a girl or a boy. Dunn and Herming (1992) showed the influence of gender in guiding the play preferences of young children. They reported that boys display more functional/solitary functional play (fantasy play and originally) than girls, who exhibit more constructive play (playing with concrete objects). Manhas *et al.* (2003: 403) found "Gender differences in the type of play activities children engaged in and even in their play behaviour. Girls were found to be more creative whereas, the boys tend to be outgoing in their play behaviour. The girls engaged in more pretend and symbolic play, whereas the boys engaged more in associative type of play". There is a strong gender differentiation in both the choice of play materials as well as the games. Manhas *et al.* (2003: 401) write that "the boys played games that involved more of physical activities and also their games required more use of space. They appeared to be more outgoing, physically active and exhibited more associative play. Whereas the girl played games, which required them to usually sit at one place and also, their games were based on themes related to household chores". Similar observations were also made in the sample areas. The girls from the beginning are encouraged to play the indoor games and the games which do not involve much running and jumping whereas boys are encouraged to play the outdoor games and the kinds of games which require much physical movement and labour. The findings of the study are somewhat similar to that of Oke (1993) who indicate that "the play behaviour of the girls is of delimiting their play spaces". By and large the adolescent girls are forbidden to play, with exception of those few who have achieved excellence in the field of games and sports and go to stadium for practice. One of the school-going girls said:

> "*I was playing a lot till 5th class. The playing time diminished a lot when I moved to 6th and 7th class. After that I am not playing at all*".

Supplementing to this yet another girl said:

> "*When we were small we were always playing. When we grew up, our workload increased manifold. That is the typical case for all girls in our* para. *Now whenever we get little leisure time, we visit neighbour's houses or gossip*".

The older children do not find enough leisure time to play. They are engaged in different work at an age when they are supposed to enjoy their childhood. The adolescent girls also like to chit chat within their peer groups. A dropout adolescent girl said:

> "*We gossip on a variety of things such as who visited where, love affairs, who quarrelled with whom and for what and a lot of other things like that*".

They are unable to gossip on a scheduled time of the day. Each adolescent girl has her own range of household and extra-household activities. The older girls find very less time to play compared to boys. Because they are subject to the restriction of time and space which the boys usually do not face. It inevitably hampers not only their physical but also their social and mental development.

Manhas *et al.* (2003: 394) write that "adults are observed to perform three kinds of roles: partial restrictive (partially telling children what to do); non-restrictive (not cautioning and protecting them from harm); non-participative (not involving in children's play activities)". Parents normally do not show any interest in the play activities of their children. Nor do they provide the children with the required play materials. Children are by and large independent in their choice and selection of play activities, play area, materials and play mates irrespective of religion. Most of the adults remain busy in household chores and hence do not play a very active role in play activities of their children.They impose a number of restrictions with regard to playing of adolescent girl children and the pre-school children. Interference of older siblings and parents in the play activities of the younger children (mainly during a dispute over any material or space) is a common thing. Parents instead of encouraging the children to spend leisure time in play or other enjoyable activities insist them (particularly adolescents) to attend one or the other household and extra-household work. Once a mother was seen telling her thirteen years old daughter:

> "*Things are lying scattered all over the house. It is expected of you to keep things at proper places as you are now a grown-up girl. You are no more a kid to play around. When will you behave like a mature girl?*"

Due to resource constraint, the sample children are deprived of modern means of leisure and recreation. However, they have their own ways and means for merry-making and rejoicing. There is insufficient space for children to play in a slum setting.

Play is a part of life and a pastime of certain age group and specific categories of the sample children. Generally, the pre-school children and children of the lower and upper primary school-going age of both the sexes spend most of their leisure time by playing different types of game. Besides the different kinds of game and sports that have a specific nomenclature, children are observed to engage in variety of other activities, which do not possess any recognition or designation. These include mud play, water play, play with garbage, etc., of the pre-school children. Adolescent girls generally spend major part of their leisure time by gossiping and watching Television. Adolescent boys spend part of their leisure time by gossiping, playing cards and watching television.

Relatively older boys assemble near the betel shops to chit-chat. They often discuss about their affairs with girls and recent sensational incidents of the slums. The discussions also at time centre on new films and stars. Quite often they organize video shows by paying Rs. 2/- for watching Hindi movies during the evening hours. Rarely do they go to the cinema hall, as tickets are quite expensive. Many young boys have completely forgotten their traditional songs, dance and music, which were integral part of Munda culture. Bose (1957) argues that "urbanization personalizes leisure and hence there is decay of the traditional modes of transmission of culture". Kaplan (1970) also analyses the institutional transformations that take place in the forms and meanings of leisure in urban context.

Concluding Remarks

Leisure should be an integral part of life of every child. Leisure leads to play or other activities which brings pleasure. It provides opportunity for recreation and enhances interaction with peer groups and thus promotes interpersonal relations which in turn help in personality development of the child. But family poverty of the sample children grabs their leisure time and deprives them from opportunities of recreation. The quantity of leisure time avail up by a child decreases when s/he becomes an integral part of the working unit of the family. Further the girls get less leisure time and few opportunities for recreation compared to the boys due to the stress of work on them. Mostly the school-going girls and wage-earning children of both the sex are deprived of adequate leisure and recreation facilities. Only the dropout non-wage-earning children get maximum leisure time. A casualty of the development process has been leisure for the child. Lack of access to appropriate means of recreation is a sad reality of the life of children living in slums.

NOTES

1. The Munda are dispersed over Bihar, Orissa, West Bengal, Madhya Pradesh and Tripura. The bulk of Munda population is found in the districts of Sundergarh, Sambalpur and Keonjhar. They are also found in Mayurbhanj, Dhenkanal, Cuttack, Phulbani, Bolangir, Kalahandi, Ganjam, Balasore and Koraput in comparatively smaller number. The tribe is sub-divided into two groups such as (1) Khangar Munda or Tamaria Munda or Pator Munda or Marang Munda, (2) Kompat Munda.
2. The Kondh are one of the largest scheduled tribe constituting 17.5 per cent of the total tribal population of Orissa. These people are found mainly in the central region of *Eastern Ghats* covering four hilly districts, viz. Rayagada, Phulbani, Baud and Kondhmal. The tribe has three main sub- tribes, viz. Kutia Kondh, Dongria Kondh, and Desia Kondh. The Kondh are well-known in the anthropological literature for their *meriah* (human) sacrifice. In recent times, man as a sacrificial object has been replaced by buffalo.
3. Gond are found chiefly in the rural areas of Keonjhar and Champua Sub-division. They speak Gondi, a dialect belonging to the Dravidian family. The Gond are immigrants from the central provinces and wear Brahminical thread. The Gond worship a number of deities of which Budhadeo, Jangadeo and Lingadeo are important.
4. Oram is one of the major tribes of Western Orissa. They are mostly concentrated in Sundargarh district. The tribe is divided into a large number of exogamous, totemic patrilineal clans.
5. *Phodi*—a kind of hockey played in the day-time in winter, *khati*—often played in summer noon, *chhur*—game of touch, *til-guti*—game of black gammon, *dundu-khel*—a variety of blindman's buff, *uku-inu*—game of hide-and-seek and hunt the slipper—European game introduced by Christian Missionary and *kantara-kantara*—jack fruit game, *didi-inu*—vulture play, and *tuyu oro sim inu*—game of the fox and hen (Roy, 1968: 272-273).
6. Those who have a lot of free time, especially as a result of having enough money not to have to work for a living.

REFERENCES

Bogardus, E.R. 1960. *The Development of Social Thought*. Bombay: Vakils.

Bose, N.K. 1957. "The Effect of Urbanization on Work and Leisure," *Man in India*, 37 (1).

Dressler, D. and N. M. Willis. 1969. *The Study of Human Interaction*. New York: Alfred A. Knoff.

Dunn, L.D. and S. Herming. 1992. "Play Pattern and Cognition," *Journal of Child Study*, 22: 34-35.

Kaplan, M. 1970. *Leisure Theory and Policy*. New York: John Wiley.

Kleemeier, R.W. 1961. *Again and Leisure: A Research Perspective into the Meaningful Use of Time*. New York: Oxford University Press.

Lancy, D.F. 1996. *Playing on the Mother Ground*. New York: Guilford Press.

Manhas, S.; A. Kaur; and R. Dhingra. 2003. "Play Activities among Gujar Children," *Man in India*, 83 (3&4): 393-405.

Mead, M. 1975. *Growing Up in New Guinea*. New York: William Morrow Company Inc.

Oke, M.; A. Khattar; P. Pant; T.S. Saraswati. 1999. "A Profile of Child Play in Urban India," *Childhood*, 6 (2): 207-220.

Oke, M. 1993. *Group Play Patterns of Children as a Potential for the Development of Management Skills*, Unpublished Ph.D. Thesis. University of Bombay: Mumbai, India.

Piaget, J. 1962. *Play, Dreams and Imitation in Childhood*. New York: Norton.

Roberts, K. 1970. *Leisure: The Social Structure of Modern Britain*. U.K: Longman.

Roy Burman, B.K. 1957. "Observations on the Effect of Urbanization on Work and Leisure," *Man in India*, 37 (2).

SECTION IV

YOUTH: LIFE STAGE, RULES OF MARRIAGE, IDENTITY AND RIGHTS

THIRTEEN

SANTAL YOUTH: Encountering Change *vis-à-vis* Life Stage and Modernity

KUMKUM BHATTACHARYA

Introduction

On June 1, 2012 the National Youth Policy 2012 unveiled the redefined youth to indicate those between 16 and 30 while the older document indicated those between 13 and 35. It has been stated that this new definition of youth reflects the United Nations and Commonwealth criteria that are 15-24 years and 15-29 years respectively. The earlier age group of 13-35 as formulated in 2003 as reported is fallacious (*HT,* June 1, 2012). From the perspective of psychobiology, youth or any life stage is not defined so definitely by age but rather by life capabilities and tasks. However, from this point of view, the standards arrived at from studies in generally mainstream population groups are problematic when applied universally across the human spectrum of diverse communities and lifestyles. Socialization, world view (perceived or viewed)[1], livelihood practices, relationship with environment, role expectations, role models and degree of isolation/ integration from or with mainstream communities are aspects that assume significance when we endeavour to understand life cycle of 'different' or 'niche' communities. Thus, though it may be possible to arrive at mutually agreed upon standards for any particular life stage that operates within known parameters of modernity and uniformity of lifestyles but to assume its universality will be fallacious as is considered when comparing the age-groups outlined in the youth documents of 2003 and 2012 necessitating the need of the latter document. Here we stress on the need for policy documents to be more in tune with various ground realities rather than being grounded in theoretical/academic understanding of social 'realities'.

Interestingly, the 2012 document has divided the youth into nine "target groups", viz., LGBT (lesbian, gay, bi-sexual and transgender); students, migrants, rural youth, tribal youth, those at risk (sex workers, drug users and victims of trafficking); youth in violent conflicts; school dropouts and youth living in institutional care (*ibid.*). Here too, it is not clear if there would be separate policies or at least the provision for achievable goals/interventions for each of the target groups according to their needs/vulnerabilities/capabilities. If we care to go a little deeper into the target group of tribal youth as an instance—the differences, sometimes glaring, become apparent say between a Khasi and Santal youths where the former may be Christian, educated and parents not practising traditional livelihood while the latter may be unlettered, somewhat isolated from mainstream society and the family observing the traditions and customs of the community to which it belongs (it may be remembered that the target group of tribes includes many diverse tribes). Likewise, there may be many common points between the rural (non-tribal, minorities, lower order caste categories) and tribal youth who live in remote villages and practise traditional livelihoods. Again, migrants as a category which include many sub-categories that have the possibility of being diverse, discrete or overlapping with other categories of target groups. It is not my intention to prolong this exercise in reasoning, neither do I decry such inclusive policies; I seek some care and caution of researchers who may premise their arguments on the sanctity of public documents and arrive at biased comparisons, e.g., of endowing, as an illustration, the Khasi youth with enterprise and describing the Santal youth as 'backward'!

Some Fundamental Issues

How do we 'see' people? Psychology trains us in seeing people as individuals and the Social Psychological approach adds the perspective of psycho social interactional model in understanding the behaviour of individuals – the emphasis being the interacting individual as the unit of study. However, on the ground we find that the interactional model can be of various types and of differing impact on the individual and often the actual interactional types are overlooked in analysis. Broadly, the types of interactional units (within the model) may be distinguished on the basis of the degree to which the sense of individuality and individual agency can operate or be activated and the nature of support the individual draws from these interactional units. Generally, the interactional units are as follows: individuals interacting with each other within the precincts of the society to which they belong; individuals forming groups and interacting within the framework of group goals, common interests and mutual attraction; groups interacting with other groups within the same society; groups coalescing to form larger structures that assume the dimension of society/community and last, communities interacting with each other across cultures or with other arcs of the same culture. The individual grows up and is socialized within these interactional units where each unit is an important link in life-cycle experiences.

It is clear that the individual is the focus of most discussions whether it is the development of personality in which much of our behaviour is rooted or in the progress from one life stage to another throughout which development of personality acts to integrate the idea of personhood within the framework of a person. Most theories of life cycle, and there are many[2], suggest that they fit description of development across the life span in individualistic, economically favoured societies as well as in those societies in which men and women are given the same options (Hoffman, Paris and Hall, 1994). The exception to this bias in some measure can be found in the Cultural contextual theories of Vygotsky (1932) and Bronfenbrenner (1989)[3] approach to understanding life-cycle development. The latter approach seems to suit the stage of life called youth or young adulthood albeit with some gaps that are to be filled. Thus, if we were to shift our attention to community-minded/oriented people who are not economically favoured or do not/cannot fit themselves in generally understood economic categories what are the available theories that would satisfactorily help us in understanding life-cycle development? We may keep the life span of people in mind while discussing the issue of the length of various life stages. The lengths are not always equal and neither is there consonance in the life tasks to be performed in particular life stages. In the last few decades we find a significant increase in longevity among the Indian population though we still lack in community-wise data. By and large it is observed that in the case of the Santals longevity may differ on the basis of their location, profession/livelihood, knowledge and clearly, access to medical services. Looking at other tribes, for example, the Jarawas – it has been established that the life span of the Jarawas rarely exceeds 45-50 years (Sarkar and Sahani, 2002: 140).

The same picture may be repeated in the case of some tribes who live in isolated conditions following traditional ways of life. The Santals cannot be compared to such isolated tribes but there are some common elements on which we can make some kind of interpolation regarding life span. Some of the factors that affect life span are nutrition, immunization, medical intervention and health awareness, on which counts, the Santals may be found falling behind national standards. Physically, the Santals look younger than their age for a fairly long time but very soon show the signs of ageing in their appearance even if not in their lifestyles. The Santals seem to be sexually active till long – it is not unusual to hear of older men finding new loves or establishing parallel families; the same is not always expected of older women who express their sexuality through singing of erotic songs, recounting of romantic stories and their love for incidences of dalliance. Indeed, romance is a source of fun and joy – *raska* – that seems to be the *raison d'ētre* for Santal life.

Thus from a life-cycle perspective, the period of late childhood, adolescence and youth[4] among the Santals seem to be telescoped into a shorter time span making a quicker transition to what we could consider as adulthood in mainstream communities. This aspect is discussed in the next section. Once again I remind the readers that our standards are drawn almost from urban communities and the risk of generalizing to all remains and we are to be cautious in drawing conclusions or relying entirely on umbrella-like policies.

Plurality[5] and cultural contact situation raise another issue demanding our attention – some sections of the communities referred above (Santals) are sometimes in greater contact through education, economy, culture with societies and communities that are often in the majority and are more individualistically driven. Under the circumstances of culture contact, these sections of the Santals appear to forge new identities and social responses with their community identity taking a back seat. These changes or transformations are rationalized as fulfilling interactional/transactional requirements. It is clear that these transformations/changes are stressful and challenging. The stresses and challenges can be understood as the conflict between 'rationalizing' and 'internalizing' social realities and circumstances within the organization of the self or personhood. It is argued that the youth is that vulnerable stage when such issues come to the forefront.

The stress on transitions in life cycles found in some theories could provide partial answers to the questions raised above – some transitions are experienced in the normal course of life while some transitions require a degree of capacity building and some transitions are unexpected and stressful requiring coping/adjusting mechanisms. In the process, there may be aberrations in behaviour.

The Santals: Life-cycle perspective

The Santals are a relatively homogeneous[6] tribe of eastern India; they are among the larger tribes of our country. According to Census (1991) report, the Santals are about 1.8 per cent of the population. Santals are found in the neighbouring countries like Bangladesh, Nepal and Bhutan (Andersen, P.B., 2002). The Santals have predominantly an oral tradition. Originally, it is believed, Santals were hunter-gatherers; for long they have been recognized by their neighbouring communities as proficient in clearing jungles and at present they are indifferent agriculturists. The Santals have been neighbours of other communities for centuries from whom they maintain both physical and cultural distance. They are known to be simple, honest, peace loving and happy-go-lucky in character, fond of their rice beer and ready to crack a joke. They are also regarded as slow and lethargic people, reluctant to accept new ideas and changes (Baski and Boro, 2012; Archer, 1974; and Bhattacharya, 1970). This is primarily an outsider's view; the Santal view of work does not conform to general ideas of work – work for the Santal is punctuated with leisure; doing as much as is necessary and possible within the context of the present rather than with any designs on the future, i.e., bound by schedule of time.[7]

In describing the growing up of a Santal, the developing years till the end of adolescence can be divided into three stages – the first five years of childhood are spent in the environs of the village around the home. They play various games, hunt small animals like frogs, rats, snakes, birds, fish while casually looking after their younger siblings. From the age of 6 onwards, boys and girls accompanying an older person are engaged in tending cattle during which time they hunt small animals that are roasted on small fires. This is a most enjoyable activity for both boys and girls giving them a sense of freedom. Santal parents often do not seek explanations of why their children are late in returning home or in enquiring if they ate anything; this is in some contrast with neighbouring communities who exercise more control over their children especially girls. The small girls are also expected to help their mothers in household duties; they also have the freedom to go to the forests with other women to collect natural fuel in the form of dry branches, leaves, cow dung, etc. It is from the older women that young girls learn the songs sung on different occasions and the stories that enrich Santal culture. They continue to go to the forests for fuel when they grow up when they can go with their compeers taking other younger girls with them – these are the economic activities in household contexts. Boys and girls or men and women do not go to the forests together for collecting fuel; men may go separately for hunting or gathering of medicinal plants; men do not generally collect dried leaves and branches for the home kitchens. Boys are encouraged to engage in economic activities at ages when many of the mainstream boys are being supported through school and preparing themselves for higher education.

The first romances spring up between boys and girls that are continued during days of festivity when there is relative freedom from adult censure or notice. Boys of 14-15 are inducted into the community rituals of worship in which girls do not play much role. Soon after, the boys and girls move into the stage when they are interested in starting their own families or at least finding their life partners. This is the traditional life and one which moves the young to take on community responsibilities and roles whereas their age peers in other communities are still 'growing up'. The transition from one stage to another is in a way telescoped. It is clear that the length of time required to pursue modern education or training for a profession is not really factored in the Santal way of life.

Therefore for a Santal to pursue the ways of the mainstream life and livelihood means making a choice between 'natural'/ traditional freedom and the relative 'bondage' to distant life goals that are viewed as somewhat 'alien' by his/her community members and even family. Why do the goals seem distant? One major reason is the time and skills/competencies needed to reach those goals and the dependence on family manifested in terms of, e.g., delayed employability. Also some of the other reasons involve the lack of necessary guidance over this long and unknown journey either at the community/family level or even at the 'nation-state' levels through policy and institutions. Learning to take advantage of state policy provisions is another kind of task helping in the passage through life cycle in the modern age.

It is not my purpose here to enter into a discussion related to the experience of the Santals with the modern education system – issues of medium of instruction, content of curriculum, quality of teaching, attitude of teachers; the infrastructure and linkages with institutions of higher learning;[8] nevertheless we can correctly surmise the enormity of the task for the Santals (and many other tribes and rural populations living in relative isolation and unexposed to opportunity) in traversing the mainstream life stages.

This brings the discussion to understanding the facets of how the world is seen (world view) as it has profound influence on the ways in which we conduct our lives. It has been explained (see note 1) that there are differences in world view when we compare literate and pre-literate societies – to the former the world is as viewed and to the latter, the world is as event (perceived). In the contemporary Indian situation pre-literate societies/communities would be difficult to locate and yet, the notion is still applicable in some degree – many tribes formally uneducated and of the oral tradition are yet exposed to and can use modern technology (mobiles, television sets, household gadgets etc.,) – thus leading to an in-between state. It will be interesting and insightful to explore if there have been changes in their world view and consequentially, on their lives.

Santals in a Variety of Settings

What are the characteristics of the Santal youth? The answer will depend on both demographic and cultural dimensions of the community as on psychological orientation of the individual. We have already seen that the age correspondence with particular life stage will not work with the Santals who are away from or unexposed to mainstream influences and are still following the traditional lifestyle. Traditionally, the Santal youth is most often a family person, if not already a father or mother; has a means of livelihood to support his family and is independent of his parents while the girl youth is starting her family and is in-charge of a household. The community usually recognizes relationships between young men and women without the rituals of formal marriage. Livelihoods do not show great variety and there is very little income disparity between them. Lives get constricted around limited dependencies.

The factors of demography, culture and individuality can be demonstrated among Christian Santals living in remote areas of the Santal Parganas who seem to have embraced Christianity and its rituals but lead their lives according to traditions. If we compare the Christian Santals of Dumka, the district capital of Santal Parganas, we see a marked change whereas with Christianity, young men (more than women) have embraced the modern way of life through education, training for a profession and have been successful in taking advantage of the policies (based on principles of positive discrimination and affirmative action) of the "nation-state". In such cases we see that the individual is psychologically prepared (aspirational) to traverse the path, the family is ready to support and the community provides the necessary cultural "broadness" (of vision) and the guidance/nurturance through modern education in the pursuit of modernity while the systems/institutions with their policies and the individual with merit meet each other half way! The youth in such a situation could easily be compared on more counts with the youth of mainstream society – albeit with some differences in cultural values and attitudes.

The issue related to physical isolation of communities is the fact that isolation is becoming increasingly limited and community spaces (physically and metaphorically) are getting constricted. We find that even niche communities are encroached upon. There is a press of 'urgent' modernity that cannot give time enough to tradition to either create the buffer to combat the changes or absorb the changes making them its (tradition) own through enculturation/acculturation[9]/reorientation. We see "urgent" modernity in the incursion of mass media, the virtual world into daily lives as well as the commodification of services and lifestyle as products that can be bought and sold; we also see the phenomenon in the blanket effect of westernization as well as the speed with which traditions are disappearing through loss of language, myths, legends and indigenous knowledge.

The individual's pace of change is not in sync with that of the community. There is bound to be a sense of alienation and discomfort – alienation from what is perceived as tradition and the discomfort that the bulwark of support is yet to be gained from modernity. In the case of the Santals the period of youth gets stretched while freedom gets curtailed; goals seem unattainable and unrealized needs arouse tension and disequilibrium.

Observing the Santals employed in large industries as they are in Jamshedpur in Jharkhand, Martin Orans (1965) has shown us the effects of push and pull of modernity and tradition in the shaping of responses. Even when parents seem to retain some of the community identity markers, their children are divested of them – they may not know the language; are not aware of their mythologies or interested in their traditions. However, they are forced to carry their community identity because of being a scheduled tribe. They face double unacceptability—from the mainstream as well as their community. It is during the period of youth that there is a stronger urge to redefine one's identity over and over again and to reflect and resolve some of the cultural issues. The ecological theory propounded by Bronfenbrenner explains the interplay between the individual and the larger systems satisfactorily.

These are the issues that not only need to be factored in the new youth policy document but supported by detailed studies conducted through the cross-sectional or longitudinal methods on samples (samples carefully chosen are to be homogeneous as far as possible; it is established that we cannot always assume homogeneity) of the Santal youth.

Discussion

Of the many theories explaining the life-cycle approach to the understanding of a life stage among some of the tribes, the ecological theory (Bronfenbrenner, 1989) and the theory of cultural relativism (Opler, 1971) seem the best suited and satisfying. Bronfenbrenner in his ecological theory proposes that development was a joint function of the person and all levels of the environment that was a system of four nested structures – Microsystem; Mesosystem; Exosystem and Macrosystem.

The latter theory proposes the idea that each culture or ethnic group is to be evaluated on the basis of its own values and norms of behaviour and not on the basis of those of another culture or ethnic group. The basic principle out of which cultural relativism emerges is a simple one: judgements are based on experience and experience is interpreted by each individual in terms of his or her own enculturation.[10]

To briefly recapitulate, government policies often do not cater as much as envisaged in their drafting stage because of assuming uniformity that is expected to transcend natural heterogeneity and with reference to the Santals we see that in the contemporary times we cannot even assume homogeneity that has for long been hallmarked as a community feature. Thus, policies need to be nuanced in their implementation.

The body of research in the area of life-cycle understanding of human development draws on western, urban metropolitan populations who share aspirations, awareness and access (to facilities and services) and needs while we are yet to build up material based on our diverse population who understandably are at various stages of development and possess differing world views. True, a large part of our youth would have more commonness than differences given the spread of modernity; yet there are large pockets in which the youth have scarcely been observed.

NOTES

1. It is posited that usually in the case of tribes with oral traditions world view is "world-as-viewed" rather than "world-as-event" (Ong, Walter, J., SJ, 1968, "World as viewed and World as event", accessed Wiley Online Library, 2009, *American*

Anthropologist, Vol. 71, Issue 4). The tribes live very much in the moment fulfilling their here and now obligations in some contrast to those who appear to lay some store by the idea that the present is the link between the past and the future and that they are interconnected consequentially.

2. Biological theories, maturational theories, ethological or evolutionary theories, psychodynamic theories (Freud, Erikson), learning theories (conditioning and cognitive social learning), cognitive theories (Piaget, Kohlberg's moral development, Selman's cognitive development theory of peer relation) and the cultural contextual theories are some of the major theories for the understanding of life cycle (*Developmental Psychology Today*, 6th edition, 1994, by Lois Hoffman, Scott Paris and Elizabeth Hall, USA, McGraw Hill). However, these theories have drawn their material from studies/research conducted on largely western urban populations with a metropolitan lifestyle from which it is difficult to generalize for the variety that makes up India.
3. Bronfenbrenner in his ecological theory proposes that development was a joint function of the person and all levels of the environment that was a system of four nested structures – Microsystem, Mesosystem, Exosystem and Macrosystem [U. Bronfenbrenner, 1989, *Ecological Systems Theory* in R. Vasta (ed.), *Six Theories of Child Development,* Greenwich, CT JAI Press]. This approach if applied to smaller communities may give us better understanding of the variations in development across cultures; also it is possible to identify the components of the four nested structures.
4. Starting from the neo natal stage the entire life-cycle is divided into age corresponding stages – infancy (early and late); childhood (early and late); adolescence (pre- and post-puberty); youth (also early adulthood); adulthood (middle and late) and old age. Each life stage has its corresponding tasks fulfilled/ achieved through physical, psychological and social-cultural resources (and these three classes of obstacles that may become significant in non-fulfilment of developmental goals). Transition from one stage to another implies a kind of mastery over previous tasks and the readiness to acquire new tasks. The tasks gain in complexity and increasingly become shaped and qualified by internalization of culture and society (for more details see Robert Kasterbaum, 1979).
5. Plurality is explained as many cultures living side by side in the same ecological niche, obviously contributing (variously) to the regional situation and using (differently) the resources of the regional situation. Fredrik Barth's (1959, Ethnic Groups and Boundaries, the Social Organization of Cultural Difference (ed.) (London, George Allen and Unwin, p.16) definition "...a society integrated economically under the control of a state system dominated by one of the groups but leaving large areas of cultural diversity in the religious and domestic sectors of activity". See also Furnivall, J.S. (1967, *Netherlands India: A Study of Plural Economy,* UK, Cambridge University Press).
6. Homogeneity among the Santals have been examined from the aspects of commonness of language, lifestyle, economy practised, rituals, festivals, traditional medicines, social structure and village organization; clan names; their situation *vis-à-vis* dominant society; however, since independence the nation-state society has exerted influence over citizenry and in response to this individuals among the Santals have per chance moved away from their traditional way of living.

Conversion into Christianity dating back to almost 150 years created a division by introducing the ideas of a 'better life' and this idea spread to many more Santals in the advent of industrialization in our country (*cf.* Orans, Martin, 1960). The homogeneity of the Santals is being qualified from this perspective.

7. Any task undertaken by the Santals is thought to have a certain inevitability or natural end not defined always by 'work-time' relationship. For details see Kumkum Bhattacharya, 2006, *Non-Western Traditions: Leisure in India* (pp. 75-92). In: Chris Rojek, Susan M. Shaw and A.J. Veal (eds.), *A Handbook of Leisure Studies*. Great Britain: Palgrave Macmillan.
8. Detailed study on these aspects has been conducted by Boro Baski, 2011 for his Ph.D. research – the findings clearly point to the challenges (levels of disadvantage) faced by Santal children in Primary Education System in West Bengal. From this study it is possible to interpolate to some degree the status of other tribes in other parts of our country.
9. Enculturation means being socialized through apprenticeship and daily life experiences and agents of socialization (M. Herskovits, 1948, *Man and His Works,* New York, Knopf). Acculturation implies learning culture through culture contact Siegal, B.J. (ed.) 1955 *Acculturation,* Stanford Anthrpological Series No. 2, California, Stanford University Press).
10. M.K. Opler, 1971 emphasized Cultural Relativism to view adolescence as an alternative approach; the nature of society has a decisive influence on what kind of person an adolescent becomes. I add to the argument that dystrophy in the society to which the adolescent belongs or his/her alienation from that society, there is risk of aberration in the organization of personhood and poses a barrier to a smooth journey through the life cycle. See also Caleb Rosado, 1994, *The Concept of Cutural Relativism in a Multicultural World*, through web search.

REFERENCES

Archer, W.G. 1974. *A Hill of Flutes: Life, Love and Poetry in Tribal India: A Portrait of the Santals*. London: George Allen and Unwin Ltd.

Barth, Fredrik. 1959. *Ethnic Groups and Boundaries, the Social Organization of Cultural Difference*. London: George Allen and Unwin Ltd.

Baski, Boro, 2011. *A Study on the Experiences of Santal Children in the Primary Education System: Some Suggested Interventions,* Unpublished Ph.D. Thesis, Visva-Bharati.

Bhattacharya, Kumkum. 2006. "Non-Western Traditions: Leisure in India", (pp.75-92). *In:* Chris Rojek, Susan M. Shaw and A.J. Veal (eds.), *A Handbook of Leisure Studies*, Great Britain: Palgrave Macmillan.

Bhattacharya, R.K. 1970. "Social and Cultural Constraints in Agriculture in Three Villages (Hindu, Moslem and Tribal) of West Bengal" in Surajit Sinha (ed.) *Science, Technology and Culture*, New Delhi, Research Council for Cultural Studies.

Bronfenbrenner, U. 1989. "Ecological Systems Theory," *In:* R. Vasta (ed.), *Six Theories of Child Development.* Greenwich, CT: JAI Press.

Furnivall, J.S. 1967. *Netherlands India, A Study of Plural Economy*. UK: Cambridge University Press.

Herskovits, M. 1948. *Man and his Works*. New York: Knopf.

Hoffman, Lois, Scott Paris, and Elizabeth Hall. 1994. *Developmental Psychology Today* (6th Edition) USA: McGraw Hill.

Kasterbaum, Robert. 1979. *Humans Developing: A Lifespan Perspective*, Boston: Allyn and Bacon, Inc.

Ong, Walter *et al.* 1968. "World as Viewed and World as Event," accessed Wiley Online Library, 2009, *American Anthropologist*, 71 (4).

Opler, M.K. 1971. "Adolescence in Cross-cultural Perspective," *In:* J.G. Howell (ed.), *Modern Perspectives in Adolescent Psychiatry*. New York: Brunner/Mazel Inc.

Orans, Martin. 1960. *The Santal: A Tribe in Search of a Great Tradition*, Detroit, Wayne State University Press.

Rosaldo, Caleb. 1994. "The Concept of Cultural Relativism in a Multicultural World", through web search.

Sarkar, B.N. and R. Sahani. 2002. "A Demographic and Health Profile of the Jarawas of Andaman Islands", *In:* K. Mukhopadhyay, R.K. Bhattacharya and B.N. Sarkar (eds.), *Jarawa Contact: Ours with Them and Theirs with Us*. Kolkata. Anthropological Survey of India.

Siegal, B.J. (ed.). 1955. *Acculturation*. Stanford Anthropological Series No. 2, California: Stanford University Press.

Vygotsky, L.S. 1932. *Thought and Language*. Cambridge: Massachusetts Institute of Technology Press.

FOURTEEN

FEASTS OF MERIT AND POTLATCHES: Similarities and Differences

ABRAHAM ROSMAN AND PAULA G. RUBEL

Earlier analysts have commented that the feasts of merit of South Asia are like potlatches, which had been identified in several parts of the world. Feasts of merit, and potlatches on the Northwest Coast show some significant similarities as well as differences. Using a comparative framework, the chapter will examine a number of societies in these two areas, commencing with the North-west Coast.

Early analysts assumed that the potlatch was the same in all of the Northwest Coast societies, and that it was characterized by competitiveness and destruction of property. The structure of marriage differed in the various North-west Coast tribes and, therefore, the structure of the potlatch in those tribes varied according to the social structure. The societies within the North-west Coast area exhibit great variations in their social structures, and as a consequence, there were variations in the structure of their potlatches. We demonstrated that givers of potlatches distributed goods to their affines (Rosman and Rubel, 1971). There are also constant features present, which include: the presence of fixed or flexible rank positions which are open to competition, and which may enter into the choice of a spouse. These features have implications for the structure.

The Haida, who inhabit the Queen Charlotte Islands and the southern tip of the Prince of Wales Island, have matrilineal descent, avunculocal residence and father's sister's daughter marriage. They have moieties and clans, lineages and houses. Each town has a dominant lineage, whose chief was the head of the tribe. Within the house, there were rank differences manifested in a graded series of "names" or titles. The political system was a flexible rather than a rigid one. However, though the rule of succession to leadership was younger brother, followed by eldest sister's eldest son, there was a great deal of competition and rivalry amongst individuals in those kinship categories. The structure of Haida society, based on father's sister's daughter marriage, is that each lineage intermarries with two other lineages in the opposite moiety. There are two major occasions for Haida potlatches. The first, *Sik*!, is the raising of a totem pole in the dead chief's honour by the man who successfully succeeded to that deceased chief, the two groups interacting at this potlatch are the lineage of the successor and deceased chief and the deceased's wife's lineage in the opposite moiety. As Swanton notes, "...when a man died, the members of his wife's clan conducted the funeral; and when his successor made a potlatch to put up the grave post, he invited them to it" (1905: 68). The guests at the *Sik*! potlatch were, therefore, the affines of the deceased chief. Given the nature of the father's sister's daughter marriage structure, this group also included father and children of the deceased chief. The second, and more important potlatch was the Walgal potlatch, held after the building of a house for the new chief, as a sign of his greatness. The sponsor of the potlatch is the new chief, and the guests are his affines, the lineage of his wife. At the house-building potlatch, the current chief's wife and her lineage play central roles, while the lineage of the previous chief's wife is not mentioned at present. Another important function performed at the potlatch is the tattooing, ear and nose piercing, and initiation of the children of the chief, who belong to his wife's lineage. As in other societies with a prescriptive marriage rule, marriage is not the occasion for potlatching or any other significant ceremonial activity. Potlatching among the Haida does not involve competition or the destruction of property.

In contrast, the Kwakiutl, who live at the northern end of Vancouver Island, and the adjacent coastal areas, are a society with an ambilateral descent structure. The largest effective social unit is the tribe, members of whom share a winter village. Tribes are divided into *numayms* which are not unilineal. Individuals can belong to one or more *numayms*, on the basis of descent from one's mother or from one's father. Among the Kwakiutl, polatches are frequent, occurring on many occasions of change or increase in status, which mark the developmental cycle of an individual. These are accompanied by frequent changes of name or ranked title rather than the acquisition of a single chiefly name. These potlatches represent the reinforcement of an individual's ties to more than one group. One Kwakiutl chief, described by George Hunt, had fourteen potlatches during his lifetime, beginning with one given by his father at his birth and ending with the potlatch commemorating the building of a house for him when he became chief (Boas, 1925). Frequent acquisitions and changes of name at potlatches represent the reinforcement of an individual's ties to more than one group. For a youth destined to be a chief, both mother's and father's *numayms* hold potlatches to give him names, and to reinforce his membership in their group. By virtue of this, he can succeed to chiefdomship in either group. By the rule of primogeniture, a female or male could succeed to the title of chief. For a chief, there was a succession of potlatches at which greater and greater names and privileges were given to the individual. Since there is no fixed rule of descent which affiliates each infant at birth, group affiliation is flexible and at critical junctures, which mark significant rearrangements of the social structure, potlatches take place at which names are given from different kin groups. This form of succession parallels the increasing incorporation of the individual into a kin group. Since the succession to chief takes place during the lifetime of the previous holder, funerals were not the occasion for potlatching, nor was there competition for succession to the chiefly position. In contrast, to the Haida, marriage defines the relationship between groups who become affines to one another, and is an important occasion for potlatching.

Among the Tlingit the groups who intermarry and become affines potlatch as opposites as they give titles and privileges to the children of those marriages. Marriage becomes a strategy involving selection of mates in order to raise the rank of children to be born of the marriage, since the rank of individuals, *numayms* and tribes is flexible. Brothers may be in affinally linked *numayms* and become "opposites" to one another in potlatching. These opposites are rivals to one another. However, in their potlatching, they make each other great. The potlatching activity of groups relates to relative rank position of those groups. If potlatches are not reciprocated, the rank of the group is reduced.

The greatest potlatches were intertribal potlatches playing out the traditional rivalry of chiefs who were affines to one another. These involved competition and often the destruction of property like copper shields.

The Tsimshian who live in the areas surrounding the Nass and Skeena rivers in the upper part of British Columbia have matrilineal descent and avunculocal residence. Titles and privileges pass from a mother's brother to his sister's son. They had four phratries which were subdivided into clans, and lineages or "houses" which was the basic residential unit. Phratries were exogamous and were the reference unit with respect to marriage. They were ranked as were clans within a phratry. There is a preferential rule of marriage with matrilateral cross cousin (mother's brother's daughter), which distinguishes wife-givers from wife-takers through the generations. Women marry up, so that wife-takers are higher in rank than wife-givers. However, tribal chiefs marry women of equal rank from other villages, resulting in a circular marriage pattern involving chiefs of different villages. Except for chiefs, affines are of unequal rank.

The Tsimshian potlatch is a ceremony which involves two sides—the host group, and the group to which it gives wives. The latter lineage, the "father's" lineage, receives gifts, and performs initiation services. The theme of the Tsimshian potlatch is to honour one's father's lineage, wife-takers, which is higher in rank. The most important potlatch include a memorial for a dead chief and the erection of his grave post, the succession to his chiefly office and the assumption of his chiefly name. With the absence of a hard and fast rule of succession, such as primogeniture, there may be several claimants, sisters' sons, within the matrilineage, for the position. Each attempt to accumulate the property necessary to potlatch, and validate the name and position. The one who succeeds proclaims his new position at a potlatch by distributing goods. Those who come to witness the accession are the father's lineage of both the new and the former chief, who are wife-takers to the chiefly lineage. At this funerary potlatch at which succession to chiefly position is confirmed, the father's lineage receives goods for the services they have performed. These include: washing the body of the deceased, wailing for him, and digging his grave. If a new house is to be built, they prepare the site and carve the house posts and the totem pole.

The only rivalry present is in the ceremonial aspect of the Tsimshian potlatch, namely the taunting songs. Among the rivals are the lineages with whom the host lineage has affinal connections as father's lineage—lineages to which his lineage gives women. The taunting takes place between host and father's lineage. The competition is ritualistic and does not involve the destruction of property. Every lineage is involved in two different kinds of potlatches. One in which they are the hosts to father's lineage, the wife-takers which is higher in rank. In the other, they are the father's lineage to whom they are the wife-givers and they are the guests.

A comparison of the potlatches of the Haida, Kwakiutl and Tsimshian reveals that there are major differences in the occasions for potlatches, the frequency with which they occur, the guests who are invited and the nature of the exchanges which take place at the potlatch. Potlatches take place at critical junctures marking the rearrangement of the social structure, when, in the absence of fixed rules relating to structural changes, the outcome of such changes is dependent upon the manipulation of individual actors. These changes always involve the matter of rank and manoeuvring with regard to rank. The guests at a potlatch serve as witnesses to the new arrangement in the structure, and their acceptance of gifts validates it. When competition for positions of rank is present, and there is an absence of a rule of succession, the confirmation of the successful claimant occurs at the funerary services of his predecessor, which is the occasion for a potlatch. In the absence of a fixed rule of descent, which affiliates each infant at birth as among the Kwakiutl, group affiliation is flexible. Potlatches occur which involve the incorporation of individuals into groups, but also at marriage, because there is no fixed rule of marriage among the Kwakiutl. Among the Haida, there is a fixed rule of marriage—one marries one's father's sister's daughter—but no rule of succession. Hence funerals, at which succession takes place, are the occasions for potlatches.

In these three societies potlatching, ranked positions and flexibility in rank are present, and represent constants. The points at which flexibility in rank are present vary and these variations are the occasions for potlatches. Potlatching to one's affines is a constant, but those who affines are—the guests at one's potlatch—is a variable.

The Feasts of Merit of Northeast India and Myanmar (Burma) have been compared to the potlatches of the North-west Coast. There are some important similarities, but also differences. Many who have written about the potlatch in the past have only stressed competitive rivalry and destruction of property. However, as we have pointed out above, potlatching differs from one North-west Coast society to another, depending on their marriage rules and social structure, though guests at potlatches are always affines of the hosts. The rivalry may be between affines, or in some cases (Haida and Tlingit), the rivalry between two kin groups, who are not affines to each other but to a third group. Typical of similarities between Feasts of Merit and the potlatch is the emphasis on the raising of social rank through distributions. As von Furer-Haimendorf observes "The most notable example of this extreme emphasis on the acquisition of social prestige are the feasts of merit, which tribes such as Nagas, Lushais and Chins perform for the express purpose of raising the donor's position in society. The conspicuous expenditure of wealth is an essential part of these feasts, and even in societies where the seeking of public recognition is less elaborately organized, generosity in the sharing of resources and particularly of food with other people ranks high among various means by which status and popularity are gained" (1967: 220). This is true of the potlatch—the donor acquires status and social prestige through the conspicuous expenditure of wealth to his affines. The societies mentioned by von Furer-Haimendorf, are, in varying degrees, societies with flexible rank, like North-west Coast societies. Some of these societies are egalitarian and the feasts of merit are the means by which individuals increase their stature and prestige.

Birket-Smith describes feasts of merit among the Nagas as follows: "Feasts of merit occur among many tribes in south-eastern Asia. Among the Naga in Assam a man's prestige and right to certain ornaments and house decorations depend on sumptuous feasts arranged for the donor's own or other villages. Such feasts generally form a fixed series with increasing expenses. The feasts are supposed to improve the existence of the ancestors in the land of the dead" (1967: 72). These feasts are arranged by the donor. A number of other features accompany these feasts. Mithuns, a domesticated version of the wild gaur, are sacrificed. Mithuns are not milked or used as beasts of burden, but serve only as sacrificial animals to be consumed at feasts. Sometimes, in order to be sacrificed, they must be "unblemished" mithuns. The Rengma Nagas say that, "The unblemished, sacrificed mithun goes straight to the land of the dead, alive" (Mills, 1937: 187). Everywhere, at sacrifices, mithuns are tethered to forked wooden posts, which are equivalent to stone megaliths, and have symbolic value. Pigs and "cattle" may not be substituted for mithuns as sacrificial animals. Among the Konyak Nagas, only a chief gives feasts of merit, and "about forty mithuns have to be killed" (von Furer-Haimendorf, 1939: 219). In some of the Naga tribes, feasts are also associated with erection of stone seats and megaliths. The eastern Angami Nagas associate the erection of "minhirs" (stone megaliths) with fertility rites (von Furer-Haimendorf, 1939: 217).

The Nagas exhibit other basic principles of exchange found in societies over the world. For example, among the Sema Nagas, "...no huntsman may eat game which he has killed himself" (Hutton, 1921: 77). The same prohibition is found among the Arapesh and the Yanomamo. As Levi-Straus has pointed out, this prohibition parallels the incest taboo. If you cannot marry your "sisters", you give them to other men, who give their sisters in return to you. Similarly if the huntsman cannot eat the game he has killed, he gives it to his "affines", who give him their game in return.

Like the huntsman, the sacrificer of mithuns at a feast cannot eat the meat of his sacrificial animal. Mills states that, among the Lhota Nagas, "Flesh of the sacrificed animals cannot be eaten by the sacrificer or any of his household" (1922: 138, 141). Among the Lhota Nagas, the sacrificer cannot eat the meat, he must give it to his "affines", from whom he receives women and to whom he gives women. At the fourth stage of a Lhota feast of merit, Mills describes the following division of the meat—the chest goes to the clan of the sacrificer (the giver of the feast), the hind quarter to his wife's clan (wife-givers), and the forelegs to husbands of women of his clan (wife-takers) (Mills, 1922: 141). This suggests a three-part structure: own clan, wife's clan (wife-givers to ego's clan), and husbands' of ego's sisters (wife-takers).

But who are the recipients of "wealth" at feasts of merit among the other Naga societies? What is the relationship between the givers of the feasts, and the guests who receive food and other valuable things? Throughout the Naga literature, there are suggestions as to the relationship between host at a feast, and recipients of sacrificial animals. For example, among the Rengma Nagas, in stage seven of feasts of merit, the father-in-law of the feast giver receives a foreleg of the sacrificial mithun. (Mills, 1937: 192) Father-in-law is wife-giver to the clan of the holder of the feast. Before putting up the skull and horns of the mithun in his house, the sacrificer must carry out "stone dragging". Most of the work is done by his "*echantyoi*". These are "husbands of the women whom the performer calls "sisters" (Mills, 1937: 141). This explicitly refers to wife-takers.

The three sided structure referred to above occurs only when there is a preferred rule of a man marrying his mother's brother's daughter. This is explicitly mentioned only for the Sema Naga, where Hutton states, "If otherwise suitable, marriage with the mother's brother's daughter, or father's sister's son, is preferred" (1921: 132). This is a statement only about Sema Naga marriage preference, so one cannot generalize to all Naga groups from this one reference. Nevertheless, this suggests that this form of social structure—mother's brother's daughter marriage, and a structure of own clan, and wife-givers and wife-takers is present among the Nagas.

The ethnographic information on marriage, social structure and who the recipients of distributions are at feasts of merit is much clearer when we turn to the Chin and linguistically related Chin-speaking tribes of Burma and Manipur State in India. These tribes all have patrilineal descent. In a recently published volume, we are provided with translation of a text, dealing only with marriage, titled *Maung Tet Pyo's Customary Law of the Chin Tribe—1884* (2008). It states that "Sons of a sister have the right of marrying the daughter of a brother" (2008: 5, 7, 11). Both the levirate and the sororate are practiced, because "the tie of relationship is not to be broken, because their descendants have to intermarry in succession" (2008: 17). This indicates that the Chin, and other Chin-speaking tribes, in 1884, had a structure of kin-groups linked to one another through mother's brother's daughter marriage.

The Purum are also a Chin-speaking tribe. According to Das, "The Purum extensively practice cross-cousin marriage of one type, namely, with the mother's brother's daughter, the other type, i.e., with the father's sister's daughter being strictly tabooed" (1945: 240-241). Accordingly, the same term, apu, is used for mother's brother and for wife's father (Das, 1945: 154). If such a marriage rule is practiced, as in the Purum case, the result is a three-sided structure consisting of one's own lineage (*sib*), wife-givers who give women to one's lineage, and wife-takers who marry the women of one's lineage. This is, in fact, what Das reports for the Purum. "For each man belonging to Purum society the *sibs* are divided into three groups, *viz.*:

1. his own, or rather his father's *sib,*
2. his mother's group of *sibs* or rather the group from which his wife is recruited, and
3. his sister's husband's group of *sibs*, i.e., the group of *sibs* in which his sisters are married ..." (Das, 1945: 125).

The reciprocal of the term *apu*, (MoBr) is *maksa* (DaHu and SiSo). This relationship is the key to services performed at various rituals. During the period of bride service after marriage, the *maksa* lives in the household of his *apu* and performs various services for him. After that, he returns to his lineage and lives patrilocally. Every Purum male, therefore, lives right after marriage with his mother's brother (wife-givers to him) as a *maksa*, and much later his sister's son, his *maksa*, to whom he is the *apu*, (wife-takers) comes to lives in his household after the sister's son's own marriage (Das, 11945: 244, 322).

Maksas perform various services for their mother's brother (their *apus*). For example, at a marriage, they kill and cook a pig for their mother's brother, and convey the bride to her new home after the ceremony (Das, 1945: 245, 321). At a funeral, the *maksas* wash the deceased's body, kill and cook a pig, dig the grave and carry the body to the grave. According to Das, "The part played by the *maksas* in the disposal of the dead is very significant" (1945: 254). At a feast of merit among the Purum, Das states "The *maksa* of the performer [the holder of the feast] then kills the mithun by spearing it above the right fore-leg" (1945: 155). One would expect that, having performed these various services, especially those involving funerals, and the killing of the sacrificial mithun, the *maksas* would be rewarded by their *apu* when he holds a feast.

Perhaps they receive a portion of the sacrificial mithun? However, Das does not tell us how the sacrificial animal is divided up, or who the invited guests are.

Chin tribes are divided into Northern and Southern groups which are territorially delineated. Tribes in both areas have the same type of patrilineal descent groupings, but differ in that Southern Chin groups are not ranked while Northern Chin groups are ranked with respect to one another. The feasts of merit among the Northern groups involve individual as well as group ranking and are a means of raising one's status. As a consequence of this difference, ceremonial structures also differ. In this comparative analysis, we will deal only with the Northern Chin groupings.

The Haka, a Northern Chin group, have a segmentary lineage structure consisting of dispersed patrilineal clans, some of which are aristocratic, others commoner, and maximal lineages within which there are various levels of segmentation. These include major lineages which are exogamic, and minor lineages, which are the units of affinal alliance (Lehman, 1963: 108, 112, 116, 117). Wealthy commoners, who pay a high marriage price are, therefore, able to marry high status women. If their descendants continue this practice they will achieve high status and many of the privileges of the aristocratic class (Lehman, 1963:108). Haka Chin prefer to marry real or classificatory mother's brother's daughters, but are forbidden to marry father's sister's daughters. This prescriptive rule of marriage results in, "The establishment of an affinal relation [which] involves corporate descent groups in a connection that lasts over time, though not indefinitely" (Lehman, 1963: 123). Social relations between wife-givers and wife-takers in the Haka Chin grouping are asymmetrical, and women, in terms of rank, marry down. According to Lehman, "This is a hypogamous marriage system, where the wife givers are often one's political superiors. The affinal relationship is then between basically unequal parties" (Lehman, 1963: 117).

Regarding feasts of merit, Lehman notes, "The series of Feasts of Merit is variously termed *bawi-lam* "the way to attaining *bawi* state", or *inn lam*, "the way to (aggrandizing) the house", because social status goes in hand with the right to build a complete house" (1963: 177-178). If a man becomes wealthy, he can perform a series of feasts of merit which then permit him to decorate his house with long platforms, carved fences, and carved forked planks to use for tying mithuns during the course of such a feast (Lehman, 1963: 178). During the several days of the *bawi* feast of merit, many people from one's own and other villages attend, being fed and entertained with drink and dancing. Status is proven by the ability to entertain all the guests on a grand scale (Lehman, 1963: 178). Those selected guests who have already performed *Khuangcawi* (the final feast of merit) are given a special ritual meal including brandy which they are forced to consume by attendants. Lehman concludes that, "The competitive forced hospitality and the attempt to validate status by public consumption of quantities of property, allies this series of feasts to the class of potlatches" (1963: 179).

Stevenson, writing about the Zahau Chin, said to be north of the Haka, are a hill tribe presumably Northern Chin, (1943: 11). "Democratic tribes and autocratic tribes" are found among the Zahau Chin, meaning that chiefs are found in the latter, along with much higher bride-price, and are absent in the former (Stevenson, 1943: 123). He states that they have a preference for mother's brother's daughter marriage, and that brother and sister are paired in that the brother receives the bride price for that sister and is paired with her husband as wife-giver and wife-taker. The three sided structure of wife-givers and wife-takers which accompanies mother's brother's daughter marriage is, therefore, present (1937a: 20, 21, 25, 27). Maung Tet Oyio, in *The Customary Law of the Chin Tribe* cited above, states that all Chin groups practice mother's brother's daughter marriage. We can, therefore, assume that the Zahau Chin do so as well.

According to Stevenson, "The characteristic difference in the reciprocities between the patrilineal male relatives and the others named [as receivers in the charts] are that ... the former [patrilineal male relatives] do not help at feasts but render assistance at all other life crises, whereas the last three [MoBr or *pu* relatives, real sisters and classificatory sisters] do help at the feasts and receive a *quid pro quo*" (1943: 143). He notes further that life crises, birth, marriage, and funerals do not serve to raise prestige or increase the status of household or lineage. This can only be accomplished by holding feasts of merit, and assistance at those feasts comes from affines. Nevertheless, at a death, the deceased's *farnu* (wife-takers) must bring a shroud and assist at lying in state and burial (Stevenson, 1943: 131). However, Stevenson contradicts himself when he states that *Pu* relatives (wife-givers) receive a specially named gift at a funeral, "...and the amount which he receives varies directly with the number of Feasts of Merit that the deceased had given..." (Stevenson, 1943: 130). The distribution of sections of meat from the sacrificed mithun at the two mortuary feasts of "mourning" and "erection of memorial post" specifically mention (1) patrilineal relatives, (2) *pu* relatives (wife-givers), and (3) *farnu* relatives (Stevenson, 1943: 132). So, there seems to be links between funerals and feasts of merit.

There are several feasts (Feasts of Merit) which involve the sacrifice of mithans, the most elaborate of which was the final feast, the *khuang tsawi* feast. At each feast, the giver's prestige was increased as indicated by the right to wear certain clothing and at the final feast, the right to change the front of one's house (Stevenson, 1937a: 24). Stevenson observes that, "The Feasts of Merit and of celebration are the basis of a system of economic exchanges between relatives and are also used as a means of payment (through distribution of flesh) of dues to chiefs, priests and blacksmiths" (1937b: 81). He presents a drawing of a mithun, divided into separate sections, which shows exactly which parts various individuals receive when the animal is slaughtered at a *khuang tsawi* feast (Stevenson, 1937a: 19). Some parts are given to relatives, others go to previous feast-givers, the cutter of the mithun, the village headman and the blacksmith. With the help of a kinship terminology chart, Stevenson notes that the relatives who receive are divided into three categories: (1) members of ego's own clan, (2) *Pu* relatives (mother's brother and wife's brother) who receive meat labelled *Pusa*, which means *Pu* meat, and (3) *farnu* relatives (1937a: 20). The last category includes sisters and sister's households (including sister's husbands), since sister's husband assists in various ways at a feast and receive mithun meat in return for this help (Stevenson, 1937a: 25). Stevenson, in a chart, notes that mother's brother and wife's brother supply two large pots of liquor (*zu*) at feasts of merit and receive "flesh dues" in return. (Stevenson, 1943: 143) According to the diagram, members in each of these three categories receive distinctly different shares of the slaughtered mithun. One can see that the distribution of meat reflects the three-fold division of relatives: ego's own group including his clan, *Pu* relatives who are wife-givers to ego's lineage, and *farnu* relatives who are wife-takers. The feast giver, who is the heir of the chief whom he succeeded, and his household, cannot partake of the sacrificial meat (Stevenson, 1937a: 17, chart).

The Haida, Kwakiutl and Tsimshian societies illustrate the different types of social structures and potlatches on the North-west Coast. Occasions, frequency, and who the guests are at potlatches vary with these social structures. Since the Tsimshian have the same structure of mother's brother's daughter marriage as the Nagas, and Chin-speaking peoples, all of whom have feasts of merit, this will be the basis of our comparison. However, there is a significant difference—the Tsimshian are matrilineal, while the Naga and Chin peoples are all patrilineal. As we shall see below, this is not really an important difference. The feasts of merit of the Naga and Chin peoples and the potlatch of the Tsimshian involve rank and status. All of these societies have their own indigenous terms for potlatches and feasts of merit. The Naga and Chin have feasts at critical junctures, i.e., rites de passage such as birth, marriage and death. These are different from feasts of merit, and do not serve to raise rank or prestige. In contrast, the North-west Coast societies carry out potlatches on the occasion of rites de passage—birth, marriage, and funerals. The Tshimshian hold potlatches at the critical juncture in their social structure, when a new chief holds a funeral, and a totem pole carved and set up, and a new house is built, at succession to the position of chief. Tsimshian succession to the position of chief, after the predecessor has died, is flexible. The individual who gathers enough goods to hold a potlatch succeeds to the position, and becomes the new chief. Rank is, therefore, flexible. Tsimshian potlatches are not held at births or weddings. Feasts of merit, however, do not occur at critical junctures in Naga or Chin structure.

There are also many other similarities between these Asian societies and the Tsimshian. The position of chief is present in both, however, in both rank is flexible. Individuals, households, lineages and clans can all raise their rank by giving larger and larger feasts or potlatches. Similarly, in both areas, individuals and groups may decline in rank by not giving feasts or holding inadequate feasts or potlatches. Another important similarity is that in both areas guests at feasts and potlatches are affines of the host. However, among the Nagas and Chins, a number of other categories of guests besides affines are also recipients of distributions at feasts of merit. Non-affine guests are also present at potlatches. These guests all serve the important function as witnesses, especially when competition occurs at points of change in the social structure. For example, among the Tsimshian, they attest to the increased rank of a clan, or the right of a claimant to be a chief.

The rule of marriage with mother's brother's daughter creates a three-sided structure. This divides the category of affines into wife-givers to ego's lineage and wife-takers from his lineage.The Nagas, Chin and the Tsimshian have this structure, though two are patrilineal and one matrilineal. The matrilineal Tsimshian honour their fathers' lineage at their potlatch for the important rites de passage services they perform, indicating that father's lineage (wife-givers) is higher than own lineage. When wife-takers make a potlatch, ego's lineage is in the position of father's lineage, performs services and is honoured accordingly.

At feasts of merit among the Chin, mother's brother, wife-giver, and sister's husband, wife-taker both receive, but are given differently named cuts of meat. The former are the more desirable, since wife-givers are higher in rank. Women marry down in the Chin system. The wife-givers lineages are one's *Pu* relatives. One's wife-givers (*Pu* relatives) play a central role in the final feast in the series of feasts of merit, the only way to raise one's rank. In return, they receive the innards of the sacrificed mithun, the best part, for the services they perform. Among the Tsimshian competition is ritualistic and rivalry is very minor, no more than one would expect between affines. Similarly, the only rivalry reported for the Chin is when hosts at a final feast attempt to force guests to eat and drink even more than they can consume. This seems more like a joke than like real competition.

Though the Tsimshian have matrilineal descent and the Naga/Chin have patrilineal descent, the structure of wife-givers, ego, and wife-takers is the same. The important difference is that, for the Tsimshian, one potlatch involves ego with wife-givers, and another with wife-takers. In contrast, at the Chin feast of merit, both wife-givers and wife-takers perform different services and receive different parts of the mithun.

REFERENCES

Birket-Smith, Kaj. 1967. Studies in Circumpacific Culture Relations. 1. Potlatch and Feasts of Merit. Kobenhaven.

Boas, Franz 1925. "Contributions to the Ethnology of the Kwakiutl," *Columbia University Contributions to Anthropology*, Vol. 3. New York: Columbia University Press.

Das, Tarakchandra 1945. *The Purums: An Old Kuki Tribe of Manipur*. Calcutta: University of Calcutta.

Furer-Heimandorf, Christoph von 1939. "Appendix 1 The Megalithic Culture of Assam," In: F.M. Schnitger (ed.), *Forgotten Kingdoms in Sumatra*. Leiden: E.J. Brill.

____. 1967. *Morals and Merit: A Study of Values and Social Controls in South Asian Societies*. Chicago: University of Chicago Press.

Go, Khup Za. 2008. *Zo Chronicles: A Documentary Study of the History and Culture of the Kuki-Chin-Lushai Tribe*. New Delhi: Mittal Publications.

Hutton, J.H. 1921. *The Sema Nagas*. London: Macmillan.

Lehman, F.K. 1963. *The Structure of Chin Society: A Tribal People of Burma Adapted to a Non-Western Civilization*. Urbana: University of Illinois Press.

Mills, J.P. 1922. *The Lhota Nagas*. London: Macmillan.

____. 1937. *The Rengma Nagas*. London: Macmillan.

Rosman, Abraham and Paula G. Rubel 1971. *Feasting with Mine Enemy: Rank and Exchange among Northwest Coast Societies*. New York: Columbia University Press.

Stevenson, H.N.C. 1937a. "Feasting and Meat Division among the Zahau Chins of Burma: A Preliminary Analysis", *Journal of the Royal Anthropological Institute of Great Britain and Ireland*, 67: 15-32.

____. 1937b. "Religion and Sacrifices of the Zahau Chins", *Man*, 37: 81.

____. 1943. *The Economics of the Central Chin Tribes*. Bombay: *The Times of India* Press.

Swanton, J.R. 1905. "Contributions to the Ethnology of the Haida", *Memoir of the American Museum of Natural History*, Vol. 8, Part 1.

FIFTEEN

"ONE, TWO OR MORE LITTLE KAFFIRS, WITH OR WITHOUT MOTHER, FROM THE TRIBE OF THE LATE MASSOUW"[1]: The Case of Sarah Taaibosch

PIET ERASMUS

Introduction

The last words of the Korana captain, David Massouw Rijt Taaibosch, as he fell on 2 December, 1885 during an attack on his stronghold Mamusa by Commandant General P.J. Joubert of the South African Republic (Z.A.R.) were, "Come out, my people, from under the Boers" (Mouton, 1957: 146). In the eyes of Afrikaner nationalism, the battle of Mamusa was regarded as rather unimportant in South African military history, except for the honourable deaths of two "brave" Boer soldiers, Captain C.A. Schweizer and Field Cornet C.N. Reneke. The fact that the battle at Mamusa led to the disintegration and disappearance of the last established Korana community in South Africa largely escaped notice.

The Taaibosch Korana inhabited the area around Mamusa since 1750 and Mamusa itself became their headquarters between 1813 and 1820 (Krüger, 1972: 452; Maingard, 1932: 121 and Schapera, 1965: 47). The Korana were one of the Khoekhoe tribes already living in the Cape Town vicinity before the arrival of the first White settlers in 1652, and are regarded as one of the indigenous peoples of Southern Africa. The Taaibosch Korana succeeded in building up considerable wealth and owned thousands of head of cattle (Bailie, 1883: 4). Mamusa's[2] situation on the west bank of the Harts River made the Z.A.R. its eastern neighbour. It was about a 100 years after the Korana had settled in the vicinity of Mamusa that the Z.A.R. came into being under the Sand River Convention of 1852. During the negotiations between the Boers and Great Britain the western border was left undetermined (Delport, 1968: 8). In other words, there was not a demarcated border between the Korana and the Z.A.R. When Britain granted the Z.A.R. independence, it was on condition that the Republic would not extend its territory nor "carry out a native policy on any other line than those adopted by Great Britain" (Bristol Selected Pamphlets, 1876: 3). However, the Z.A.R. did not take much notice of these two terms. Regarding the first, it can be said that two consecutive state presidents, that is, M.W. Pretorius in 1868 and T.F. Burgers in 1872, tried to extend their territory by means of treaties with indigenous leaders such as Massouw Rijt Taaibosch (David Massouw Rijt Taaibosch's father). The Z.A.R. succeeded through two further agreements with Britain, that is, the Pretoria Convention signed 3 August 1881 and the London Convention signed 27 February 1884, in extending its territory. The Korana who were directly affected by these agreements were refused participation in the deliberations and their protests against the terms fell on deaf ears. With each new agreement the western border of the Z.A.R. shifted further to the west to include more and more Korana territory until Mamusa eventually fell inside the Z.A.R. This entailed that the Korana were hereafter subjects of the Z.A.R. and had to bow to the authority of the Republic (*cf.* Bester and Van Eeden, 1999: 415; Birkhead & Groenewald, 2005: 8; Delport, 1968: 18 and Liebenberg, 1990: 21). Naturally, this had dramatic consequences for the Korana. Before, David Massouw Rijt Taaibosch and his people were free and independent. In consultation with his council, generals and field cornets, Taaibosch wielded the sceptre, entered into or broke off treaties, declared war or peace and exercised his power everyday. With the proverbial stroke of a pen, this was taken from them. It goes without saying that the Korana would not put up with this state of affairs that was forced upon them.

An important aspect of the "native policy" of the Z.A.R. (the other term referred to above) that caused great dissatisfaction under indigenous communities regards the demarcation of their residential areas (also referred to as reserves, locations or stations). This was done in order to restrict inhabitants and to prevent them from settling outsides reserves. It was also designed to facilitate taking census, the basis on which taxes to the State were determined. The Z.A.R. ensconced the principle of no equality between Whites and Blacks in their constitution of 1858 and the vote was reserved for Whites only. The legislative implication for the indigenous groups was that they were not entitled to any rights that go hand in hand with citizenship; they had, in fact, no legal rights. They could not own any property, enter into a civil marriage, nor bring a civil action against a White in court (Butler, 1900: 48-49). The right to own a firearm was taken away from them (Atmore, *et al.*, 1971: 547). Strictly speaking then, the Korana were not allowed to be in possession of firearms. But the Z.A.R. did not have the capacity or the will to enforce this term (Leśniewski, 2010: 108), while smugglers like J.W. Honey took advantage of the state of lawlessness and established a flourishing trade with, often stolen, firearms. David Massouw Rijt Taaibosch was one of Honey's clients (TAB SS V1110-R4867-1885).

It is not difficult to understand why the Korana did not want to give up their freedom and land rights and simply continued to exercise their traditional claims and rights regarding freedom and land. But the Z.A.R. interpreted this as unlawful occupation of what was now regarded as Boer farms and they decided to act against the Korana by force of arms. Some other reasons the Z.A.R. gave for the war against the Korana were alleged stock theft and a refusal to pay taxes. In terms of the typical colonial discourse of the Z.A.R. these were interpreted as misdeeds (Maree, 1952: 9), insolence (Hoon, 1950: 7) and irregularities on the part of the Korana (Grobbelaar, 1957: 203).

Sarah Taaibosch experienced this war as a girl of about ten years. She was one of the children that were wounded during battle; she was wounded on the right side of her head. In order to understand her story, the run of events before, during and after the war must be reviewed.

"A Hard Furrow ..."

There are uncertainties as to how the battle started, how long the shooting lasted and about how many people were wounded or died.

It is, however, certain that there was no command from Joubert to start shooting. There are two different versions of the events, one from the Boer forces and one from independent observers.

From the sworn statements of Joubert and Commandants J.H. De la Rey and P.A. Cronjé (commanders of the two commandos involved) the course of events that Joubert said was a "hard furrow to plough"[3] can be reconstructed as follows. Joubert's plan was to deploy his forces so as to cut off the Korana from their source of water, the Harts River, and to force them to surrender in this way. In order to execute his plan, Joubert ordered De la Rey on 2 December, 1885 to move camp to the other (eastern) side of the river. De la Rey took 40 of his men to explore the place where they had to pitch camp. While De la Rey was busy with this, Cronjé turned up with 150 cavalrymen, all young men, at Joubert's camp. Apparently Cronjé did not know what was expected of him, because one of his adjutants dismounted swiftly (Delport, 1968: 67-68) and went up to Joubert to ask what Cronjé's orders were. Joubert replied that De la Rey first had to take in position in order to cut off the Korana from water, as has been decided.

Cronjé understood this differently. He stated in his affidavit after the battle that he had received, on Wednesday 2 December, 1885 half an hour after sunrise, orders from Joubert to keep the Korana away from the water (TAB SS, V1141-R6231-1885-part 1). He took position on the northern side of Mamusa and gave his field cornets the order to keep the Korana away from the water. Cronjé went to assess the situation and came across De la Rey who was on his way back along the Harts River and whom Cronjé informed about his orders to his field cornets. When Cronjé arrived back with his men, he found that a great crowd of Korana and "Kaffirs" were thronging together before them. He then ordered one of them that he later identified as a son of David Massouw Rijt Taaibosch that they lay down their arms to which he replied, "I'll be damned"[4]. At that stage he heard shots ring out from the front of his lines. As he turned his horse to see what was going on, shots were fired simultaneously from his left and right and his horse was hit. Then shots were fired from all sides at the Boers.

Meanwhile, De la Rey and his men were coming over a ridge from the south and saw from the crest how Assistant Field Cornet Gert Olivier of the Cronjé commando was trying to disarm a Korana.

The Korana resisted and a scuffle broke out. A "Korana meid" (Korana woman) came to the man's assistance by hitting Olivier with a marrowbone against the neck. P.J. Delport, Olivier's adjutant, then nudged her "gently" away with the butt of his rifle. This according to De la Rey: Four shots hit Delport at once and he was the first casualty. These were apparently the shots Cronjé reported to have heard and which had led to shooting from all sides (TAB SS, V1141-R6231-1885-part 1).

According to Joubert the fighting lasted about 50 minutes (TAB SS, V1142-R6231-1885-part 2) at which point the Korana left cover and fled into the open fields around the koppies. This gave the burghers a chance to shoot at them or to go after them on horseback. H. Pretorius and his artillery were among those who went on horseback after the fugitives and shot five of them. The Korana fled through a narrow pass. When H. Pretorius and his men had just passed through as well, he realised that the surrounding ridges were full of Korana. Renewed shooting broke out. H. Pretorius himself shot and killed an armed Korana while one of his men lost his arm. The Korana in the open fields could not resist much and so were either shot or taken prisoner. By ten o'clock that night, fighting still continued, but Mamusa could not be taken in. Joubert ordered that double watchmen be placed out to prevent anyone from escaping (TAB SS, V1142-R6231-1885-part 2 and Delport, 1968: 69-70). Sarah Taaibosch related how they had been told to lock the doors and not to make fires or light tallow lamps that could give their positions away. The children lay fearful in the dark. The grown-ups were quiet. From afar they could hear the hustle and bustle in the Boer camps. They did not know what tomorrow would bring.

The next day Joubert sent Schweizer out with the order to withdraw the cannons from their position so that they could be used more effectively. Schweizer, together with three artillerymen, disobeyed the order and decided to take in Mamusa. They progressed up to just before the defences where a Korana bullet hit Schweizer in the head. One of the cannons was set up about 300 paces from the stronghold, but the cannon fire was so ineffective that this was eventually stopped (Delport, 1968: 69-70 and Mouton, 1957: 146).

When Joubert realised at 14h00 that the bombardment was of little help, he sent a Korana prisoner of war, Jeremia, with a white flag to Mamusa. He warned that it would not help to continue fighting and said that he undertook not to shoot on the women and children coming to surrender. At 16h00 120 men, women and children, among whom the wife of David Massouw Rijt Taaibosch and two of his children aged 13 and 20 (TAB SS, V1142-R6231-1885-part 21), surrendered. A single cannon shot signalled the end of the fighting.

The numbers cited for persons killed or wounded (on both sides) vary. Joubert states that nine "brave" burghers were killed and 14 were wounded[5]. Joubert does not, however, state in his report that some burgers fled and were later fined (TAB KG, V15-CR782-1886), nor that some deserted or were dishonourable and thus discharged for misconduct (TAB SS, V2860-R6639-1891 and R2380-1891). Seven of the fallen were buried near Joubert's camp on 4 December (TAB SS, V1142-R6231-1885-part 2).

On the Korana side, according to Joubert, there were 130 fallen[6], among whom about four or five women and three or four children (TAB SS, V1142-R6231-1885-part 2). Kateibe, the son of David Massouw Rijt Taaibosch, was among the fallen, as well as second-in-command David Links, four field cornets (among whom Hans, Simon and Koeraan), two councillors and an ex-general (TAB SS, V1142-R6231-1885-part 2, Mouton, 1957: 146, Maree, 1952: 10 and Delport, 1968: 73). The fallen Korana lay for a week in the warm summer sun before they were buried by the local inhabitants under supervision of the Z.A.R. artillery on 8 December. In order for the government to avoid expenditure for the care of the wounded Korana, Joubert ordered field cornets Bender and B.J. de Beer to place them out under the care of Boers (Liebenberg, 1990: 23).

The independent reports mentioned above contain insightful, but disturbing information. First, there was a Reuters report, dated 5 December 1885 (TAB SS, V1142-R6231-1885-part 2), based on "reliable information from an eyewitness of the fight which took place at Mamusa". The report stated that: "At Wednesday Joubert with about nine hundred men surrounded kopje the possession of David Massouw and hundred natives. Some forty Boers advanced and stated to natives they had come to disarm them. One Boer seized a native's gun, accidentally a shot went off whereupon remaining Boers at foot of Kopje opened heavy fire. Fifteen Korana took possession of Kraal and opened fire caused Boers to retire; remaining Kaffirs fled on to flat at foot of Kopje and were shot indiscriminately without regard to age. Several Boers rode upto them actually blistering them while firing so close were they. About thirty natives and forty women and children were shot. One child about twelve years old was found with five bullets wounds in him. Nine Boers were killed and fourteen were wounded but only three killed by Korana, the rest being killed by cross firing as stated by men of Potchefstroom Laager. Thus has caused bitter feeling between them and Bloemhof contingent. Supply of water running short, natives surrendered after holding out twenty four hours – David Massouw was found shot. Dr Allport who attended from Vryburg was refused permission to render assistance to the wounded and several Englishmen who gave water to wounded natives were insulted by Boers. Appears natives had no intention of fighting as Boers were allowed on Kopje and they shook hands with them, and guns and ammunition were afterwards found stored away inside their huts in usual peaceful manner".

There was a second report by Captain George Puzey to Colonel Carrington (dated 4 January, 1886 – Imperial Blue Book C.-4839, 1886:9-10). He gathered his information from people who were present at the fight. Puzey reported that:

"The natives had no intention of fighting".

(1) This is shown – (a) by their sending their cattle to graze the morning of the fight[7] ... ; (b) by the natives allowing the Boers to come on the Kopje mixing and talking with them ...; (c) by the number of guns found in the huts after possession was taken by the Boers'.

(2) "That there was no occasion for fighting, and that was known to the Boer leaders who had made arrangements for taking possession of the water supply ..."

(3) "That women and children were shot, though the actual numbers vary. ... [I]t was impossible to distinguish male and female in the rush, but as all who rushed down the hill were unarmed, there does not seem to have [been] any cause to have shot any. ... [O]ne who was there shortly after the fight ... overheard two young Boers disputing as to which of them hit the woman. ... Another told me that some miles from the Kopje he saw the dead body

> of a boy about 6 years shot through the back. ... I was told by one who went over the field the day after the fight, and again after a week that during that time bodies of women and children that he had noticed had been moved, and afterwards found they had been buried. The bodies of the men had not been touched."

In *De Volkstem* (10 December 1885)—that was subsidised by President P. Kruger of the Z.A.R. (Botha, 1900: 23)—the claims of the Reuters report are rejected. Delport (1968: 75) also casts doubt upon the correctness of Puzey's report. He bases this on the opinion of Lieutenant Lochner that *a couple* of the Korana were indeed armed, as well as on the version of H. Pretorius that he had shot and killed *an armed* Korana. But Delport shoots himself in the proverbial foot by finding evidence of only a few armed men. "A couple" and "an armed" clearly imply that the vast majority of the fallen were unarmed. Sillery (1971: 138) came to the same conclusion.

Another burning question relates to the women and children that were shot, deeds that had indeed taken place in earlier skirmishes between Boers and Korana (Manson, 1998: 504). That Joubert was uncertain about the exact number of children and women who were shot, throws suspicion on the numbers he referred to. In fact, Metrowich (1970: 54-55) is certain of the fact "that a large number of women and children" were among the dead and wounded. The explanation given by Rev. Radloff why women and children were shot, namely that various Korana men put on women's clothes to mislead the Boers (Delport, 1968: 76), does not make sense at all. For, if they were disguised, how did the Boers know when shooting at these "women" that they were in fact men?

Nevertheless, as will be shown in the next section, the considerable number of deaths was not the only loss suffered by the Korana.

"Without Form and Void"

Because all the Korana huts or homesteads were burnt and broken down by the Boers (Conder, 1887: 77-78), and because thousands of heads of cattle, all the crops on the lands, all household goods and personal belongings were taken by the Boers as spoils of war, Mamusa was after the fighting, in the words of Joubert, "without form, and void"[8] (TAB SS, V1142-R6231-1885-part 2). On a council of war meeting on 4 December, 1885 the Boer leaders decided to divide the prisoners of war into two groups: those who were guilty of riot and resistance and those guilty of lesser crimes. The underlying assumption being, therefore, that all were guilty; the only difference lay in the degree of guilt. The first group consisted of 210 men, women and children and they were sent to trial in Pretoria. The wife of David Massouw Rijt Taaibosch and his son, Klein-David Massouw (David Massouw Junior), were in this group. The second group consisted of 369 women and children who did not participate in the fighting. Nevertheless, this group did not get off scot-free, but were booked in with Boers from the Lichtenburg and Potchefstroom districts as so-called "apprentices". More about this system will follow later.

The first group departed on 9 December, 1885 in three wagons for Pretoria which they reached eight days later. From the group of 210 only five men, among whom Adonis, Dawid Links and Klein-David Massouw, were prosecuted for "insurgency and resistance against the law" (TAB SS, V1141-R6231-1885-part 1). They were found guilty on 19 May, 1886 and sentenced to two years imprisonment with hard labour. While the rest of the prisoners of war in the first group were not prosecuted and found guilty, the government decided that they had to be booked in as apprentices with Boers, like the other 369 people in the second group. The day of booking the Korana in was scheduled for 8 January, 1886, but there were so many requests that grants were decided upon by the drawing of lots (Delport, 1968: 86-88).

In order to understand the system of apprenticeship, one has to take into account one of the terms set by Britain during the Sand River Convention for the Z.A.R. to become independent: slavery had to be stopped (BSP 1876:3). Although the Z.A.R., under President Andries Pretorius, had agreed to prohibit slavery (Articles 10 and 224 of the Z.A.R. Constitution incorporated the abolition of slave trade), slave raids took place on a regular basis in the Z.A.R. (Butler, 1900: 17). Z.A.R. officials, such as, President M.W. Pretorius, the then Commandant General P. Kruger and Commandant Cronjé, led several raids against the indigenous peoples and owned hundreds of slaves (Morton, 1992: 99 & 104). This practice was so rife that, in the first ten years after independence (in 1866), the landlord of Potchefstroom had estimated the total population of apprentices to be at least 4,000 (Morton, 1992: 104). This system came down to apprentices being "unfree servants of white households" (Morton, 1992: 100). The so-called "Black Ivory" or apprentices were sold at between £5 and £20 per person (Morton, 1992: 100 and Butler, 1900: 5). They were legally entitled to good treatment and, ultimately, their freedom – children were supposed to remain in service until adulthood – but they were often abused and seldom manumitted (Morton, 1992: 105). Moreover, an individual Boer's absolute authority over his apprentices was legally recognised (Morton, 1992: 105). The Z.A.R. had adopted the system of apprenticeship in order to "supply the lack of field labour" inside the Z.A.R. (Butler, 1900: 15). However, apprentices from the Z.A.R. were also traded in the then Delagoa Bay (Maputo), Mozambique (Morton, 1992: 103), that is, "apprentice" raiding were not necessarily conducted to meet Boer labour demands.

To conclude this section, it must be asked whether the placing of the Korana on Boer farms, which meant they found themselves spread out over the whole of the Z.A.R., had had such a salutary or wholesome influence on them as Mouton (1957: 146) claims. Certainly not. This brought an end to the last Korana community that was still functioning as a socio-political unit; it destroyed their inter-communal cohesion and kinship; it meant the end of their independence (*cf.* also Birkhead & Groenewald, 2005: 9 and Metrowich, 1970: 54-55).

The Comfort of an Old Pair of White Socks

Sarah Taaibosch was "fortunate"—she was placed with her parents, three brothers and a sister as apprentice on a farm in the Bloemhof district[9]. They possessed only the clothes on their bodies; the rest had been taken by the Boers. Sarah Taaibosch passed away in 1964 on the farm Tafelkop, near Bloemfontein. Her two grandchildren, Mrs. Tiger (née Taaibosch) and Miss Taaibosch still recall how their grandmother related how her little feet had hurt from the cold as she walked barefoot across the frost-covered fields to take the sheep to graze. In the afternoons, she had to lead them back to the Kraal.

When her feet were later almost too sore to walk, she got a pair of old white socks from the farmer's wife to protect them against the cold.

The family could no longer take the abuse on the farm and they decided to escape that very first winter. They left under cover of the night, without food. Because they knew the Boers would organise a commando to go in search for them, they fled into the ridges, where they hid in the day and, come night, they went further on foot. As in the time of the siege of Mamusa, they dared not make a fire by which to warm themselves. They were on their way to relatives living on the farm Tafelkop, a distance of about 260 km away. They lived on veldkos (wild fruit) and when they approached the local people they had to take care that the Boers did not see them.

The hardships of the war and the flight were too harsh for Ouma (Grannie) Sarah to speak too much about that time. When the children kept on nagging for more stories, she became angry and chased them away. She also decided that the children would not learn the Korana language, !Ora, as she feared they would be stigmatised and prosecuted for having fled from the farm in the Bloemhof district. In order to hide their Korana identity, the people from Tafelkop presented themselves as Griqua or Coloured.

Grobbelaar (1956) was looking for Korana in the Free State and the then Western Transvaal in 1948 for his research on their physical characteristics. Wherever he went he took photographs as illustration material. One of the photos he took on Tafelkop was of Sarah Taaibosch. During an interview on 3 November, 2011 while I was told the story of Sarah Taaibosch, I asked the family to show me a photo of Sarah, but they had none. Two months later, I discovered her photo in Grobbelaar (1956: 137) and I immediately had an enlargement made and returned to the family. I asked, "Who is this?" At first there was only the silence of disbelief. Then followed surprised shouts and cries. Tears flowed freely as the photo was gently and lovingly touched.

Discussion

Where the Z.A.R.'s work of destruction of the Korana left off, apartheid took the relay. The implementation of the apartheid policy of racial segregation implied the following for the Korana: The *Population Registration Act* 1950 (Act 30 of 1950) required South Africans to be identified and registered from birth as belonging to one of four distinct racial groups: White, Bantu (Black), Coloured and "Other". Those who were not Whites or Blacks were regarded as Coloureds[10] – the umbrella concept for the "residue" – those who did not fit in anywhere else. The Korana were stigmatised as "Coloureds" and were politically, socially and economically forced to renounce their origins. Lee, (2003: 97) estimates that, "up to 2.5 million Coloured South Africans would identify themselves as Khoi or San, but until recently the opportunity for these peoples to explore their roots has been compromised and thwarted by the distortions of Apartheid".

The *Constitution of the Republic of South Africa*, 1996 (Act 108 of 1996), addresses the historical injustice committed against the Korana. It affords the Korana, other Khoekhoe groups and the San constitutional accommodation and recognition, the right to self-determination, and it makes provision for the promotion and development of their indigenous languages [Chapter 1 on languages, section 6, subsection 5a (ii)]. The intellectual and political space that the Constitution opened up gave people who claimed a Korana heritage the right to determine their own means of linguistic and cultural development, as well as the right to determine their identity. Korana people have become increasingly active in asserting their respective identities, in reclaiming their culture and challenging the previous definitions imposed upon them. In effect, as various other authors confirm (Lee, 2003: 100; Ruiters, 2009: 104; Besten, 2011: 176 and De Beer, 1998: 38 and 2001: 109), the ending of apartheid provided opportunities for people to determine self-identity as they wished and to experiment with their identities.

Different independent Korana organisations have been established over the last couple of years. To mention a few: There is the Free State Korana Community Committee (FSKCC), led by Mr. R. Beddy. The FSKCC's constitution was approved by representatives of the Korana Royal Family on 22 January, 2000. The activities of the FSKCC are mainly centred upon the recording and reinterpretation of Korana history. J. Taaibosch-Davids registered the Free State Korana Culture and Heritage Council (FSKCHC) on 14 May, 2002 and the issues of Korana identity and religion are regarded as important. R. Dodds founded the movement known as "Die Kinders van !Kora" (The Children of !Kora). Its members focus strongly on what they regard as authentic cultural activities. In the Northern Cape the Korana South Africa First Nation organisation was established during 1994 by Messrs H. Hoogstander and J. Kats.

Of all the various Korana movements, the Taaibosch family of Bloemfontein is probably at the forefront of organising a renaissance under the Korana. To them, Sarah Taaibosch is a role model of Korana perseverance and their will to survive. Her photograph is displayed proudly against the wall of their headquarters.

NOTES

1. This is how a Boer worded his written application for slaves or 'apprentices' to the Government of the Z.A.R. (TAB SS, V1144-R6356-1885). The archival documents of the period contain terms such as "kaffer" (Kaffir) and "meid" (referring to a Black or Coloured woman servant) that are offensive and unacceptable today. These terms do not only reflect a specific historical context, but reveal definite elements of the world vision of the Boers of that time (*cf.* Van Onselen, 1990:101-102 and Butler, 1900: 48). For this reason, it has been decided to retain the original terms, but to place them in inverted commas because of their offensiveness.
2. The etymology of the name "Mamusa" is not entirely clear. Some sources explain that it is of Tswana origin and derives from "Mma" (noun = mother) + "amusa" (verb = to breastfeed).
3. Joubert used the expression "in harde gekrap" suggesting that the Boers were in a scrape, in a difficult situation or even in a predicament, or had a hard time winning the battle (TAB SS, V1142 R6231-1885-part 2.
4. The report states: "Dit verdom ik" (TAB SS, V1141-R6231-1885-part1).
5. Maree (1952:10) makes mention of 10 fallen on the Boer side.
6. Delport (1968:73) estimates that the number of fallen on the side of the Korana was between 130 and 140, Mouton (1957-146) projects the numbers between 130 and 150, Sillery (1971:138) records that 80 Korana died and that 20 were wounded, while Metrowich (1970:54-55) records that about 150 were fatally wounded and another 100 sustained less serious injuries.
7. This was, according to Stow (1905:302), normal, daily practice under the Korana.
8. It is ironic that Joubert quotes from the *Bible* when he describes the areh as "woest en ledig". The text is Genesis 1:2 from the King James version. Joubert would have referred to the Dutch version, *De Statenvertaling*.
9. By contrast, the nine-year old girl, Perzena, was placed alone, without family or friends with H.R. Lemmer of Potchefstroom (TAB SS, V1148-R61-1886).
10. According to Erasmus and Pieterse (1999: 169), the notion of being "Coloured" originated among freed slaves and their descendants between 1875 and 1910. In Jung's (2000:168-169) opinion, the process started much earlier, as the social

and political identities that had been created during the era of slavery were responsible for the development of Coloured identities. Although the term was thus used long before the apartheid era, its meaning was more fluid in the nineteenth century (Lewis, 1987:7-10).

REFERENCES

Atmore, A., J.M. Chirenje, & S.I. Mudenge. 1971. "Firearms in South Central Africa," *The Journal of African History*, 12 (4): 545-556.

Besten, M.P. 2011. "Envisioning Ancestors: Staging of Khoe-San Authenticity in South Africa," *Critical Arts, South-North Cultural and Media Studies,* 25 (2): 175-191.

Bailie, A.C. 1883. *Annexure to Votes and Proceedings, House of Assembly*. Papers *re* Stellaland: A58.

Bester, S.J. and E.S. Van Eeden. 1999. "Grondregte in die proses van dorpsontwikkeling vir swartes in die Schweizer-Reineke gebied tot 1962 [Land Rights in the Process of Town Development for Blacks in the Schweizer-Reineke Area Until 1962]," *Historia,* 44 (2): 409-423.

Birkhead, H. and J. Groenewald. 2005. *The Pseudo-Siege of Schweizer-Reneke. Anglo-Boer War Centenary Series, No. 2*. Johannesburg: Philatelic Foundation of South Africa.

Botha, P.H. 1900. *From Boer to Boer and Englishman*. London: Hugh Bees, Ltd.

Butler, J.E. 1900. *Native Races and the War*. London: Gay & Bird.

Conder, C.R. 1887. "The Present Conditions of the Native Tribes in Bechuanaland," *The Journal of the Anthropological Institute of Great Britain and Ireland,* 16: 76-96.

Bristol Selected Pamphlets. 1876. *The Transvaal*. Bristol: University of Bristol Library.

De Beer, F.C. 1998. "Ethnicity in Nation-States with Reference to South Africa," *South African Journal of Ethnology*, 21 (1): 32-40.

____. 2001. "Nation-Building in South Africa – Exploring the Ethnic Landscape," *South African Journal of Ethnology*, 24 (4): 105-112.

Delport, A.B. 1968. *Die Korana-oorlog in Wes-Transvaal 1885*. Pretoria: UNISA. (Ongepubliseerde M.A.-verhandeling) [*The Korana War in West-Transvaal 1885*. Pretoria: UNISA (Unpublished M.A. thesis)].

Erasmus, Z. and E. Pieterse, 1999. "Conceptualising Coloured Identities in the Western Cape Province of South Africa," (pp. 167-187) *In:* M. Palmberg, (ed.), *National Identity and Democracy in Africa*. Cape Town: Human Sciences Research Council of South Africa, the Mayibuye Centre at the University of the Western Cape and the Nordic Africa Institute.

Grobbelaar, C.S. 1956. "The Physical Characteristics of the Korana," *South African Journal of Science*, 53 (4): 97-159.

____. 1957. *The Origin and Distribution of the Living Korana Collected for a Somatological Study*. 3rd Pan African Congress proceedings. London: Chatto & Windus.

Hoon, M.G. 1950. *'n Geskiedenis van die onderwys van blankes in Schweizer-Reneke en omstreke (1889-1945)*. Pretoria; UNISA. (Ongepubliseerde M.A.-verhandeling)

[*A History of the Education of Whites in Schweizer-Reneke and Surrounding Areas (1889-1945*). Pretoria; UNISA. (Unpublished M.A. thesis)].

Imperial Blue Book C.-4839. 1886. *Further Correspondence Respecting the Affairs of the Transvaal and Adjacent Territories*. London: Printed by Eyre and Spottiswoode.

Jung, C.E. 2000. *Then I was Black: South African Political Identities in Transition*. New Haven: Yale University Press.

Krüger, D.W. 1972. *Dictionary of South African Biography*, Vol. II. Cape Town: Tafelberg.

Lee, R.B. 2003. "Indigenous Rights and the Politics of Identity in Post-apartheid Southern Africa," (pp. 80-111) *In:* B. Dean and J.M. Levi (eds.), *At Risk of Being Heard: Identity, Indigenous Rights, and Postcolonial States*. Ann Arbor: University of Michigan Press.

Leśniewski, M. 2010. "Review of Story, W.K. Guns, Race, and Power in Colonial South Africa," *Werkwinkel Journal of Low Countries and South African Studies*, 5 (1): 104-110.

Lewis, G. 1987. *Between the Wire and the Wall*. Cape Town: David Philip.

Liebenberg, M.M.B. 1990. *Schweizer-Reneke*. Pretoria: RGN.

Maingard, L.F. 1932. "Studies in Korana History, Customs and Language," *Bantu Studies*, 6 (2): 103-162.

Manson, A. 1998. "Christopher Bethell and the Securing of the Bechuanaland Frontier, 1878-1884," *Journal of Southern African Studies*, 24 (3): 485-508.

Maree, H.P. 1952. *Die geskiedenis en ontwikkeling van die dorp en distrik van Schweizer-Reneke: 1870–1952*. Ongepubliseerde dokument waarvan die kopieregte oorgemaak is aan die Ned. Herv. of Geref. Gemeente, Schweizer-Reneke. [The History and Development of the Town and District of Schweizer-Reneke: 1870–1952. Unpublished Document with Copyright Transferred to the Dutch Reformed or Reformed Congregation, Schweizer-Reneke].

Metrowich, F.C. 1970. *Scotty Smith*. Cape Town: Books of Africa.

Mouton, J.A. 1957. "Genl. Piet Joubert in die Transvaalse Geskiedenis," *Argiefjaarboek vir Suid-Afrikaanse Geskiedenis*, 20 (1). ["Genl Piet Joubert in the Transvaal History", *Archives Yearbook for South African History*, 20 (1).]

Morton, F. 1992. "Slave-Raiding and Slavery in the Western Transvaal after the Sand River Convention", *African Economic History*, 20: 99-118.

Ruiters, M. 2009. "Collaboration, Assimilation and Contestation: Emerging Constructions of Coloured Identity in Post-apartheid South Africa," (pp.04-133) *In:* M. Adhikari (ed.), *Burdened by Race: Coloured identities in Southern Africa*. Cape Town: UCT Press.

Schapera, I. 1965. *The Khoisan Peoples of South Africa*. London: Routledge & Kegan Paul.

Sillery, A. 1971. *John Mackenzie of Bechuanaland/1835-1899: A Study in Humanitarian Imperialism*. Cape Town: Balkema.

Stow, G.W. 1905. *The Native Races of South Africa*. London: Swan Sonnenschein.

Van Onselen, C. 1990. "Race and Class in the South African Countryside: Cultural Osmosis and Social Relations in the Sharecropping Economy of the South Western Transvaal, 1900-1950," *The American Historical Review*, 95 (1): 99-123.

Transvaal Archive Depot, Pretoria.
TAB SS V1110-R4867-1885.
TAB SS V1141-R6231-1885-part 1.
TAB SS V1142-R6231-1885-part 2.
TAB SS V1144-R6356-1885.
TAB KG V15-CR782-1886.
TAB SS V1148-R61-1886.
TAB SS V2860-R6639-1891 and R2380-1891.

BIO-NOTES OF THE CONTRIBUTORS

Behera, Deepak Kumar is presently the Vice-Chancellor of Berhampur University, India. Prior to that he was Professor and Head in the Department of Anthropology, Sambalpur University, India. He obtained both his Master's degree (Gold Medalist) and Ph.D. from Sambalpur University, India. He has been in the teaching profession for more than 30 years. Professor Behera was a Fulbright Visiting Scholar at California State University at Long Beach during the Fall semester 2007. He was also a Visiting Professor at the Department of Social and Cultural Anthropology, Tuebingen University, Germany during the Summer term (April-July 2013), at Department of Anthropology, University of Free State, Bloemfontein, South Africa (2001, 2003), Department of Anthropology, University of Durban-Westville, Durban, South Africa (2001), Institute of Psychology, Federal University of Rio de Janeiro, Brazil (2004) and Maison des Sciences de L'Homme, Paris and CNRS-EHESS, Toulouse (2006). He has to his credit more than 100 research publications in reputed journals and edited volumes. Most of his publications are in the fields of tribal studies and children and childhood. Professor Behera has in total authored/edited eighteen volumes. Of those, nine published volumes of *Contemporary Society: Tribal Studies* (Concept Publishing Company Pvt. Ltd., New Delhi) are jointly with Professor Georg Pfeffer of Institute of Ethnology of Free University of Berlin, Germany. He has brought out five volumes jointly with overseas scholars. Professor Behera has participated more than 25 different international conferences held in Mexico, Germany, Belgium, Sweden, Israel, Denmark, USA, South Africa, China, Japan, Italy, Norway, France, UK, Bangladesh, Brazil, France, Egypt, Singapore, Australia,

South Korea, Ireland, etc. He had delivered several invited lecturers in different overseas universities and research institutes (like Hebrew University of Jerusalem, Israel; Tel Aviv University, Israel; University of Orange Free State, South Africa; University of Durban West-Ville, South Africa, University of California at Santa Cruz, University of Illinois at Chicago; University of Utah, Logan, University of Tuebingen, Germany, etc.). He was the Editor of the *Journal of Social Sciences* during 1997-2002. Professor Behera was elected as a member of the Executive Board of International Union of Anthropological and Ethnological Sciences (IUAES), the apex anthropological body at the international level, in the year 1997 and served in that position for two consecutive terms, i.e. for the period 1998-2009. He is the founding Chairman of the IUAES Commission on Children, Youth and Childhood. Professor Behera is a member of Permanent Council of IUAES and in this capacity he represents India. He is a member of the International Advisory Board of the Journal *Sociological Analysis* (North Carolina, USA), *Boyhood Studies* (New York, USA), and *Practicing Anthropology* (USA), *Acta Academica* (South Africa). Professor Behera is in the Executive Board of the Centre for India Study at Aarhus University, Denmark. He was the Director of the UGC Centre for the Study of Social Exclusion and Inclusive Policy of Sambalpur University. He is also presently a member of the Advisory Committee of the ICSSR-ERC, Kolkata and Governing Council, Association of Indian Universities, New Delhi. He is the Vice-President of the Institute for Social Research and Applied Anthropology, India. Professor Behera was the Chief Convenor of the IUAES Inter-Congress on "Children and Youth in a Changing World" held in Bhubaneswar in 2012. Fourteen scholars have already received their Ph.D. degree working under the supervision of Professor Behera.

Mailing Address: Vice-Chancellor
Berhampur University
Bhanja Vihar
Berhampur
Ganjam, Odisha
Email: <behera.dk@gmail.com>

Bhattacharya, Kumkum teaches Psychology in the Department of Social Work, Visva-Bharati University (founded by Rabindranath Tagore) since 1979 where she is a Professor. She has worked in Tagore's programmes of Rural Reconstruction in the university as part of extension activities. She has extensive experience of working with the Santals. Her doctoral work was on the comparative aspects of socialization of children among the Hindus, Muslims and Santals in a plural situation. She looked after the publications of the University from 2006-2011 during which time she became interested in the creative works of Rabindranath Tagore. Her recent book (2014) *Rabindranath Tagore: An Adventure of Ideas and Innovative Practices in Education* has been published by Springer in the series "*Key Thinkers in Education*".

Mailing Address: Deer Park
Shantiniketan
West Bengal-731235

Bowen, Zazie is a researcher at the Australian National University (ANU), where she taught in the School of Archaeology and Anthropology in 2012 (*Culture and Person*, course convenor/lecturer) and 2013 (*Belonging, Identity and Nationalism: Community at a Large Scale*, Assistant Lecturer). She obtained her doctorate at the Australian National University in 2012 based on an ethnography of children and play in Mayurbhanj District, Odisha. In 2012, she was a post-doctoral fellow in the Research School of Humanities and the Arts at the ANU while researching education in rural Odisha. In 2013, she organized the conference, *Childhoods in South Asia: Contemporary and Historical Perspectives* and is currently guest co-editor of a special issue of a journal based on the conference papers.

Mailing Address: Zazie Bowen, PhD
School of Archaeology and Anthropology
ANU College of Arts and Social Sciences
The Australian National University
Email: <Zazie.Bowen@anu.edu.au>

Carrin, Marine is Director of Research emeritus (CNRS) at the Centre d'Anthropologie Sociale, Toulouse. She has published extensively on *adivasis* in India as well as on the *bhuta* cults in Karnataka. She is the author of *La Fleur et l'Os :symbolisme et rituel chez les Santal,* EHESS, 1986) ; *Enfants de la Déesse : prêtrise et dévotion féminine au Bengal* (CNRS, 1997) and co-author of *A Peripheral Encounter, Santals, Missionaries and their Changing Worlds* (with H.Tambs-Lyche, Manohar, 2008). With P. Andersen and S. Soren she wrote *From Fire Rain to Rebellion Reasserting Identity through Narratives,* Manohar 2011 (An edition and translation of Santal Texts). She has edited *Managing Distress :Therapeutic Cults in South Asia,* (Manohar, 1999), and co-edited *Tribus et Basses Castes: Resistance et Autonomie dans la société indienne*, Purusartha 23, (with Ch. Jaffrelot, 2002), *People of the Jangal: Reformulating Identities and Adaptations in Crisis* (with H.Tambs-Lyche, Manohar 2008), *Voices from the Periphery: Subalternity and Empowerment*, (with L. Guzy), Routledge, 2012 and the *Politics of Ethnicity in India, Nepal and China* (G.Toffin and Pralay Kanungo), Primus 2014. She has a book in press on Santal Ritual Discourse, and is currently working on indigenous knowledge in India. She is also co-editing *Remaking Knowledge: The Agency of Youth* with H.Tambs-Lyche and D. Blanc (*in press*), Primus.

Mailing Address: 16 rue des Fontanes
Toulouse-31300
France
Email: <marinecarrin@hotmail.fr>

Erasmus, Piet is Head of the Department of Anthropology at the University of the Free State, Bloemfontein, South Africa. His academic interest is focused on issues pertaining to the Khoekhoe and San, identity discourses, transformation and land reform. He has authored numerous publications (articles/chapters/books) and delivered congress papers on all of these topics, both nationally and internationally. He also serves as an editorial advisor and reviewer for a number of national and international professional journals.

Mailing Address: Professor of Anthropology
P.O. Box: 339
University of Free State
Bloemfontein-9300

Republic of South Africa
Email: <erasmusp@ufs.ac.za>

Finnan, Christine is a Professor at the College of Charleston in Charleston, South Carolina, USA. She holds a joint appointment in the Teacher Education Department and the Sociology and Anthropology Department and currently serves as Program Director for the Masters in Teaching, Learning and Advocacy program. Her doctorate in education and social sciences was awarded from Stanford University in 1980 following completion of a dissertation examining the role of the ethnic community in occupational identity development among Vietnamese refugees. At the College of Charleston, she teaches courses in education and anthropology, issues of race, class and gender in education, educational policy, and language and culture. In 2012, she organized a study abroad trip to India focusing on comparative childhoods in the US and India. In 2014, she will return to India as a Fulbright Scholar to conduct research at the Kalinga Institute of Social Sciences in Bhubaneswar. In addition to university based teaching and research, she worked for SRI International in Menlo Park, California engaged in large-scale research and evaluation studies of refugee resettlement and education policy and with a national school reform initiative, The Accelerated Schools Project, as a regional program implementation director and director of research. Along with articles in several journals and chapters in edited books, Dr. Finnan authored *The Upper Elementary Years: Ensuring Success in Grades 3-6* in 2009, co-authored *Accelerating the Learning of All Students: Cultivating Culture Change in Schools, Classrooms, and Individuals* in 2000 with Julie D. Swanson, and co-edited *Accelerated Schools in Action: Lessons from the Field* in 1996 with Edward St. John, Jane McCarthy, and Simeon P. Slovacek.

Mailing Address: 104 Wando Reach Ct
Mt Pleasant, SC 29464
USA
Email: <finnanc@cofc.edu>

Guzy, Lidia a social anthropologist and scholar of religions, is currently Lecturer in the Study of South Asian religions and cultures at National University of Ireland, University College Cork (UCC).

She specialises in (i) anthropology of South Asian cultures and religions (popular Hinduism, indigenous Adivasi religions, ascetic and ecstatic traditions, goddess worship); (ii) media anthropology with special focus on music, and (iii) museum anthropology. Since May 2002, Lidia Guzy holds a binational PhD in Social Anthropology from Freie Universität Berlin and École des Hautes Études en Sciences Sociales, Paris. Her doctoral thesis focused on ascetic and ecstatic traditions in rural Hindu and indigenous India: "*Babas and Alekhs – Between Asceticism and Ecstasy. A comparative socio-anthropological study of the ascetic Mahima Dharma tradition in two districts of Orissa (Dhenkanal and Koraput) / Eastern India*". In January 2011, Lidia Guzy finished her post-doctoral thesis ("Habilitation") at Freie Universität Berlin with her work "Marginalised Music—Music, Religion and Politics in Western Odisha" (published in 2013, by Lit Verlag). This work presents the results of her anthropological documentation of hitherto unknown traditions of sacred music performed by marginalised musicians and priest-musicians of the *adivasi* (indigenous) Bora Sambar region of western Odisha. The work is based on more than 30 months of ethnographic research in rural and urban regions of western Odisha.

Mailing Address: Lecturer in Contemporary South Asian Religions
Study of Religions Department
Marginalised and Endangered Worldview Study Centre
University College Cork (UCC)
National University of Ireland, Ireland
Email: <l.guzy@ucc.ie>

John, S. Simon has a Masters and PhD in Folklore. He worked in Anthropological Survey of India and Indira Gandhi National Centre for the Arts, New Delhi. At present he is an Associate Professor and Director-in-Charge of Arunachal Institute of Tribal Studies, Rajiv Gandhi University, Arunachal Pradesh, India. He received the Presidential young scholar award from the President of India at Rashtrapati Bhavan, New Delhi in the year 2010.

Mailing Address: Dr. S. Simon John
Associate Professor
Arunachal Institute of Tribal Studies
Rajiv Gandhi University
Rono Hills, Itanagar
Arunachal Pradesh
Email: <simonjohn19@gmail.com>

Marak, Quinbala is an Assistant Professor in the Department of Anthropology, North-Eastern Hill University, Shillong, India. She has a BA in Anthropology Honours (1997) and an MA in Anthropology (2000), both of which she topped in the University of Gauhati, Assam (India) and was, therefore, a double gold medalist. She is the recipient of the B.S. Guha Medal, Janaki Devi Memorial Prize, Dhiren Sharma Memorial Prize and Renuka Das Memorial Award. She has a PhD in Anthropology from North-Eastern Hill University, Shillong titled "Food, Identity, and Difference: An Anthropological Study". Her research areas have mostly been concentrated on the Garos of India and Bangladesh. Her published papers in different journals and edited books represent her research interests on gastro-politics, anthropology of children, and ethno-archaeology.

Mailing Address: Department of Anthropology
North-Eastern Hill University
Shillong-793022, Meghalaya, India
Email: <qmarak@gmail.com>

Nath, Nibedita is presently working as a Lecturer in Government Women's College, Sambalpur. She has completed her M.A., M.Phil., NET, Ph.D. (Social Anthropology), MBA (HR and MKTG) from Sambalpur University. She stood first class first in Graduation and has received OSANY award for being "Best Graduate in Humanities". She also received gold medal for being first class first in Post-Graduation in Anthropology. Dr. Nath has qualified UGC NET and is also the recipient of Doctoral Research Fellowship of ICSSR (Indian Council of Social Science Research, New Delhi). She has visited University of Oslo, Norway, Europe for presenting paper in the international conference Childhoods 2005. She has to her credit published a half a dozen of papers in International level and a dozen of papers in national level in different journals and edited books. In the development sector she has worked in National Alliance of Women (NAWO) (ORISSA CHAPTER) and Regional Medical Research Centre, Bhubaneswar. Dr. Nath has worked as part time lecturer in Department of Anthropology, Sambalpur University and JISSAR, Bhubaneswar as guest faculty. She has also served as full time Lecturer for around 3 years in KSSS, KIIT University, Bhubaneswar.

Mailing Address: Dr. Nibedita Nath
C/o Mr. Nandlal Nath
At and Near Check Gate, Golgunda
PO – Jagruti Vihar
Burla, Sambalpur
Odisha, India
Email: <nibedita_nath@rediffmail.com>

Ranjan, Geetika is Associate Professor of Anthropology at North Eastern Hill University, Shillong, India. She graduated and post graduated in Anthropology from the University of Lucknow. Her doctoral research is on "Panchayati Raj and Bhoksa Political Organization". She carried out long term fieldwork among the Bhoksa of Uttaranchal. She won the Young Scientist Award from the Indian Science Congress (2001) for her paper, "Role of Elites for the Development of the Bhoksa Tribe". She has published over 15 papers in national and international journals. Her published works range from ethnography, epistemological discourses on "Tribe" to folklore.

Mailing Address: Department of Anthropology
North Eastern Hill University
Shillong
(Meghalaya)
INDIA
email:geetikaranjan19@gmail.com

Reichel, Eva read English language and literature at the Free University of Berlin. She taught at a grammar school and offered courses in the field of in-service training and school-management. After retiring she started from scratch and read Social and Cultural Anthropology at the Free University of Berlin as a regular student. Her M.A. thesis on

Notions of Life in Death and Dying. The Dead in Tribal Middle India was published as a book in 2009 by Manohar, New Delhi. She carried out long term fieldwork among the Ho in Middle India. While doing her doctorate, she worked as a senior lecturer at the Institute of Ethnology at the Free University.

Mailing Address: Marlenestr. 09
13505 Berlin, Germany
Email: <eva_reichel2002@yahoo.de>

Rubel, Paula G. and **Rosman, Abraham** are Professors Emeriti of Barnard College and Columbia University. Professor Rubel received her PhD, based on fieldwork with the Kalmyk Mongols, an émigré group living in the United States. Professor Rosman received his PhD from Yale University based on field research with the Kanuri in Northern Nigeria. They have jointly published nine editions of *The Tapestry of Culture: An Introduction to Cultural Anthropology*. They did a comparative study of the potlatch of Northwest Coast societies publishing it as *Feasting with Mine Enemy* in 1971. In 1978 they published *Your Own Pigs You May Not Eat: A Comparative Study of New Guinea Societies*. They have done fieldwork together in Iran, Afghanistan, and Papua New Guinea, including New Ireland. They have published many articles on their fieldwork and comparative research. They are the coeditors of *Translating Cultures: Perspectives on Translation and Anthropology* (2003). They have also done research on the collecting of ethnographic artifacts in the nineteenth century and have recently published *Collecting Tribal Art: How Kwakiutl Masks and Easter Island Lizard Men Became ART*. The present paper relates to earlier research comparing potlatch type societies in different parts of the world.

Mailing Address: Email: <pgr4@columbia.edu>

Srivastava, Vinay Kumar had his Ph.D. from University of Cambridge, United Kingdom in the year 1994. He taught Sociology at Hindu College of Delhi from 15th September, 1976 to January 1985. He joined the Department of Anthropology, University of Delhi, as Lecturer in Social Anthropology on 21 January, 1985. He became a Reader in Social Anthropology on 15 September, 1986, and Professor on 14 January, 1997. He was on lien from the Department of Anthropology, University of Delhi, where he was employed as Professor of Social Anthropology, and joined as Principal, Hindu College, University of Delhi, from 10 March, 2010. He works on comparative religion, caste system, family dynamics, medical systems, and anthropological theory and methods.

Mailing Address: B-349 Chittaranjan Park
New Delhi 110 019
Email: <vinaykumarsrivastava.vks@gmail.com>

Subramanyam, V. is U.G.C. Emeritus Professor (Fellow) at Department of Anthropology, Andhra University, where he taught from 1986 to 2010. His doctorate was earned from Andhra University in 1985 and was based on field work among Rural Muslims of Andhra Pradesh, India. He taught the courses of Social and Cultural Anthropology to Post Graduate students of Anthropology at Andhra University since his joining as Assistant Professor. He became an Associate Professor in 1994 and a full Professor in 2005. He established Centre for Study of Social Exclusion and Inclusive Policy at Andhra University in 2007 with the financial support of University Grants Commission, New Delhi. He served as Director for CSSE&IP, Andhra University from 2007 to 2010. He conducted several major and minor research project studies throughout his academic career. He has carried out field work in rural and tribal areas of Andhra Pradesh, India. He has received grants from U.G.C, I.C.S.S.R., Ministry of Tribal Affairs, D.S.T., T.C.R. & T.I. and A.P. Tribal Welfare Department. He has associated with India INCLEN. He has conducted several empirical research studies on various health issues. He has carried out collaborative research work with the Centre for Mass Communication Research, Leicester University, U.K. and contributed a case study of "Mandur Village in Andhra Pradesh" for the edited volume of *Mass Media and Village Life* published by Sage, New Delhi. He has published sixty research articles and four books. An edited volume on *Social Exclusion, Integration and Inclusive Policies* with K. Sekhar, Published by Rawat, Jaipur, which is one of the sources of reference for future research in the field of social exclusion and inclusive policy studies. His recent book titled

Environment, Livelihoods and Sustainable Development of Tribes in India, accepted for publication by Rawat, Jaipur, India.

Mailing Address: U.G.C. Emeritus Professor (Fellow)
Department of Anthropology
Andhra University
Visakhapatnam–530003
Andhra Pradesh, India
Email: <vsubramanyam23@rediffmail.com>

Tulebaeva, Baktygul is a Ph.D. student in Social and Cultural Anthropology at the Eberhard-Karls University of Tuebingen (2011-). Her research project is called "Between Development, Soviet Science and Traditional Healing: An Ethnography of Childhood and Child Health in Kyrgyzstan". In autumn of 2012, she went to Kyrgyzstan to study childhood and a healthy growth of children. The aim of the project was to research what Kyrgyz people understand by a child, a healthy child and what they do in order to ensure health and well-being of their children. She earned her Master's degree in Social Anthropology at the University of Edinburgh in 2009 and wrote her thesis on the cross-cultural study of the concept of child well-being. After obtaining her undergraduate degree at American University in Central Asia in 2005, she worked at a Cultural Research Center Aigine and was involved in projects on the role of mass media in political participation in Kyrgyzstan, sacred sites and traditional knowledge. Her articles *Let's Learn to Express Our Thoughts* and *Belief and Knowledge in Healing Practices* were published in the Open Society Foundation Journal *ScholarForum* and edited book of G. Aitpaeva *Sacred Sites of Issyk-Kul: Spiritual Powers, Pilgrimage, and Art* respectively. She is awarded scholarship by Open Society Foundation and a joint DAAD-UCA (German Academic Exchange Service—University of Central Asia) Scholarship.

Mailing Address: Fichtenweg 9, 207-208
72076 Tuebingen
Germany
Email: <tulebaevab@gmail.com>

INDEX